SKY
CLOUD
MOUNTAIN

SKY CLOUD MOUNTAIN

DAVID ANIRMAN

iUniverse, Inc.
Bloomington

SKY CLOUD MOUNTAIN

The information, ideas, and suggestions in this book are not intended as a substitute for professional medical advice. Before following any suggestions contained in this book, you should consult your personal physician. Neither the author nor the publisher shall be liable or responsible for any loss or damage allegedly arising as a consequence of your use or application of any information or suggestions in this book.

iUniverse books may be ordered through booksellers or by contacting:

iUniverse
1663 Liberty Drive
Bloomington, IN 47403
www.iuniverse.com
1-800-Authors (1-800-288-4677)

Because of the dynamic nature of the Internet, any web addresses or links contained in this book may have changed since publication and may no longer be valid. The views expressed in this work are solely those of the author and do not necessarily reflect the views of the publisher, and the publisher hereby disclaims any responsibility for them.

Any people depicted in stock imagery provided by Thinkstock are models, and such images are being used for illustrative purposes only.
Certain stock imagery © Thinkstock.

ISBN: 978-1-4759-4841-7 (sc)
ISBN: 978-1-4759-4882-0 (ebk)

Library of Congress Control Number: 2012916336

Printed in the United States of America

iUniverse rev. date: 09/05/2012

Contents

Part I.   Sky 1
   Introduction...3
   Atlantic Crossing...16
   Gathering Together 68

Part II.   Cloud...95
   Conceptual Interlude 97
   Dispersion...104

Part III. Mountain 115
   Historical Interlude 117
   Prologue...143

First Day
   Timothy's Waterfall 151
Second Day
   Hidden Lines...156
Third Day
   Birds in the Saddle...162
Fourth Day
   Mirrors 170
Fifth Day
   The Mountain Lady 179
Sixth Day
   The Lion...187
Seventh Day
   The Serpent Tower...193
Eighth Day
   Arrogant Dragon 198

Ninth Day
  The Maze 206
Tenth Day
  Gooseberry Springs 217
Eleventh Day
  The Kings of Old 222
Twelfth Day
  Birds and Bees 232
Thirteenth Day
  The Lady Iboga 239
Fourteenth Day
  His Serpency 256
Fifteenth Day
  Tourmaline Castles 266
Sixteenth Day
  A Summons 273
Seventeenth Day
  Atop the Hill 279
Eighteenth Day
  The Ancient Wanderer 284
Nineteenth Day
  Return 307
Twentieth Day
  The Final Oracle 313

Epilogue 317
Works Cited 327

Part I
SKY

Introduction

For those to whom time is not an illusion, I might say that this story begins a long while ago. When precisely, I do not know because in trying to remember, I recall a panoply of times past and wonder if this was more relevant than that, an event more promising than a hope, or if birth or death was the newer beginning. Incessant change erases the boundaries of memory, and I find no place of entry more fitting than another. Perhaps this is unimportant, for in a tale such as this, the past and the present are a moving couplet whose reality is itself of no moment. The melody I hear mingles with those I have heard, and even this that I write is already past and hardened into words; words which, like time itself, spill out and have no more stability than the dreams they awake.

Since much of this story is concerned with a sacred mountain, a colossal relic from great antiquity sleeping quietly in the back country of southern California, I can think of no better starting point than to recount the events of a day several years ago when this mountain opened for a moment and whispered of her secrets. It was May, perhaps early June, nineteen hundred and seventy-some years into the era of our thrice-tried calendar. The day began at a ranch tucked in a narrow valley below Spitler Peak, a mountain whose modest dome is one of many similar crags in the southeastern ridge of the San Jacinto Mountains. The ranch was a retreat founded by the Brotherhood of Eternal Love so that its people could turn away from the polluted incompetence of modern technocracy and re-establish their human bonds with the earth.

Two miles below the ranch along the dirt road that winds its way up from Garner Valley is a small creek that has, over the seasons, cut a miniature sub-canyon through the alluvial plain of the mountains. The creek tumbles for another two miles through a twisting gorge in a series of waterfalls and deep pools sculpted from bedrock granite. Because the creek is so small, and not unlike the many others that tap the mountains, it was known among us only as the Waterfall. I had often gotten very high there, and by wandering among the great boulders and cliffs of the gorge, been taken much higher.

So it happened one early spring day that I left the ranch shortly after first light and walked to the Waterfall. At the place where the gorge dropped away from the higher plateau, I took a few hundred micrograms of crystalline LSD (lysergic acid diethylamide), and meandered with the stream until my legs would carry me no further. I put my pack and poncho down, and crumpled beside them in a steep hollow between rock walls. The creek poured from a smooth stone spout into a pool at my right, ran through the grasses and brambles about me, and twisted around a large rock to fall out of sight. The sounds were of birds calling and moving water and an occasional breeze that stirred the pines to murmuring among themselves. The smell was warm Gemini and flowers, and the sky was the color of lapis lazuli save where the molten sun pierced its earthly consort with the radiance of heaven.

I sat facing stone walls, staring in fascination as my mind dissolved the realities of its normal perception. Across the stream stood several huge slabs of sandstone, two of which opened out like a book. They were caressed and erased by time, silenced by eternity, but, as I gazed, intricate glyphs from some ancient calligraphy assembled on their pages. Before my eyes, the sandstone began to shimmer, then came alive with the words and flowing patterns of a long-forgotten language. Strangely familiar symbols echoed from the past, appearing on the stone as though engraved by the hand of a consummate craftsman. Each character enclosed and connected others; each radiated a separate tone. The whole expanse of rock was covered in minute detail, offering many levels of interpretation, many meanings to be explored. Every line was distinctly formed, every mark concise, but neither the alphabet of the writing nor the direction of its intelligible sequences was known to me.

I moved about the area, seeing the slabs from different angles. From lower and higher elevations I could see the ideographs clearly from every perspective, but on close inspection I found that the rocks themselves were smooth and unchiseled. It appeared that the whole cliff was embossed with wonderful hieroglyphics, which over the centuries had been effaced by the wind and water of this hidden place, and were now visible for a moment only because I gazed through a crack in time. There was no understanding in me, either for the glyphs or the tongue whose motions they sought to express. The perception merely sparkled at its own level, presenting me with a masterwork of art; for such is the wonder of the profoundly stoned consciousness—that beauty is its architect.

I scintillated in that space for hours, punctuating the day with Ulysses-like excursions to other universes within. Coming back, I had but to open my eyes, and the gift of intuitive seeing was there to be enjoyed. Toward evening as I made my way out of the gorge, I found other rocks that bore the same designs. By this time my body was growing tired, and the glyphs were subsiding, soon to vanish from the reality of sight and fade to the dim mirror-eye of memory.

I sat to watch the sun crest the western mountains with gold and lingered in the after-light to wonder about the objective validity of what I had seen. There were different ways to interpret the sensory data. I had long known that LSD was a physiological as well as a psychological sacrament. I could assume that it had greatly clarified my vision, enabling me to see impressions left by effaced engravings that still radiated their presence in a spectrum visible to my acid-opened eyes. But I discounted this line of argument, for I also knew that my mind was capable of creating these illusions of ancient purpose from its own dream-stuff. At other times in my life I had seen similar designs radiating from the face of the sun-speckled ocean, or from evening cloud forms, or from moonbeams in a midnight forest. I had learned that the enlivened mind plucks from its environment the pieces it needs to fulfill its pleasure and arranges them as it pleases. For such a mind, a universe may lie within the sparkle of a stone, an ocean in a drop of dew, a poem in a fragrance.

While I pondered these things, an insight began to grow and stayed with me as I drifted back toward the ranch now nestled in a shadow beneath its sharp ridge of mountain. The insight was not concerned with the objective reality of what I had seen but rather with the projecting power of this extraordinary environment: how it could so finely fashion my intuition. The place itself was sacred and long ago had perfected the art of speaking to people. I could associate no historical time with what I felt, and yet I clearly understood that this was a place of royal lineage that now slept in the bosom of the everywhere watching and protective earth. As darkness closed about me, I sensed myself walking the avenues of a city of gold: a city of real gold for which gold is but a metaphor. And I wondered if this was one of the fabled Seven Cities of Gold that European man, in his insatiable greed, could never find.

The mind that creates such experiences is the mind that reaches out into its own cellular and electromagnetic potential. I, who ride this mind but watch, marveling at its wonderful simplicity and at the unending alterations that mask its passage through life. Time fashions each point in my mental matrices, fixes it, and replaces it with void. I perceive one reality, only to have it dissolve as another forms. Each has its moment of recognition. It is a process of which my ego is only a part, for my ego is but a discrete entity continuously reborn as the awareness of other things. What I am and what I confront are the two aspects of every situation. The consciousness that informs them both is the creative function of the universe, which as the essential nature of the totality, precedes their existence and activates their differences. To awaken as this consciousness is to come to an ancient understanding and cross the threshold of freedom, for perfect awareness dwells beyond images, and knows everything as itself.

Many are the books written about this consciousness, many the ideas that precede understanding. They come from every race, culture, and epoch of humanity, for what they say is intrinsic to the human mechanism itself. All tell of the same thing in their bold and varied metaphors: this consciousness, with its finger of time and its thumb of space, is everywhere centered and, being beyond the lesser understandings it creates in us, rests in perfection. The pathways to this consciousness are as many as the stars of heaven, as complex as the people who would follow them. There are religions and yogas, meditations and disciplines, bibles and scriptures, all acclaiming the same memory, articulating the same hope. Sometimes an intuition of the way arises spontaneously, sometimes after years of effort. Fasting may lead this way, as may diet or drugs. For some, it is found in sex, for others, in abstinence. We may stand on our heads or walk firmly planted in our obstinacy. We may mutilate the body, cherish it; be fanatic or tractable, daring or docile. We may desire this consciousness above all things or flee from it, and still it hides itself before us, untarnished among the thoughts we think to think in private, and is ever the guide that leads the way we direct, even when we deny or debase it.

To maintain this understanding is to maintain high consciousness, and the maintenance of high consciousness, like every other human skill, is something that may be learned. Over the past fifteen years, I have taken two approaches to this learning and developed complementary sets of tools for the undertaking. One set contains classics in the study of high consciousness, the other, a small assortment of psychedelics. I have used both, as far as possible, in compatible environments and in the company of turned-on friends. A real world peopled with karmic companions is indispensable, for without it, life has no source from which to renew its energies, and this failure to be nourished manifests as boredom, frustration, and hatred—the antitheses of that which is sought.

Movement is a function of life, its direction, a matter of choice. When I first took LSD, I was engulfed with undreamt-of profusions generated through my nervous system by the universes it confronted. At the same time, I felt a need to reduce these overwhelming experiences to some set of useful and ego-relevant concepts. And so, over the years, I dabbled with many systems and listened to many learned voices. Concurrently, I continued my psychedelic exploration, thereby renewing the remembrance of what it was I sought, for what I was able to experience when profoundly stoned I was able to conceptualize when my mind retreated to its more familiar haunts. During these periods, I let the memory of high consciousness guide me among the writings and people who described it.

The world and books, good friends and psychedelics, which are mutually reinforcing, and my life flowed in a manner that the insights they generated prompted. Along the way, I was befriended by many, including the most ancient book that our species, in its fascination with words and concepts, has preserved. This book is the *I Ching,* a classic from the Chinese cultural tradition, known to us in translation as the *Book of Changes.* It is a work whose antiquity is less than its profundity and, since the events of this story are intimately connected with the counsel derived from it, let me speak for a moment of the reasons why I hold it in such high esteem and say something of the methods by which it operates.

The *I Ching* is a compilation of experience taken, not from centuries, but millennia. It functions on three levels: as an oracle, a manual for correct behavior, and an integrated presentation of conceptual wisdom.

Ultimately, the three are one, for the wisdom displayed in conduct is the structure of the future, the womb of the next moment. The book is a set of commentaries on a series of six-line figures called hexagrams. Each hexagram is a structure of firm and/or yielding lines; the firm being represented by an unbroken line, the yielding by one broken line in the middle. A firm line indicates an advancing and penetrating force; a yielding line refers to a field whose qualities are receptivity and acceptance.

In all their combinations, the six lines form a total of sixty-four hexagrams, but every hexagram contains the possibility of altering its structure into that of any other hexagram. This alteration embodies the projective power of the *Book of Changes*, and stems from the observation that both firm and yielding situations, when pushed to their polar limit, will reverse themselves, i.e., those that have reached their maximum firmness will yield, and those that have yielded completely will become firm. The firm and the yielding are the fundamental, complementary principles of the universe. In the hexagrams, these principles display themselves metaphorically, just as they do in the actuality of human experience. They express the polarities innate to us and detail the manner in which these manifest and alter themselves to reflect the invariable patterns of our uniqueness.

In functioning as an oracle, the *I Ching* responds to questions by presenting one or two hexagrams specified through some sort of random process, such as the division of sticks or the throwing of coins. The person inquiring of the oracle first poses a question in the manner he or she would have it discussed and then carries out the random process to construct the hexagram line by line, from bottom to top. This process determines the sequence of firm and yielding, lines and whether any given line will change into its opposite. If no changing lines occur, a single hexagram is produced; one or more changing lines result in two hexagrams.

In themselves the hexagrams are analyses of the sixty-four experiential categories through which human life expresses its infinite variety. These categories are the fundamental behavior patterns available to us as human beings. Their expression is what we mean by conduct. In this life we are path-following animals accustomed to trailing our emotions and reason, but the paths depicted by the *I Ching* lead nowhere, for the one consciousness which the book elucidates is everywhere and eternally present. The pathways through the hexagrams merely express this fact within the matrix of freedom and choice.

The *Book of Changes* calls one who is capable of moving correctly through the situations of life the superior person, and it is this person to whom it speaks. The ethic that one lives, and in which one is guided by the book, is the empirical ethic of action in accord with the nature of each situation. But this is not the empiricism of the independently scheming ego. Nor is it an ethic that can be abused by one who might use the book to deceive others, for in the one universal consciousness there are no others, and all deception is of the deceiving ego itself. The *I Ching* refers to such an ego as the inferior person, and all the advice in the book is directed toward forestalling the development of such a deceptive state within ourselves, or, more positively, toward developing our inborn and innately superior qualities. For one to ask advice concerning the ways of deceit is to receive an answer that, if followed, would lead to the unmasking of the deceiver. Presumably such a person would not follow this advice, therefore he could not properly use the book. Thus the ethical universe of the *I Ching* insulates itself from the machinations of the inferior person, while clearly expressing the manifold ways of the superior person.

The wisdom of the *I Ching* is the wisdom of the earth, for the book, like the people who conceived it, is eminently practical. Besides telling us the essentials of correct behavior under any circumstances, it supplies us with conceptual tools for building the framework of all successful action. In its supremely embodied conception of creative heaven and receptive earth, its ever valid metaphors of thunder and rain, mountain and wind, fire and lake, it delimits a universe of exquisite perfection. In using these metaphors to describe the mottled way of the superior person, the *Book of Changes* indicates the structure of the situation into which he will move, even as it shows him the one in which he finds himself at the time of the inquiry. A relationship is developed between the present and the future, but this is not a relationship of simple causality. The connection between time segments is more fundamental that this. Its only intrinsic attribute is change, for it is neither evolution nor devolution, but change alone which is the defining characteristic of process.

Fortunately, the attitude of mind that sees continuous change as the primary fact of existence, does not cast man adrift amid the storms of an aleatory universe. The harmony implicit in change is the perfect harmony of every sphere, from the sub nucleonic to the supracosmic. The Chinese call this harmony the Tao, and to live freely within its patterning is to enter the realm of the Buddhas and Christs who have peopled our past. The *Book of Changes* specifies some pragmatic aspects of this harmony and teaches the superior person, resident in each of us, how to fashion life in accordance with them. It is capable of telling us when to speak and when to keep silent, when to act and how to act precisely, and of no ness importance, when to forbear, when to say no to the world or ourselves, even though pride or precedence crumbles.

Since it is attuned to the physiological structure of life, the *I Ching* speaks properly whether we listen or not. Accepting its advice provides consistency to living, but this acceptance itself is an act of faith: faith founded on the excellence of the Tao, and based on a knowledge of the extraordinary perceptual state called enlightenment. Correct conduct is neural growth into more comprehensive levels of experience and feeling. Consistent action is the only firm basis for this growth. Smaller patterns are permeated and encompassed by larger one. Ultimately, the Tao—the supreme pattern—may be perceived; but this is no ordinary perception, any more than the genetic coding which gives us our eyes is itself visual sight. We must grow to it ourselves, but the *I Ching*, like our DNA, points us in the right direction.

Some maintain that the *I Ching* works by magic. I agree with them, stipulating only what Carl Jung rediscovered for Westerners, that magic works for those who believe in it. Magic is not something we do, but something that happens around us. What occurs is a product of our own actions and those of everything else in our environment. The intangible total is more than the sum of its parts, and the difference is magic. It requires nothing but our capacity to notice it: to see it out of the corner of the eye or to recognize it head on. To partake of the magical is to open to it, to be receptive to the flux of time in the unadorned discreteness of now, and to the myriad patterned realities it projects. Life is tentative in that we cannot foreclose every event by categorizing it in terms of the familiar, for the recognizable is but a designation for our personal past. This is not to deny the beneficial operation of our rational minds. Like our arts or sciences, they become more complex within and beyond their limits. They are guided by their own synchronistic functioning to expand and create new perceptible universes, but this aggrandizement is also the realm of magic—that vast space that seems to surround and yet to retreat from our current understandings but from which these understandings themselves may be seen to flow. To believe in magic is to be free from erroneous certainty.

One of the more delightful forms that magic has assumed in my life is the ability I have rediscovered to anthropomorphize my many environments and the objects within them. I do so as an intermittent game that has no more meaning that the simple enjoyment it arouses in me. I let the things of my world speak to me through their manifold modes of communication, for everything within the Tao radiates its own significance. Sometimes I merely bask in these radiations, asking nothing more. At other times my world speaks to me as friend, or teacher, or lover. A tree may wave its branches and brush its tendrils through my brain; a flower may sing as sweetly as ever I heard a human voice; a clump of dirt may dance from beyond the confines of my time sense, belying its insentience even as it moistens itself into roots and fruits and ultimately me. In the Tao, all things are alike, but for me to presume that all things are like me is to wrap myself in illusion. Nevertheless, I anthropomorphize as I will, and find in it the genesis of a friendly illusion: life to be respected, an earth to be cherished, and a universe to be comfortably at home in.

It is this home that the *Book of Changes* describes in its wonderful way, so it is not too surprising that I also anthropomorphize the book. I have met the *I Ching*, with its many authors and myriad commentators, as an old Chinese friend and dabbler in virtue. Written by men, it speaks to men, and I have encountered that mind as a robust sage musing on the busyness of things, contemplating the sequences of change as the great forces of the cosmos play out their games as earth life and all the possibilities therein.

Over the years, I have come to love the *I Ching* and other classics of high consciousness. Stoned, I have studied them, for they structure my trips superbly, while the psychedelics, with an elegant reciprocity, display and explain their wisdom. Scripture and sacrament have always been complimentary symbiotic vehicles for the human drive toward perfection. They arise together and flourish as lovers. During the past thirty years, while new sciences and arts appeared everywhere, many of the great Eastern spiritual classics reached us in good translations, and all sorts of psychedelic substances exploded into prominence. Each of these phenomena is an aspect of the consciousness that is exhibiting itself as our history. It is a new consciousness, so it has brought forth new things: LSD as well as space probes. But it is also an ancient consciousness reawakening, so it has brought back the secrets and mystical sacraments of antiquity: the *I Ching*, and peyote, psilocybin, and cannabis.

My life with psychedelics began in the summer of 1964, on a California side hill, when I swallowed a sugar cube to which one-hundred-millionths of a gram of LSD had been added. As with nuclear energy whose birth twin it is, the tiniest amounts of LSD are spectacular, logarithmically expanding consciousness through the multilayered mysteries of mind. I was among the fortunate. Early statistical research indicated that about 5 percent of those who tried LSD without psychic preparation were enabled to experience a profound level of consciousness, generally characterized as mystical. However, this percentage rose dramatically when the set of the individual and the setting of his environment were prepared for this possibility. Thus it became evident that high consciousness was the implicit promise of our humanity. LSD provided a glimpse of this consciousness, but it also demanded the hard work of restructuring ordinary awareness in terms of its insights, for if this process was not undertaken the sacramental value of the drug was soon nullified.

My first few trips were amazing. Subjectively, each lasted many lifetimes, and even the frightening parts were often quick, unambiguous steps to high consciousness. But after fifteen or twenty trips, spaced out over several years, the character of the experience changed. My ego had learned to play games with the new levels of awareness. Its agility became a trap, for it could skirt my hang-ups and avoid dying at the appropriate moment. I became adept at not letting go and hung like an apple rotting on the tree. I suffered because I knew what I wanted, but was blocked and diverted by a complex of factors that could only be called me.

During these years, I was in the navy, but as my insights deepened, so, too, did our involvement in Vietnam. After an eye-opening tour in South East Asia, I left the service in 1967. I stayed with LSD but, despite my best efforts, the experiences continued through a long period of psychic adversity. Trip after trip, I slogged by way through gray hellish storms and roamed endlessly through trivial worlds of tinfoil and plastic. My consciousness imploded, paused, and exploded in the super-sensuous pulsations of the Tao, but blockages in the neural circuits were swamps, habit patterns were kaleidoscopes, prejudices were demons, and hatreds were the assassins of love. Seeds sprout in the dark, bacterial earth, and our lineage is no different; but for either tree or man to come forth, consciousness must abandon the seed and seek the sun.

By 1969, though I used LSD frequently, it seemed as if certain parts of my being had calloused over, and that the sacrament could no longer gain me access to the deep levels of consciousness that my earlier trips had revealed. By this time, a great deal of experimental work had shown that LSD was completely non-toxic. It could be taken in large doses, and frequently, with no ill effects. All that was needed was healthy body and an easy mind. So, along with many others I experimented with massive doses.

The results were ambiguous, for higher dosages were no guarantee of higher consciousness. For a while, I took LSD three times a week, doubling the dosage each day to overcome the effects of tolerance, then waiting five days for the accumulated tolerance to dissipate before repeating the cycle. These too were ambivalent trips, but I discovered that the highest point of the three days usually occurred on the first day, no matter how large the subsequent dosages. Unfortunately, the first day was also the least stable, for my psychosomatic blocks were then at their strongest. In order to circumvent this problem, I set out to investigate the synergistic relationships between LSD and other psychedelics, hoping to undermine the blocks while still retaining the soaring power of the acid. I tried drugs in combination and in sequence. In both cases the results were excellent and, when I held the LSD until the second day, its full power dawned on a tranquil inner space.

At first, I experimented in this way with mescaline and STP, but in July of 1969, that portentous month when our Apollo astronauts first stepped out on the moon, an old friend gave me some ground-up Iboga root and told me it was a mysterious sacrament. Iboga is a shrub native to equatorial Africa. *The Merck Index of Chemicals and Drugs,* a technical reference work on pharmaceuticals, mentions only that it is used by tribal hunters when they stalk game since it enables them to remain motionless for up to two days while retaining their mental alertness. I had first heard of Iboga a year earlier from Claudio

Naranjo, a Chilean doctor who was professionally interested in the use of psychedelics for psychotherapy.

He considered Iboga without peer for his purposes because it made it possible for a person to re-experience episodes from the past in all their original clarity and immediacy. This allowed traumas and the imprinting of behavior patterns to be explored directly. During the months that followed, I met several others who had experimented with Iboga. The descriptions they gave were vivid, but hedged with warnings. They spoke with awe of the drugs profundities, but also of its power to arouse terror; they told of its topological distortions and new spectrum hallucinations, but also of its devastation of the nervous system. A drug to be cautious with, they said, but one seemingly worth the dangers.

I decided to take a two-day trip using first the Iboga and then, if this proved successful, LSD. On the day before the historic moonwalk, while the command vehicle and lunar module were orbiting the still-virgin lady, I swallowed two large capsules of brown Iboga root. As was my custom, I threw an *I Ching* to interrogate my energy levels, and drew a single hexagram: "Innocence", or "The Unexpected". It left me somewhat bemused, innocent I might be, I thought, but after the lurid stories of my friends there was nothing I did not expect. But the *I Ching* read me aright, for none of the dire predictions materialized. The day was unexpectedly serene: the gentle rush, a smooth ascent through trance levels, and hours of dipping in and out of an unending, unrolling tapestry of lovely visions.

The action came on the following day when, fully refreshed, I dropped 1000 micrograms of an LSD called Sunshine and, with the help of our space program, regained access to the cosmos. It was a day of stupendous intensity. Never before in history had so much human consciousness been emotionally and intellectually excited by exactly the same thing at precisely the same time. Several hundred million of us concentrated on one object, an object that all could see simultaneously and each could see with equal clarity: the moon, ancient goddess of love, mystery, and magic, whose fateful courting was being dramatized in electronic words and phosphorescent pictures for an audience of nations. With such energies coursing our species' consciousness, I was swept out into the vast reaches of space and floated as primal idea in the mind of creation. Revelations assembled themselves as galactic spores and burst in the womb of my seeing. It was a perfect day, perfectly orchestrated, yet how quickly it slid back into itself and disappeared.

During the same months, the last of the waning sixties, I also began to experiment with the psychosomatic explosive called DMT (dimethyltryptamine). Alone, it is a remarkable sacrament. When used in conjunction with LSD, a psychic synergy beyond compare may be brought to birth. One inhalation of the concentrated smoke, and the world melts into its patterning constituents. A second inhalation, and the body becomes transfixed with a silence so deep and so startling that within it a tear would fall as a torrent. A third inhalation, and sentience visibly radiates itself from everywhere: plants and animals are transfigured to their sacred essence and pebbles sparkle like self-conscious, magical jewels. But the balance is delicate. The vision can detonate along with the nervous system that falters before it.

I remember one trip when my head disappeared, but not the rest of me, and for an excruciating half hour I lay in smoldering ruins. With DMT's quick, uncontrollable rush, I simultaneously expanded and contracted. My body bloated, my head shrank to nothing, and an unshrieked scream disappeared with my vocal cords. Sometime later, after murky contortions through the tar pits of addled time, I re-emerged as a disjointed, amoeba like thing, putting itself back together with psychic pseudopods. Such experiences, though often quite horrible, are no more than a widow's mite in the table stakes of consciousness, for under the guidance of the LSDMT synergy, vast realms of perfect attunement may also occur, and the stellar brilliance of the clear-light void shine from everywhere, from everything, inside and out.

Unlike the heavier psychedelics, which are best taken occasionally, the cannabis twins, marijuana and hashish, can be used frequently for the learning of high consciousness. But with these, too, tolerance levels build quickly, and the drugs have to be managed intelligently to maintain an optimum high. During the high, the mind may be utilized, or not, to equal satisfaction. When there's something to be accomplished, a small amount of grass can relax the body and concentrate the mind on its task. When contemplative chores are undertaken, a joint or a few tokes of hash can marvelously structure several hours of productive time. Whatever it is, cannabis makes it better, a little clearer, and a lot more fun, so if you have the wherewithal, light up, and join me on a trip.

Atlantic Crossing

Somehow, very near, in the endless vault of space through which we move, a creative intelligence of unutterable comprehension dwells, dreaming the vagaries of life:

children, she dreams, and kings
sacred and secret things
mothers, lovers, fathers, suns
the radiance of shining ones
forests growing, cities churning
rivers flowing, pyres burning
strange designs that thinkers flee
and all things borne within the sea
pioneers who pride the land
and fools who scribble in the sand
hopes of men who make libations
and crones who screech the death of
nations
stranger are we, and stranger she
who calls upon the void to be
space revealing, time concealing
standing proudly, bending, kneeling
lost beyond the realm of thought
beyond the galaxies thus wrought
where what is seen is left behind
in secret confines of the mind
where dreamers play to win at dreams
the universe and all it seems
while he who takes the dream to wife
may wake the dreamer up from life

The small pipe of hashish grew cold in my hand. The night was still. Across the room a redwood fire burned low, and the fog pressed against the window, calling to the candle within to glitter its droplets on the glass. I awoke from my reverie, my eyes wandering the room, settling on objects at random like bees among blossoms, seeing each clearly without seeing anything at all. My hashish-enhanced vision played with the patterns of darkness, with the fire spirits and shadow goblins of the corner, then slowly, very slowly, came back across the rippled wood floor to my old copy of the *I Ching* that lay waiting before me.

I shook the pipe, stirring the dead ashes, then set it aside to wander the corridors of my memory, seeing myself as I had been years before: young, impatient, curious, possessed of a wanderlust that being in the navy and flying about the world had increased rather than stilled. So long ago it seemed, so many ages past. I wondered if the abilities I had then developed still lingered in some secure backwater of my being, or if they had slipped off to the realm of fanciful remembrance, not quite forgotten but irretrievable as practical skills. I had not flown the ocean for six years and then only in large aircraft with thoroughly trained crews. But I now had the opportunity to take a small Beechcraft Turbo-Baron across the North Atlantic from Canada to England. The possibilities of the trip excited me. They reenergized old, neglected circuits in my brain and reanimated learned tissue in my muscles. I felt a little shot of adrenalin. But I had misgivings too. Time had edited my life, removing whatever was unneeded in day-to-day living, and I had no idea how thoroughly I had been decomplicated. Thoughts that would not focus tingles my brain stem, while those intangible emotions that underlay my ability to think seemed ready to tremble and drop me to the abyss below.

Again my eyes circled the room. The shadows wove themselves into a shape, a vagueness of mountains, and a small aircraft buffeted by a turbulent sky. The fire, barely crackling, roared in my ears, thick clouds rose with its vapor, and the window turned to ice. I shook my head and the shapes dissolved, leaving a strange calm about the aerie of my seeing.

Sometime later, I picked up the *I Ching* and took from it a small cloth sack containing three Chinese coins. I moved the coins in my hands, enjoying the feel of the old bronze and the sensation of cold metal warming in my fingers. When the temperatures equalized, my mind left my hands and returned to my throat where, with words, it sought to frame a proper inquiry concerning the proposed flight. I played with the phrasing of my question, saying it one way and then another, tossing it back and forth between the lobes of my brain, from the active to the receptive modes, polishing it, until I knew what I was saying, what I meant by the words I chose, and what I wanted to ask. With this accomplished, I let the question and its probings drop away while the ritual of consulting the oracle infused my mind and concentrated it within the familiar, formless patterns of respectful silence.

Six times I shook the coins, and six times dropped them before me. After each throw, I laid wooden matches on the floor, broken or unbroken as the coins directed. The figures of sticks and shadows seemed to grow out of the wood and, when completed, constructed the hexagram called "Waiting (Nourishment)", which by virtue of a changing line in the place of the ruler, became that of "Peace".

I lit another candle, and in its flickerings perused the answer of the oracle. In the first hexagram "strength follows on danger". Under these conditions, says the book, "sincerity leads to success". "Perseverance brings good fortune", and "it furthers one to cross the great water". But do not push events, for a period of waiting is indicated. Success may be expected but, like rain, it will come in its own time. "Eat and drink, be joyous and of good cheer: peace will follow when the course of heaven and earth has been completed."

The *I Ching* settled my mind, and I accepted the challenge. I expected to leave in a day or two, but six weeks were to pass before the trip came together. The problem lay with the aircraft, which sat in Montreal awaiting both minor maintenance and the installation of extra fuel tanks to extend its range sufficiently to fly directly from eastern Canada to Iceland. The shop in Montreal was understaffed and, as I was to discover, had other problems as well. Consequently, it was late June before I received assurances that the work would be completed in four or five days. But by then, the problem of time was intruding itself. I had to be back in San Francisco on the 18th of July. This only allowed me about two weeks to iron out the various details of the trip and complete the crossing.

On the Fourth of July, no holiday in Canada, I again checked with Montreal, expecting the work to be complete. It was not, and the service manager was ambiguous. The job had started, or was about to start, and was being rushed, or would be rushed. I hung up, not sure what was happening, and decided to leave for Montreal immediately. Early the following morning, a Wednesday, I embarked on an Air Canada 707 and jetted off on the first leg of my journey.

It was a relief to be underway. Getting started cleared my head and put me in a happy frame of mind but, as the blue skies of the western United States gave way to storms east of the Mississippi, I thought more seriously about the trip ahead. I knew that the Baron was a reliable aircraft, and I assumed that it would be in good condition since it had undergone periodic maintenance in the fall. The tachometer on the starboard engine was broken and the cabin heater was inoperative, but both systems were easy to repair. Everything else presumably was in order, but I was prepared for surprises because all complex machines have moods, unique temperaments, and particular gremlins.

I also recalled the moods of the North Atlantic and the many melodies of her siren's song. In past years I had had a lot of experience with the lady. She angered easily. She cried voluminous tears. She could be as cold as a witch's tit and as thunderously outspoken as Kali herself. But I also knew that she was a queen by birth, a mother of legends and secrets, a voluptuous lover awash with inconceivable delights, and a moist, womanly consciousness shaded with depths of communicable wisdom. For my part, I had both loved and feared her. Now, like a court magician of old, I meant to insinuate myself into her good graces with a touch of arcane knowledge—in this case, the artful science of predictive meteorology that would tell me the days of her beneficence.

My plan was to leave Montreal as quickly as possible and wait at one of the international airdromes in Newfoundland until good weather prevailed along the route to Iceland. These airports are on the eastern periphery of North America and serve as continental arrival and departure points in the complex web of the North Atlantic air transport network. I had not flown through the area in a dozen years, but I remembered it clearly for it was tinged with the excitement of my early flying days. My first operational squadron had been part of the Navy's Fleet Logistic Air Wing, flying military versions of the four-engine DC-6 transport to Europe and Africa. Our primary departure points had been Argentia and Stephenville in Newfoundland, with an alternate, when these were socked in, at Goose Bay, Labrador, 300 miles to the north. I had greatly enjoyed the area and was eager to return and confront it half a generation later. I hoped to spend no more than a day or two in Montreal to check out the aircraft, acquire the extra gear that the flight would entail, and do whatever preliminary paperwork might be required.

The 707 bumped through rolling black storm clouds and landed in a downpour of warm, sloppy summer rain. By the time I got my luggage and hailed a cab, the rain had stopped, and the sticky afternoon was perking up. The Baron was at a hangar on the far side of the field. I went to the adjoining office and introduced myself to the service manager. Although somewhat surprised, he greeted me warmly, sat me down, and was profuse in his apologies. The work of the additional tanks had not been started, nor had anything been done to the tachometer or heater, but he was sure I would understand. The problem was the French. A month earlier, his shop had installed similar tanks in the cabin of the Beech craft D-15. The work had still not been certified by the civil aviation authorities who were all French Canadians, so the aircraft was administratively grounded. Each time the airworthiness inspector came by, he found some minor correction to be made. The work was done, but on each subsequent visit he found something else that needed doing. The D-15 had become a hangar queen, her pilot angry, and the maintenance people fed up with the inspector. The chief mechanic said that the installation was more than adequate to meet the government specifications, and the manager heatedly accused the authorities of trying to drive the British out of business by bureaucratic fiat.

I was somewhat disgruntled when I walked out to look at my aircraft. The wet field sparkled with afternoon sun and clouds of steam rose from the puddled blacktop. The Baron, pale blue and white with streaks of faded gold along the fuselage, was at the end of the parking mat, sitting as it had through the long winter and spring. She looked worn and disheveled: mud-splattered, caked with dirt, with one tire flat so she tilted to port like a crippled goose. I walked around her slowly, letting my eyes rove over her surfaces, checking her antennas, peering into her air scoops and vents, trying blindly to reach her innards and awaken her heart. Here and there, specs of corrosion peeked through chipped paint, and I unhappily discovered that a rudder control cable had sheared in a storm, leaving the rudder to flap in the wind and tear the thin aluminum skin of her tail. I climbed up the low wing and slipped into the cabin. Everything inside was dry and shipshape. The battery was dead, so I could not check the electrical systems or radios, but I knew I would have ample time for that during the next few days.

It was now late in the afternoon, and no more could be done, so I returned to the terminal, rented a car, and went off for dinner.

Before going to bed I threw another *I Ching*. I was clearly still involved in the "Waiting" of two months earlier, but I needed some information about the current situation. The book replied with two hexagrams and two changing lines. The names of the hexagrams, "Deliverance" and "Pushing Upward", told me pretty much what I wanted to hear; the second was particularly welcome because I had received it in connection with a successful flight I had made previously. "Deliverance" says obstacles have been removed and difficulties are being resolved. Hastening would bring good fortune, and I could expect success. But the first changing line was not as fortunate as the rest of the hexagram. It says:

> If a man carries a burden on his back
> And nonetheless rides in a carriage,
> He thereby encourages robbers to draw near.
> Perseverance leads to humiliation.

The second line told me cryptically what to do in order to secure help, but nonetheless left me baffled:

> Deliver yourself from your great toe.
> Then the companion comes,
> And him you can trust.

Taken as a whole, the reading was something I could rest easily with.

When I arrived at the hangar on Thursday morning, the Baron had already been pulled inside. A radioman was in the cockpit testing the electronic gear. The side panels on the nacelles were open and the engines warm. The chief mechanic came over and told me they had checked out well. This was good news, but I was primarily worried about the sheared control cable and the possibility of structural damage to the fuselage. We spent a half hour going over the airframe, but beyond the ripped skin of the tail and the broken cable linkage, nothing was damaged.

Another mechanic came out of the stockroom. He had been unable to find a replacement tachometer or spare parts for the heater system. The chief said that they could be ordered from the States, but I knew that would take too long. I did not really need a second tachometer since the two propellers could be synchronized and the rpm of both read from the operative instrument. The cabin heater, however, was crucial. I planned to fly between 15,000 and 20,000 feet to take advantage of the prevailing westerlies (strong winds that can be counted on for a tail wind when going east). On the ground, the arctic summer can be unpleasantly cool, and the temperature drops quickly with altitude, so the heater was required for my operational efficiency as well as comfort. I needed it fixed, and asked if something could be jury-rigged. The mechanic said he would try.

The extra fuel tanks were another matter. They were not a stock item, nor had they been ordered from the States, so they would have to be specially built. The installation would take five days and would still have to be certified by the intractable inspector. The D-15 sat next to us in the hangar, disassembled for inspection. The plumbing was simple, and the tanks solidly constructed. The inspector was due again by that afternoon. If he approved the work, the plane could be buttoned up and gotten out by Friday morning, and the full attention of the shop could turn to the Baron. I told the chief to go ahead as soon as possible and asked if they would consider working on Sunday. He sounded dubious, but said he might be able to get a metal smith to work after noon.

My plans were beginning to disintegrate. In the office, I talked over the situation with the service manager. Assuming no delays and the unlikely compliance of the inspector, the airplane could be ready and certified by the following Thursday. Thursday evening I could fly east, and spend Friday preflighting the oceanic routes. If the weather permitted, I could leave Newfoundland Saturday morning and be in London by Sunday night. This gave me two days to spare: two days awaiting favorable weather, or two free days in London doing whatever Londoners do.

In the meantime, I had other matters to attend to in Montreal. The Baron was a foreign registry aircraft, so I needed permission to fly over Canada on the first leg of my journey. This was a formality but, since much of the distance was wilderness, I also required certain items of survival equipment. I already had an inflatable raft, food, and personal survival gear, but I needed more. The service manager told me of a Scotsman who supplied such things, and, as it turned out, the man materialized while we were discussing him for he was also doing business with the pilot of the D-15. I explained my problem. He said I required a water ration, aircraft signal flares, and an emergency radio, all of which he could supply.

The Scotsman was interested in seeing the Baron, so we walked out to the aircraft talking aviation. During the Second World War, he had been a pilot in the Royal Canadian Air Force and flown supplies to beleaguered Britain. He told of the route they had taken through Greenland and Iceland, then down to Scotland and northern England where they off-loaded beyond the range of the German bombers. Their only enemies had been equipment failure and the long arctic winter, when icy winds swept out of the north. The then unnamed jet stream dipped low, driving them off course, and unreported frontal systems buffeted them along the way. Radar was a thing of the future, and the low-frequency radio beacons that marked their destinations were as fickle as the nearest thunderstorm whose static masked their signals. I had known similar problems in the navy, for the large propeller transports of both the forties and fifties operated under much the same constraints. Both faced obstacles that subsequent jet aircraft avoided with their long range, high speed, and ability to operate at altitudes well above the storms through which their predecessors flew.

We discussed the D-15, and my chances of getting out in five days. He mentioned the proverbial snowball in hell and figured three weeks at best, maybe two if I spoke good French. He asked the Baron's range, and whether I had considered going via Greenland. I told him I had, and had discounted the possibility. The aircraft could make the crossing without the additional fuel tanks, but the only air fields I knew about were the SAC bases at Thule and Sondrestrom; both were much further north than I wanted to go, and lay within the vast area of magnetic unreliability, where a special gyroscopic compass system was required. He agreed that Thule was out of the question and Sondrestrom marginal, but said when he had flown the route he had refueled at an airstrip called Bluie West One, fifty miles up a fjord near the southern tip of the island. As far as he knew, the field was still in operation. He thought it had been renamed after the war and suggested I check with the Danish consulate since Greenland belonged to the Danes.

After lunch, I went to the Civil Aviation Branch of the Transport Ministry to fill out several forms and see what I could learn about Greenland, particularly Bluie West One. My question drew a blank, so when I finished the paperwork and the office hopping it entailed, I drove downtown to the Danish consulate. Here too, I was stymied. No one in the office had ever been to Greenland, nor had they any information about it. The best they could do was have me fill out the immigration forms that would be required should I go there, and give me the phone number of their military attaché in Ottawa. I called the embassy and caught the attaché as he was leaving for the day. He too, had never heard of Bluie West One, but thought it a colorful name for a place in Greenland. He suspected it might refer to an airstrip near the town of Groennedal, a hundred miles northwest of Cape Farewell. In any case, he said, I would have to get permission from Copenhagen to enter Greenland, so he gave me the telex address of their air ministry and told me what information they required.

Friday dawned with thunderstorms and the mugginess of another frontal system. I went first to the hangar. The D-15 sat as she had, wide open for inspection and still three or four hours from completion. Make it six days, I thought, and scratch one in London. The metal smith was working on the Baron. The heater malfunction was in the thermostatic control unit. If the unit were by-passed, I would still have manual control of the heater. The system had a fuse if it overheated, so I told him to go ahead.

The chief mechanic came over from the metal shop where he had been working on the sheared control linkage. He did not have a replacement in stock, so he was modifying a Cessna linkage to fit. While he was installing it, the Scotsman arrived with flares, an emergency radio from the Neolithic days of aviation, and olive-drab cans of army surplus distilled water. The radio was a ponderous affair energized by hand-cranking a generator. Its antenna was a long wire attached to a deflated weather balloon. A cylinder of helium was included to inflate the balloon, which was then whisked off with the wind, antenna in tow. The radio only transmitted, and then on but a single frequency: the international distress call at 500 kilocycles. There was no provision to talk; it merely squawked SOS. I remembered the units as rugged and reliable, but no more pretentious than their balloons and virtually impossible to operate in a one-man raft.

The supplier also brought his *Aircraft Captain's Book,* circa 1942, which was the RCAF's en route manual for the transatlantic connection during the war. There were three pages on Bluie West One, and three dim photographs. One showed a very adequate airstrip running up a steep slope toward a glacier. Another depicted the approach to the airport from beyond a rocky promontory at the entrance to the sub fjord wherein it lay, and the third was of three islands in the mouth of the major fjord. They were important for identifying the seaward approach, but in the old photograph I could distinguish little more than jagged ridges against a leaden sky. I asked about the weather in the fjord. He said it could be turbulent, but that there were usually two or three hundred feet between the water and the bottoms of the clouds. Fog was frequent, but generally predictable; icing was bad.

He had given me enough to go on. If the strip were still operational it would be adequate for my needs. The rest depended on the Danes. I drafted a telex message to Copenhagen giving the relevant information on the aircraft and flight and requesting permission to refuel at Groennedal; adding in parenthesis, Bluie West One. Since Danish time was five hours ahead of Montreal, the Danes were already closing up for the weekend by the time I got the cablegram off, and I could not expect a reply before Monday.

I spent the afternoon in the pilot's flight planning room and weather briefing facility at Montreal International Airport. I had a variety of charts and approach plates for the areas through which I would be flying, but many of them were outdated and required corrections. I also needed to know the current en route and terminal radio frequencies and the procedures for oceanic position reporting. I had hoped to find someone familiar with the problems I faced but was disappointed, for the only information they had concerned the jet routes from Montreal direct to Europe. I was also disappointed with the weatherman. Since Montreal is a major weather station, I had expected a thorough briefing on the seasonal weather patterns along my route, but here too, data was sparse and expertise lacking.

By five o'clock I was back at the hangar. The service manager said they could begin work on the tanks in the morning, but I told him to hold off until Monday. Sometime during the afternoon, I had decided to cut loose from my big toe and to bet on the Scotsman.

I left the hangar and drove downtown on the freeway that winds along the St. Lawrence River. I had checked out of my motel after breakfast in hopes of a more pleasant weekend adventure, so I went to the cobblestoned heart of old Montreal and took a room in an inconveniently authentic hotel. The building faced a long, grassy mall that was a conspicuous center of activity. It ran downhill toward the river, but the view was blocked by a huge grain elevator that dominated the waterfront and the city above. The mall was flanked by narrow roadways and these in turn by restaurants, open-air cafes, and more hotels while galleries, curio shops, and music halls lined the side streets. Most of it was authentic, but here and there the natural charm of the old architecture was giving way to studied, picturesque replacements, or simply disappearing with history; boarded up, condemned, and awaiting demolition beneath the feet of new Montreal whose concrete high rises, like giants, stalked the city.

Dinner and a good wine mellowed my head. When I finished, night but not darkness had come to the mall, so I wandered the warm evening enjoying the smells and noises of French America. Gypsies, students, and tourists relaxed on the grass, and flower stalls bedecked in summer colors, did a brisk business. Music was everywhere. I reflected that a country unravaged by a divisive war enjoys itself easily, but here too, there were flyspecks in paradise. Several times I asked for something in English, only to get a curt reply in French. When I explained that I was from California, however, the feeling of piqued hostility changed abruptly, and I quickly learned to preface my questions with my origins.

I was early to bed and out again with the dawn. Street cleaners and produce trucks rumbled down empty avenues, dripping water behind, but the city still slept, and only the semiconscious hum of its electromechanical vitals pulsed through the pavement. Later, when morning strollers appeared, replacing my aloneness with anonymity, I dropped into Montreal's subway system and discovered how well civic things may be done. Each station was different, each was designed by a different national artist, and the trains themselves were quiet and efficient. I went to the Isle of Man where Expo, the dazzling remains of the 1967 World's Fair, was still happening. Unfortunately, it was closed for repairs, so I went instead to an amusement park on the other end of the island and spent the afternoon caught up in a child's delight of roller coasters and carnival, frozen custard and merriment.

Sunday dawned much as Saturday, but another front was moving into the area and the air was heavy with impending storms. I had breakfast in a sidewalk café, and afterward, settled over coffee with the Sunday paper. It contained mostly Canadian news, but the headlines and front page were dominated by events in the States. On Saturday afternoon, President Nixon had announced a $750 million wheat deal with the Soviet Union. It was his campaign carrot to the Russians and corporate grain speculators, timed to make the Sunday editions. It also undercut the hullabaloo building for the Democratic National Convention, scheduled to begin on Wednesday. George McGovern, the front-runner for the presidential nomination, had landed in Miami, but hardly on the front page in Montreal. The Nixon Supreme Court, overturning a lower court's ruling, had denied him 153 California delegates, so the nomination, which had seemed to be his, was still up for grabs.

Henry Kissinger was in Paris again, awaiting the North Vietnamese with one of Nixon's sticks. The war was not to be turned off yet, and the stage was being set for intensified violence, a proven vote getter over the past generation. In South Vietnam, the Vietnamese army was claiming massive enemy assaults in Quang Tri Province. They also claimed major victories. The American command headquarters in Saigon knew nothing of either, and called them figments in the political consciousness of General Thieu. Nonetheless, the Secretary of Defense used the information to brand McGovern's proposals on military spending a white flag surrender budget.

A rash of skyjackings had occurred during the previous month, and the President finally grasped the nettle by editing the Bill of Rights. He authorized searches of aircraft passengers and their baggage and began setting up an expensive bureaucracy for official control of personal movement. In Los Angeles, the chief of police declared that skyjackers should be publicly hanged at airports, while across town, jury selection for the Pentagon Papers Conspiracy Trial was to begin on the following morning.

On another front, Bobby Fischer was maintaining the strategic offensive in his brilliant match with the World Chess Federation. The Federation was in a shambles before his onslaught, and Boris Spassky, his Russian opponent, was beginning to show signs of testiness. The first game of the match had been scheduled for a week earlier, but was still being delayed, although it was now set for Tuesday. After months of combat, Fischer was still hassling his opposition, quibbling over every point, refusing to yield a single pawn. The lighting was incorrect; the audience sitting too close; the television cameras distracting; the playing board itself the wrong size. It was good copy, superb gamesmanship, and a brilliant exercise in Machiavellian chess, but the battle was being joined in Reykjavik, the capital of Iceland (one of my en route stops) and a city, said the newspaper, without an available hotel room.

Another piece of relevant information concerned an eclipse of the sun that was due to occur the following afternoon over eastern Canada. It would be 85 percent full at Montreal and total over the Maritime Provinces. I had known about the event for some time and was disappointed that I would be unable to view it from Newfoundland. I had seen partial eclipses before, but never the truly awesome spectacle of the moon completely covering the sun, whose fiery corona blazes out of the blackened sky and dances with space in the eternal drama of fusion.

I finished my second cup of coffee and left the newspaper on the table. The weather front was moving in from the southwest, so I spent the day driving north into the Laurentian highlands through low, forested mountain country dotted with glacial lakes. The city had provided an enjoyable interlude, but I felt happier leaving it behind. The driving lulled me into a quiet space, and my brain contorted the landscape with memories of wilderness, of the wild terrain toward which I was heading, and of the all-consuming, restless ocean over which I would pass.

Monday began with thunderstorms, drizzle, and wind, but clear skies were forecast for early afternoon. At the hangar, much to my surprise, the telex reply from Copenhagen was waiting. There was a classic terseness to the message:

RE YOUR TELEX CONCERNING
LANDING IN GREENLAND STOP THERE
IS NO AIRFIELD IN GROENNEDAL STOP
YOU ARE WELCOME TO LAND IN
NARSSARSSUAQ STOP

I was delighted but as yet had no charts for Greenland, nor any idea where Narssarssuaq was. I presumed it was Bluie West One, but that was not much help. With something of a start, I realized that I was all set to go. Until then, I had been expecting a few more days of delay, and I was completely unprepared for a speedy response from a government bureaucracy.

I asked the hangar crew to pull the Baron out to the mat and fuel her while I went to the terminal to file a flight plan and, incidentally, to find out where Narssarssuaq was. Flight planning had the information I needed. The airstrip was in southern Greenland, fifty or sixty miles from the coast in a cul-de-sac near the end of a labyrinthian fjord. There was a low-frequency radio beacon on an island near the entrance to the fjord, and another at the airfield, so navigation did not look difficult. It was clear from the North Atlantic charts that the best departure point in Canada was from Goose Airdrome at Goose Bay, Labrador, rather than any field in Newfoundland.

I had never been to Labrador. The routes I flew in the navy lay more to the south, and Goose was a distant alternate that I had never needed. Nevertheless, I figured I knew it pretty well because all of those northern airfields had a sameness about them. They had been built simultaneously for the wartime airlift and were stamped out of the same mold. Here would be the enlisted men's mess hall, over there the barracks; here the commissary, there the chapel; identical administration buildings would be clustered about an identical tower; and all would be built of clapboard, painted the same white and green, the same shades of gray. They also offered the same excellent services: well-lit runways, radar approaches, comprehensive weather forecasting, thorough flight planning, good food, movies every night, and drab, overheated rooms insulated against the long winter cold.

I was excited by the idea of going to Labrador and Greenland, and equally excited to be leaving so quickly, for it meant I could now view the total eclipse of the sun from the air. On the ground, I was at the mercy of the weather, but in the sky I was free, the clouds my dancing partners. I worked out a flight plan to Goose Bay. Airtime was a little less than four hours. The eclipse would be full at 4:42 pm, so if I left Montreal at one o'clock, I would be near Goose Bay when it occurred. I could circle at altitude off the airway until it passed and then land giddy with its energy.

The frontal system buffeting Montreal was predicted to pass by noon. It was moving to the east, which meant I would have to penetrate it shortly after takeoff. I needed clear weather during the initial portion of the flight so I could test the aircraft systems and return visually to Montreal if there were any serious problems. I also wanted a little time to settle into the aircraft before flying it irretrievably into the clouds.

I filed a flight plan for a one o'clock takeoff and returned to the hangar. The Baron was fueled and ready. The sky had been clearing for over an hour, and the visibility at the field was excellent. I said good-bye to everyone and took my luggage out to the aircraft, but while checking its external readiness for light, I noticed gasoline leaking around the filler cap of the port main tank. A peculiarity of the Baron's fuel system was a twelve gallon auxiliary tank mounted in the engine nacelle above the main tank in the wing. It gravity-fed the main, and until it was emptied, put pressure against the main tank filler cap. The leak indicated a shot gasket, so I went back to the hangar hoping for a replacement, but a half-hour search of the stockroom uncovered nothing. It was getting close to one o'clock, so I decided to leave with the leak, knowing it would stop as soon as the auxiliary tank was drained and pretty sure I could replace the gasket at Goose Bay.

I returned to the aircraft and strapped in. The engines started easily and sounded good, but when I was ready to taxi, I was unable to raise the tower on the radio. I tried both radios at several frequencies without success, and I finally had to shut down the engines and go back to the radio shack. A radioman removed the units from the plane and bench tested them in the shop. They checked out perfectly. He replaced them in the Baron, and again they worked. I took it that another gremlin was getting paid for his long winter's work.

By now it was after four o'clock. The eclipse had started, but was still indiscernible in the blaze of the sun. A squall line had appeared in the west, blowing rapidly toward the field. It looked ominous, and I hurried to get out before it, but the first drops of rain struck while

I was still preflighting the plane. I jumped into the cockpit and sat undecided as the fury of the storm hit. Sheets of water beat down on the canopy and a leak above the compass dripped on the console. My spirits flagged, but I knew the squall would pass quickly, and its raucous interlude gave me a moment to think. I would miss the eclipse no matter what I did, but it still made sense to leave, for I would gain a day by flying at night. As I mused on this, however, the sky began to darken. Above the clouds, the moon slid in front of the sun, and my rain-restricted vision shriveled further. The nearby hangar faded to a dull, looming shadow, and the lights that came on in its offices seemed dim and distant. I held out for a moment, but then the eclipse took hold of my psyche, and I grew restless and unaccountably anxious. Only a damn fool, I thought, would take off into a storm at night under the auspices of a solar eclipse. So I changed my mind, jogged back to the hangar, suitcase in hand, and said hello to everyone again.

That night, inadvertently, I got drunk. Tuesday dawned more brightly than I, but aspirin and breakfast solved my problem, and I was soon more excited than on the previous day. The flight would take me 700 miles to the northeast, over water and unbroken forest. I savored the prospect of watching the wilderness unroll below, disappear behind. My memories of it were all good and had recently been augmented by the stories of a brother, Yellow Bear, who had spent four years with the Eskimos of Hudson Bay and told me of strange happenings at the top of the world.

I went first to the terminal and filed for a nine-thirty departure. I lost an hour of clock time in transit, so would arrive at Goose around two. The frontal system of the day before was a hundred miles to the east of Montreal, between Quebec and Riviere du Loup. Beyond the front it was clear, but Goose was forecasting heavy thunderstorm activity for the afternoon.

The Baron looked beautiful in the morning sun. The engines started smoothly and the radios worked. The tires had become square from sitting, so I bounced rather than rolled down the taxiway to the run-up area. I tested the communications and navigational radios, then ran up the engines and checked the derivative systems. The last action on the checklist was to align the directional gyro with the magnetic compass. Since the gyroscope precesses, it must be frequently reset, and it is usually aligned just before takeoff with the airplane pointed down the runway. Runways are numbered according to their magnetic headings, so a rough check on the accuracy of the magnetic compass is made at the same time. I had aligned the gyro in the run-up area, expecting to check it on the runway, but in the excitement of the moment, I forgot to do so and took off into a warm blue sky presuming it correct.

I turned onto course, climbing to my assigned altitude of 7,000 feet. The fuel seepage was like skywriting. The siphoned gasoline was vaporized by the air rushing over the wing, and extended as a rainbowed contrail to the tail. When I was steady on my heading, I switched the valves of the fuel system so that both engines were being fed from the left wing, thereby draining the auxiliary tank more quickly.

I was talking to Montreal Departure Control Radar on the radio. A controller was monitoring my takeoff and climb. To him my dazzling world of aircraft and sky was only a silent electronic spark blinking across a radarscope in a darkened room somewhere below. Shortly after I steadied on course, he reported that I was drifting rapidly to the north. I made a correction of ten degrees to the south. He said it was not enough. Another ten degrees did not stop it nor ten more, but I held my own at forty. The compass was a disaster, but not unusable once I knew the magnitude of its error. The gyro was working properly, and could be aligned by radio bearings, so I got a final compass check from Montreal and continued on my way.

The engines ran well, but the automatic synchronization system between the propellers was inoperative. Occasionally I had to resync them manually. When the propellers ran at different speeds, an annoying beat frequency appeared in the drone of the engines: at its worst, it was an intolerable WA-WA-WA that drowned out the radios. With these, I needed all the help I could get. Departure Control sounded fuzzy on both of the VFHs and faded too quickly as Montreal dropped behind. Both sets of navigational radios were also exasperating. My automatic direction-finding equipment was not homing well, and the OMNIs appeared limited in range. Generally, the two systems are complementary. Both provide directional information for flying to and from radio beacons, but the ADFs operate at a lower frequency. Although they have a longer range, they are susceptible to atmospheric interference, while the OMNIs are static free but limited in range to the line of sight.

The autopilot was erratic. It held the wings level, but drifted in heading and would not hold altitude. It was a luxury, though, and not having it was no hardship. I could trim the plane well enough to fly, with but occasional finger-pressure corrections. Generally, there was not much else to do anyway. The deicers on the wings, tail, and propellers were in good order. The cabin heater worked fine. I switched it on and got hit with a blast of warm air. At 7,000 feet, I did not need it, nor did I need oxygen, but the tank was full, so I checked the system. It worked as advertised and smelled clean.

As I moved from one set of testing procedures to another, I could feel my old abilities reasserting themselves. I was aware of dominating the space that was my world as a pilot. It was a world that moved with the aircraft, both within and without the cockpit. The controls at my fingertips and the instruments before me formed a sensual matrix embodying my ability to deal with concerns beyond the confines of the plane. My eyes roved ahead, scanning the distance-near future out of which could come danger, and from which my track materialized. I passed Quebec in the clear. Far ahead, I could see the backside of Monday's frontal system lying like a gray-white wall across my course. Soon the view was overwhelmed by cloud, and scud built around the aircraft. I penetrated the storm like a projectile, and instantly found myself in a turbulent twilight of muted translucence, a mother-of-pearl sky splattering the windshield with streams of water.

My awareness refocused itself in the cockpit and I concentrated on the task of scanning the instruments. A dispassionate aspect of my mind formed their information into a picture of how I, and the aircraft, moved through the air: a conceptual picture hardly inferior to seeing itself. Gyroscopic devices sensed aircraft motion and displayed it against the background of their spatial stability. One provided an artificial horizon; another, a needle indicating the aircraft's turning rate; a third, its compass heading. I could tell if I was level or climbing, turning or upside-down. Barometric instruments translated air pressure to altitude and noted changes in it, while the antennas that sprouted outside the aircraft channeled their inputs to various electronic receivers, providing me with the purposeful ears I needed. The Baron was like a bat homing to the call of its kindred. But as the aircraft drove deeper into the cloud, I became uneasily aware that my bat had a touch of deafness.

Over Riviere du Loup, I had trouble getting my position report through to the ground. All of the radios were malfunctioning. Sometimes one, sometimes another would go out, and I was constantly fiddling with them. Five minutes after I passed the beacon, the flight service station called with what sounded like an amended clearance. I was not sure because the radio faded badly, but it seemed that I was being rerouted around some heavy storms in the area. I was on an airway defined by a series of radio beacons and was being turned to intercept an alternate airway. The beacons involved had French names that sounded nothing like how they read, and the fellow on the other end of the radio, though speaking in English, was thinking in French Canadian. He made the translation with difficulty, but he sounded urgent, and this made me uptight. He wanted me to turn and after a bit of hassling, I got the name of the next beacon to fly to. But while I was fumbling with the airways chart, trying to retune the radio and copy down the rest of the amended clearance, I dropped my pencil. I fumbled and found it behind my foot, but missed what was being said, and then noticed I had already turned twenty degrees past my new heading. I steadied up and brought the nose back to the correct course. The heading needle on the OMNI centered, but then, almost immediately, a red flag saying OFF dropped across the face of the instrument, indicating it had gone dead. I switched to the backup, but it, too, was out. I managed to copy the rest of the clearance while fine-tuning the ADF in an attempt to get a fix on a nearby low-frequency beacon, but the ADF needle hunted uselessly from storm cell to lightning flash.

I took several deep breaths and told myself that everything was under control. Altitude and heading were steady, and the engines purred. I maintained the course I had when the radios went out and busied myself calculating how soon I would be over the beacon, when suddenly I remembered the horrendous compass correction. For a moment I freaked out and could not remember if it was to the right or left. I cleared my head, got it straight, and responded with the aircraft. I turned smoothly and added a further correction to compensate for my error. As I rolled out on the new heading, however, it dawned on me the first course had indeed been correct, and correction unnecessary, because I had been flying a radio bearing, not a magnetic heading, when the OMNI quit.

Suddenly, I was furious, incredibly pissed off at myself. Rage grabbed at my brain but I intercepted it at birth and throttled it. A familiar, authoritarian voice that had long dominated such situations for me, crackled electrically from the depths of my subconscious: "Cool it!" My body began automatically to comply but much to my amazement, and so hard on the heels of the commanding voice as to be almost an echo of it, came an even more insistent feeling inviting me to let go. The psychic battle was instantly joined. I was wrenched between the two commands, and the feelings won. With a bellow of frustration, I screamed my rage. I yelled myself hoarse, railing at my stupidities, and roaring like a bosun. At the same time, the dispassionate aspect of my mind kept track of what I was doing and flew the aircraft back to the correct course.

The yelling unblocked me, and I soon settled down to heavy breathing. While I contemplated my next moves, the OMNI, with no more warning than the disappearance of its red OFF flag, came back on and pointed ahead to the beacon at Sept-Iles. A few moments later, the Baron broke from the clouds into a bright afternoon. Below me, the mouth of the St. Lawrence River opened wide to its gulf, while somewhere else, on a twilit edge of consciousness, I knew that my energies were responding to events much as the first changing line of the *I Ching* had predicted four days earlier.

Beyond Sept-Iles, my course turned north, and the St. Lawrence dropped behind. The afternoon was cool. Scattered, puffy cumulus clouds lay along the route and gave me an occasional marshmallow to pop through. Below, the forests of eastern Canada stretched away in every direction, unmarked by roads, railroad tracks, or power lines. Clear lakes, reflecting the sky, shone blue and sparkled like scales on a celestial trout. Within the Baron, a host of similar reflections glittered. The instrument dials were glass-faced, the radios shiny Bakelite, and the various control handles brightly painted, color-coded by function. Like a bird, the Baron moved through the air, its nose hunting slightly to the left, then to the right, changing the shadow patterns in the cockpit, flashing the sun from one piece of glass to another, dazzling the windshield, and throwing rainbows into odd corners. The patterns varied with the vibrations of the engines, which caused the reflections to jiggle, the shadows to dance, and the bony structure of my body to buzz with their insistence. They were as much a part of the aircraft as its wings or tail, and an aspect of flying that I often enjoyed, but as the settlement of Lake Eon passed beneath, I busied myself with my position report while the vibrations, sounds and shifting lights faded into the background.

As I approached Goose Bay, afternoon thunderstorms were building inland from the coast. From sixty miles away, I could see several large ones in the vicinity of my destination. I contacted Goose on the VHF and requested a ground-controlled radar approach for landing. This required me to follow instructions from a ground controller who monitored my progress on carefully calibrated radarscopes. When I told him that my compass system was unreliable, he switched to a no-gyro approach. I was not given compass headings to fly but merely told when to start and stop each turn.

The controller took me around one storm cell and through the edge of another. A third was over the field. I entered it 2 miles out and exited through its bottom at 300 feet. The runway was dead ahead, partially in the clear, and just beyond it was another black storm. The runway was four or five times longer than I needed, so I landed far down it, and still had a lengthy roll out. It gave me time for my first look at Goose. Parallel to the runway, about a hundred yards back across a concrete matting, was a long row of huge hangars and, beyond this, the whole administrative and social complex. Everything was closed. There were no aircraft to be seen, and tall weeds grew from the cracks in the concrete.

The tower directed me to the far end of the field where a cluster of smaller buildings and hangars fronted a subsidiary runway. The second storm hit as I taxied in. Two other aircraft were parked in front of an old terminal building. No taximan appeared, so I pulled up next to them, cut the engines, and waited for the rain to slacken. It was coming down in such sweeping torrents that I closed the cowl flaps and oil-cooler doors to seal the hot engines. From the pilot's seat, I could just see the corner of the port oil-cooler door. It did not move when I threw the switch. I tried several times, then added it to the list of malfunctioning items I had discovered on the flight.

When the storm let up, I sprinted to the terminal. There were several people inside, one of whom was the customs and immigration inspector who stamped my papers. He confirmed the fears triggered by the closed hangars and overgrown mats: the world of a dozen years earlier had disappeared. The large hangars, the administration buildings, the shops and barracks, all stood vacant and abandoned, technological casualties of the jet age. A city had folded up, and its people had returned to the heartlands. The world they had serviced was gone, and gone too, were the things I had expected from that world. Few, save an occasional itinerant like myself, flew the North Atlantic from here. The traffic at Goose was mostly local except for the evening shuttle flights that plied the provincial periphery of Canada, bringing supplies, hunting parties, and fishermen from Montreal. There was no longer an oceanic briefing facility here, no transient maintenance service, and no one, as far as the inspector knew, conversant with the problems that lay east of Canada.

He mentioned two places on the field that might provide some help: the Goose Flying Club and a seaplane outfit based in a hangar adjacent to the terminal. When the storm passed, I went to the hangar and spoke to the maintenance boss. I told him I needed a compass and assistance with the oil cooler door and radios. He was forthright. He had no parts for the Baron and could not spare a compass. His men had their own work to do during the day, but if they wanted to work for me on their own time, that was their business. I scouted around and found a mechanic and radioman, who were willing to help that evening.

It was only mid-afternoon, so I walked over to the flying club hoping they might have an extra compass. The building was locked and empty, but a member happened by while I knocked. They had no compasses but I did find out that the shuttle flight did not leave Montreal until 6:00 pm, so there was a possibility I could have one sent out that evening. I called the hangar in Montreal and told the service manager my problems. He had no spare parts for the oil cooler, but did have a compass and would try to send it on the shuttle. I hoped it would be enough and that the difficulty with the oil cooler would be no more than a loose connection. I felt certain my radio problems were in the antennas, and the radioman had assured me that he could get all the antenna wire I needed.

I checked at the terminal for a place to spend the night. There was a hotel in town but it was filled with fishermen, so I was allowed to have a room in a reactivated barracks on the field. It was only a few hundred yards from the terminal. I got my luggage from the plane and walked over. The old building had an air of utter familiarity about it. The room had a creaky metal bedstead with a sagging mattress, and down the hall was the communal toilet and shower. I cleaned up and went to the snack bar in a small building halfway back to the terminal. The mechanic who had agreed to help me was having dinner. I joined him, and we discussed my troubles.

Later we walked out to the Baron. The radioman was checking the antennas. As hoped, my problems lay in the wiring and connections. Some of these had corroded over the winter, and the ADF antenna was the victim of a bad repair. I unlocked the cabin for the radioman while the mechanic and I looked to the oil cooler. The motor and drive gear were located in a single factory-sealed unit; if this was malfunctioning, the flight would have to be aborted until a replacement unit came from the States. For fifteen minutes, we fiddled with it and tightened all the connections, but nothing we did helped. The radioman joined us under the wing. He said he could do the necessary work on the antennas during his lunch break Wednesday. He asked about the oil cooler. The mechanic said it looked hopeless and, while explaining what was wrong, tapped the offending unit with his wrench. It started right up. Airplanes are like that. We lubricated the screw assembly and ran the door through its cycle several times. It worked fine.

The mechanic had an aligning instrument from his shop, so I was able to partially correct the errors in the compass. We first taxied to the far end of the mat, moving the aircraft away from the buildings whose electrical equipment and mass of metal distorted the earth's magnetic field. I lined the Baron up at each thirty degrees of heading and corrected the compass by adjusting two compensating screws. Each turn of the screw altered the adjustment for all headings, so the process was one of balancing extremes. We managed to get it within tolerances for some directions, but on others it remained as much as fifteen degrees off—technically unusable and not good enough for a transatlantic flight.

We quit for the night and had a beer at the snack bar. The shuttle arrived around eleven. I checked at the terminal, but the compass had not arrived, so I was faced with an extra day at Goose. I wandered back to the barracks in the clear, palpable night. The crescent moon had set and the northern constellations sparkled just out of reach. I looked for the aurora borealis, but the summer sky, though alive, was undisturbed by dancing fires. In my room, I broke out the *I Ching*. Having reached my oceanic departure point, I was anxious to have the book tell of the crossing itself. As I sat pondering a quilt of questions, however, I dozed off and woke later with a start. The day had been long enough, so I put the book aside until morning and sagged with the mattress.

The Labrador morning was cool and the air was fresh after Montreal's city breath. I got up around eight, showered, and did the *I Ching*. The hexagrams were "Peace" changing to "Pushing Upward". Surprisingly, I had already received both of them in regard to the trip, so I took it to mean that everything was on time and progressing nicely. The changing line foretells success and indicates that something additional would be thrown in:

> When ribbon grass is pulled up, the sod comes with it.
> Each according to his kind.
> Undertakings bring good fortune.

Breakfast at the snack bar was powdered eggs and weak coffee. Afterward, I walked to the seaplane hangar where a crew was waiting for a ride to the ramp. I tagged along and spent the morning watching their operations from the wharf where their twin Otters were moored. Around noon, an old Ford with a cardboard TAXI sign in the window arrived full of fishermen bound for a lake two hundred miles away. I asked the driver about a ride into town after they took off. He was happy to wait, so we stayed until an Otter splashed off across the choppy bay and lumbered into the air.

The settlement at Goose Bay was a creature of sea and air. On the way into town we passed a dirt road heading south where a sign said it was 173 miles to the next paved road, and the driver added that it was washed out a hundred miles down. The town was a few blocks of clapboard houses on hard, dry ground. Built for snow, it looked naked in the summer. It was civilization one step back from nature: a few stores, a cafe, a hotel, a church, and a cemetery. I ate lunch and settled my stomach with a smoke on a bluff overlooking the town and bay. Later, I checked the inventory at the Hudson Bay Company store, bought some postcards, and filled them out over a beer at the hotel. The bar was a large room, empty except for a table of laughing Indians who were drinking beer from pitchers. They reminded me of Yellow

Bear, and his stories of the Arctic, so I wrote him my last postcard and pushed back my chair, remembering what he told me.

The Eskimos of upper Hudson Bay live north of Canada's great northern forests. According to Yellow Bear, some had never seen a tree, for permafrost nips life a few inches below the surface of the soil, leaving only stunted tundra. The Eskimos ate only meat, for few edibles grew, and then but briefly. They hunted seal, polar bear, caribou, and, during the summer thaw, narwhale that surfaced among the fissures in the ice. During the long winter night, the men carved fetishes from the sacred black-green stone of the Belcher Islands, which lay far out in Hudson Bay. They said that the bay itself was the site of a great meteorite impact, and they too, had legends of the Deluge. Yellow Bear said they were a happy, austere people, everywhere being civilized to tin houses, tobacco, and alcohol. I drank my beer. The Indians across the room ordered more pitchers.

I stopped in the hotel lobby to mail all the postcards except Yellow Bear's. He had no address, so I stuck his in my pocket for personal delivery later and caught the taxi back to the airfield. Dinner was dry hamburgers and reconstituted milk. The radio in the snack bar was on, the local station broadcasting news from the ticker tape. In Miami, Senators Humphrey and Muskie had dropped out of the presidential race, but neither offered to support McGovern. In Reykjavik, Bobby Fischer, on schedule, was late to his opening, but his favorite chair had arrived the previous afternoon, so presumably, he was comfortable. Not so the defense lawyers in the Pentagon Papers Trial who complained, futilely, that fewer than ten of one hundred prospective jurors were under forty, none were under thirty, and only two were black. It appeared that the cards were being stacked on every front, and even at Goose, the movie for the evening was disappointing, so I spent my time reading. Twice I walked to the terminal to meet the shuttle flight, but it was delayed in Montreal and did not reach Goose until well after midnight.

The compass arrived in the night, hand delivered by the pilot of the shuttle, no charge—a courtesy of aviation. After breakfast, I took it to the aircraft and spent an hour building a level platform for it above the magneto switches. It still needed aligning, but that had to wait until evening when the mechanic was free.

I spent the afternoon preflighting the navigational legs from Goose to Narssarssuaq and Narssarssuaq to Reykjavik. Narssarssuaq was centrally located, each leg was about 700 miles long. From Goose I would fly steadily to the northeast. My first reporting position over the Atlantic was at a hypothetical point called Capelin, 200 miles from Goose and 50 miles east of the Labrador coast. It was a mandatory checkpoint for all traffic arriving or departing from the continent. I would get my last radio fix there, and my last voice contact until Greenland.

An ocean-station vessel manned by the French was located midway between Labrador and Greenland. It provided navigational and meteorological information to passing aircraft, but my course would take me more than a hundred miles north of the ship, and I doubted if I would be able to contact it. My destination was marked by two low-frequency radio beacons. The first was off the coast on the island of Simiutaq, and the second at the airfield 50 miles up the fjord.

After Narssarssuaq, I would fly more directly east. My track would cross the ice cap of southern Greenland and the cold, empty Denmark Straits. With an early start, I could be in Narssarssuaq for lunch and in Reykjavik for dinner. The twenty-four hour weather forecast for the northern Atlantic looked fairly good. A weak frontal system was off the coast of Labrador and moving slowly toward Greenland. Hopefully, I would penetrate it en route and get to Narssarssuaq first. For two days, Narssarssuaq had reported fog in the morning and clear by noon. The pattern was not expected to change until the front hit. Beyond Narssarssuaq, I would be in the clear until close to Iceland.

I remembered Iceland for its peculiarly bad weather. One of the stable features of the North Atlantic is a meteorological phenomenon known as the Icelandic Low, a circling storm system that rarely dissipates. Like a pirate ship, it roves loose in mid-ocean and continuously storms the battered coasts. At the moment it was relatively weak, standing stationary over Reykjavik.

At five o'clock, I went to the seaplane hangar. The mechanic was busy elsewhere, so the radioman and I did the compass alignment. The new instrument was not much better than the old. We worked on both for some time and finally got them to tolerances; the old compass being more accurate to the north and east, the new compass, to the south.

The engines were working well and the radios checked out loud and clear, so the Baron was ready for the crossing. I made arrangements at the terminal to have the aircraft gassed at seven o'clock in the morning. After dinner, I took in the movie. It was a war film. The first ten minutes were of a camouflaged British bomber flying low through the Alps at night. It made it to wherever it was going, which I took as a good omen. The rest was about a bored Richard Burton taking on the German army. It must have worked, for I slept well afterward.

I awoke at five-thirty. It was cold and getting light. The terminal duty officer took me by truck from the barracks to the flight-planning building on the other side of the field. It was the only one in the old complex still operational, and the drive through the deserted streets was strange, almost eerie. Two men were on duty. One gave me the latest weather information from the teletype. The front from the day before was somewhere in mid-ocean, reported to be a mild system nothing more than a couple of hundred miles of wet, sloppy cloud, promising ice. Narssarssuaq was reporting fog, but forecasting clear. The Icelandic Low was still over Reykjavik, but beginning to move. I requested a flight altitude of 15,000 feet, hoping for a strong tail wind, but the winds were out of the northwest. On the first leg, I would have a hefty crosswind from the left, and none behind; and on the second leg, where the winds were somewhat diminished, only ten knots of help.

I completed my navigational problem and used the information it produced to fill out my flight clearance request with estimates for each reporting point. Since I would not be getting any fixes over the ocean, accuracy was crucial. I took my time. The duty officer signed my clearance, wished me a cheery flight, and reminded me that no search and rescue operations would be launched in the event that I did not reach Narssarssuaq.

The gasoline truck was finishing with the aircraft as I arrived. I walked around the perimeter, checking externals. The Baron was all set to go, but somehow I was not. The morning was still nippy, and I was headed north, so I dug into my suitcase for a set of long johns and put them on in the terminal.

The roar of the first engine startled the morning stillness, and echoes bounced from the buildings. I taxied to the nearest end of the active runway and did the run-up. The engines and radios checked out well; the compasses read ten degrees apart. I called for takeoff and requested a left turn to my departure heading. I was taking off to the west, so a right turn through north to course would have been more expedient, but the judgment on the hexagram "Pushing Upward" includes the phrase: "Departure toward the south brings good fortune," and I saw no reason to fly in the face of the oracle.

The Baron accelerated smoothly and lifted from the continent with a touch of grace. On the turn, I steadied momentarily to the south, called it my departure heading, and continued around to the northeast. The southern end of Goose Bay was clear, but the coastal areas were blanketed by a morning overcast. The cloud topped at 10,000 feet and extended well out to sea. By the time I leveled at 15,000, put on my oxygen mask, and reduced power for long-range cruise, it had closed in below. The Baron flew into a bichromatic world: above, a deep blue sky sustaining the sun; below, rolling white cloud tops. I settled into the aircraft and responded to its way of flying. It spoke to my body, to my balancing ears, to my eyes, and I felt the air rushing over its surfaces as if its skin were my own. Like a bird, I delighted in the sensual sky and loved the mysterious into which I flew, where air brushed space and magnetic contortions emblazoned the embrace.

My mind darted about its airy playland, and my body fell into the habit patterns of guiding the aircraft without me. Flying, like driving, is an assemblage of learned routines best handled subconsciously; simultaneously rather than in sequence. A routine is learned when it can be performed automatically, but a lingering ego likes to pretend that it is in control and substitutes a series of memories about how to do something for the uninhibited doing of it. It demands to know what is going on before it acts, and so, merely by thinking at the wrong time, misses the moment. For me, flying had become a nearly instinctual response to recurring, complex patterns. Thinking obscured the pattern, so I aborted thoughts and trusted the vast dynamism of the universe that constructed my every environment.

I got cross-bearings over the coast and reported the position to Goose radio. Seventeen minutes later, I reported Capelin. It was still undercast, but far ahead I could see the cloud mass breaking up. My first glimpse of the turbulent north Atlantic was a surprise and snapped me out of my reverie. Through a small, mist-filled break in the cloud, I caught sight, not of the ocean, but of coastline. In a moment it was obscured again, but I was sitting bolt upright with thoughts tumbling through my head. Was there a freak wind from the south, or were both compasses off, and was I tracking north along the coast rather than out to sea? I waited until the undercast broke again. The coastline reappeared through the mist, but it was not the real thing, merely the outer edge of the coastal ice shelf. The whole shelf now spread out behind me, cracking in the intricate design of a summer thaw. Below was an intensely dark blue sea, dotted like the constellations of heaven with a thousand great icebergs migrating to their watery destinies in the south.

The last of the undercast disappeared behind and a vast blue world of ice, sea, and sky engulfed me. I tried the autopilot again without success and fiddled with my oxygen mask. I wished I had my old navy mask, a sophisticated piece of equipment, custom fitted to my face. This one was a little plastic cup that pinched onto the nose and leaked oxygen around my sunglasses.

The heater was operating well. I had already used it three or four times and, as the temperature dropped, I cycled it again. A few minutes later the temperature was still dropping, and I had not detected the faint odor that accompanied the heated air. I flipped the switch a couple of times, and hoped. The temperature continued to drop. The sun warmed me in my Plexiglas greenhouse, but unpressurized aircraft always leak, and eddies of cold air built around my legs. I fumbled with the suitcase on the seat behind me and pulled out a ski sweater, wool socks, a knotted hat, and gloves. I put the socks on first, then struggled into the sweater. There was still a draft on my knees, so I broke out a blanket and draped it over my legs. The temperature settled to comfortably crisp, but the sun was beneficent, and the whole magnificent sky mine to enjoy as though from a mountaintop.

The Baron spun itself out into a world ruled by ice kings and thunderheads. Time became the substance of dreams, a kaleidoscope of vapors. From inside, I watched streams of consciousness cascade through my passivity. Gradually, I quieted my mind and fell into a meditation that fronted as a door for another state of consciousness. The perfection of the moment dissolved my thinking about it, and something else shone through, lightening all about.

This meditation is one practiced regularly by Zen Buddhists and others. It is an excellent way to ravish time while guiding a vehicle through space. The Zen people trace its origin to an Indian monk named Bodhidharma who traveled to China with a thousand years of Buddhist teachings hung uselessly, like beads, around his neck. The Chinese themselves had been stirring their classics with the Buddhist sutras for several hundred years, so there was little need for Bodhidharma to explain anything. For the most part, he just sat in a cave, eyes open, facing the wall. A lot of people came by, full of questions, but left with them unanswered, quoting quandaries to essence with essence. Every now and then, someone would sit down next to him. Occasionally, somebody stayed, so his insight spread—slowly perhaps, but inexorably—and now, a millennium and a half later, in a lonely, lovely sky above a sea of ice, the essence of Bodhidharma lurked like a dragon, for piloting the Baron was like facing a wall, nothing was seen, nothing missed.

I returned to myself flying the aircraft, staring at the unmoving instruments, with my ears tuned to the droning engines and the radio that would not speak for hours. I reached out to the power controls and adjusted them slightly, smoothing the sound. I was conscious of my breathing, aware of its calmness. I knew I was hovering on the edge of a magical space and remembered the first time I had drifted beyond the confines of an airplane, to roam free in the sky: It was spring, 1959, between midnight and dawn. I was copiloting a flight from Cuba to Puerto Rico. The pilot was aft, asleep in a bunk, and the flight engineer, beside me in the cockpit, dozed away a long day of delays. Four engines rumbled methodically. All through the cockpit, the instrument lights were turned low, so only a dim red haze marked the face of each, while beyond the aircraft, the stars and a slice of waning moon shone more brightly. Sixty miles north of the Dominican highlands we entered an area of tropical thunderstorms. Immense cumulonimbus, many miles in diameter, built upward to 50,000 feet—three times the altitude of the aircraft. I moved us as a snake through the clear air among them, skirting the edge of a towering rampart, or sliding beneath the blown turban of an anvilled top. The storms were alive with electricity. Lightning sliced through their vitals, branching into a hundred jagged streaks that turned the churning cloud incandescent with fire. From every quarter the storms flashed noiselessly, and the sky twinkled like a garden hung with paper lanterns. Suddenly, I was pulled from the aircraft and joined to the dancing energies beyond it. I seemed to hover above the night itself, for great storm cells stood tall beneath me, and the airplane, like a tiny silver gnat at my knee, flew between them.

My mind blinked like a strobe. I was simultaneously in the cockpit and far above it. The magic of the night sucked me into itself, and my heart pumped a fountain of luminescence. Lightning spewed from my nowhere-existing, all-seeing eyes, and reached like slow-growing roots for the grounding sea below. The sky was tangibly alive, wise with wordless intelligence and traces of forgotten sentience. Everywhere I looked, it was beyond and below me, above and within me, for I was the field of night resplendent with jewels.

Back in the aircraft, I felt the field contract and reverse itself, until I was again contained in my body looking out at what I had just been. Strange energies pulsed from my stomach and surged through my chest, until I was awash with sensuous joys, throbbing with astonishments. I was panting slightly. My forehead was damp. My eyes stared at my hands that in the shadows, seemed to be staring back . . .

For all of its beauties, the experience had left me with a classic conundrum. I had seen another aspect of mind and called it mine but the eye that I was, was not the I that I saw. At the time, I knew little about relativity, or how the ever-recurring patterns of life expressed their richness through my physical mechanisms. I wanted to learn. I knew how to see, to hear, almost to touch, how to mold these into awareness and infuse the bundle with socially acceptable ideas. But I did not know what made the processes of consciousness happen; which factors were vital, which trivial. Like an infant learning to see, I was again in the undifferentiated field in the upside-down world of the eye's concave, intruding side.

When I finally tried LSD, I was transported into the same areas of consciousness and then beyond those, to realms of unsurpassable beauty and presence. Later, having more practice with both psychedelics and mind disciplines, I reached a point where unusual states of consciousness did not interfere much with the normal acting out of my life. They came and went with hardly a ripple to mark their passage. Finding myself in an airplane for an hour or two, it was not difficult to disappear from my own consciousness for a while and, on returning, to be aware of a fading visionary sequence or the tail end of some subtle-seeming thought already drifted away. During these times of ego absence, everything that needed to be done was done, simply and correctly.

So it was as the Baron and I rumbled toward Greenland. For short periods, I was released from the world's reality without losing it. Lulled to a tranquil place within by the steady, reliable hum of the engines, and confronted by the immensity of nothing wherein I was moved, my thoughts quieted. Images drifted across the sensitized plate of memory until a visionary sequence arose that, like an epic movie, caught my interest and swept me along unaware of my capture.

It began gently enough: a sequence of thoughts, a flowing stream of consciousness, mildly directed, and effectively focused on the Indians I had seen at Goose Bay. The thought pictures were of forest dwellers and northern mysteries, of tundra and ice floes, of shamans, and strange rites. I enjoyed them for a few minutes, until they evaporated as an engine fluctuation caught my attention.

Moments later, a glint of sunlight from the propeller hub pulled my eyes beyond the aircraft. The wing seemed surreal against its backdrop of empty blue, as cold and insubstantial as the ice castles three miles below. Suddenly, I lapsed with wonder at the splendor of the sky, and, without warning or confusion, became aware of my seeing into a different order of perceptual reality. I gazed from out a great spherical space, one that was neither inside nor outside myself, but composed of both dimensions. My eyes were droplets balanced between them, almost irrelevant appendages, and yet, flowing from their confrontation with this strange space, images arose into cognition. I saw the earth from a distant vantage as a liquid crystal saturated with life, spinning endlessly through heaven. She seemed a goddess, alive as a glove of glowing colors, forever spinning time on the loom of eternity. As a living jewel, her waters sparkled in the sun, shining like wind-polished mirrors to reflect her lord. Continents, seas, and warm islands, rich and bountiful, appeared and rolled away. I wafted beyond them, caught in my own fancy, remembering the stories that Yellow Bear had told of Hudson Bay. North America hove into sight and I looked for the watery eye of the continent whose tears were great lakes, but to no avail, for a shield of haze covered the Laurentian Highlands, and the north lay swaddled to my view.

Yellow Bear, and tales told in a tipi, filled me with images of the Eskimos, and their belief that a gigantic meteorite had struck the earth here. The thought was enough to guide the vision, and new images crackled into consciousness. I grew cold, and the space from where I watched became rigid as though compressed. I felt an alien presence penetrate, and a projectile of galactic iron appeared, fast falling into the gravitational vortex of the earth below. It screamed to a momentary incandescence, then plunged flaming through the mantle of air, deep into the sleeping planet. The meteorite exploded. A mountain vaporized, and the bedrock granite below was squeezed to plasma that spurted up like burning oil. My head shook with the impact, snapping me back to myself in the cockpit, wrapped in the constant drone of engine staring out through patches of Plexiglas windshield. I steadied in the no-man's-land between reality and vision. All was well with my surroundings, so I stifled an arising ego before it locked its thought-teeth into experience, and re-entered visionary space. The earth wobbled from the blow it had received. Smoke and steam exploded from wounded America. Cracks sliced out from the impact crater, and torrents of ocean rushed in. Waters poured into the blazing cauldron and were thrown off as tumultuous clouds of superheated steam writing with primal violence. Earth stuff and molten meteorite blasted out with the steam, and black tornadoes raged around the hole. As the planet reeled, stupendous storms drove toward the ocean, stampeding like buffalo through the same sunny sky where now I, and my fragile machine, sped eastward. I again came to with a start. The day was bright, calm, seemingly together. I looked back over the tail of the aircraft, but no clouds were in hot pursuit. Ahead, all was as it should have been: clear blue above and below, fading to haze in their distant joining. I settled myself for a third excursion to the catastrophic space and drifted back into my exotic theater, now no more than the thinnest veil away. Time was compressed. The steam storms cooled to a vast, surging cloud, endlessly generated from behind, rushing toward Greenland. The cloud jammed against the coastal mountains, pushed upward, and froze. As it poured inland, it was squeezed by the icy fingers of the western peaks. The sky pumped freezing water to the ground, and days and nights were indistinguishable in an unending fall of gray slush from the utter blackness of the enveloping fury. Slowly, the distant wound was cooled by the ocean's persistence, and the gaping sore was soothed with sediments. The great cloud weakened. Tentatively, the sun reached for the surface of its third borne, now reeling and haloed in snow. The mountain peaks of Greenland glistened in a sea of white, and whatever might have been below them before was obliterated beneath a hundred trillion tons of ice, to sleep the millennia through as a continent of snows.

A call on the radio brought me back to the aircraft. Far to the south a transatlantic jet was talking to the ocean-station vessel. I had the ship's frequency tuned in on the VHF, but I could only hear the pilot of the jet talking because the ship was over the horizon, while his aircraft flew somewhere above it. My ADF needle was homing on the ship's beacon, so I calculated a time-distance measurement and came up with an approximate range of 120 miles. This put me close to my navigational preflight estimate, so I knew I was on schedule, and that my compasses were satisfactory. I tried to raise the ship on the VHF, but without success, so I transmitted my position in the blind and flew onward, to the northeast, searching for the frontal system that lay somewhere ahead.

I stamped my feet a few times to keep up my circulation. The cabin was not uncomfortable in the sun, but my legs were as cold as though I were sitting at a December football game. I needed to jump around, wave my arms. Instead, I tensed and relaxed muscle groups, then slipped off the oxygen mask and sang an old navy fight song. Fight songs are designed to warm the body by boiling the blood, so I tried to sing very loud and forcefully, but my voice was creaky and high-pitched due to the thin air at altitude. I sounded like an angry Donald Duck. Amused, I persisted, and after a few stanzas started laughing at myself, then giggling. I felt lightheaded, completely happy, almost intoxicated, and knew, much to my own good humor that I was suffering from hypoxia. I let out two good yells in order to clear my throat, then slipped the mask over my nose, and pulled at the ice cold oxygen.

When my breathing steadied again, I removed the mask and fell into the rhythmic strains of a simple chant. I was still lightheaded, so I alternated the mantra and the oxygen, spacing out behind both, watching them structure each other. Below, on the intense blue surface of the ocean, I watched infinite patterns form and dissolve as swells and white-capped wind waves reverberated from nodes of ice. Upon this pattern, my mind superimposed fanciful pictures from its own infinite contents, while the ocean spirit decoded my DNA and with an invisible finger crafted its designs on my forehead.

I continued searching for the front ahead. The longer it delayed, the more cause for worry, for then it could only be socked in over Greenland. One ADF was tuned to Simiutac; the other to Narssarssuaq. Neither was homing, but the Simiutac needle wandered back and forth, not quite locking in, but sniffing at something. At the fiftieth meridian, I altered course a few degrees in accord with my preflight estimates. I also reduced engine power because I had already burned several hundred pounds of fuel, lightening the aircraft to a point where I could get maximum cruise efficiency at a lower horsepower. In the distance, I began to make out the front as a slight rising in the haze level.

The haze grew whiter and took shape as a cloud mass extending out of sight to the north and south. It rose to an altitude considerably above my own. As I approached, the air lost clarity and warmth, and an undercast filled out, patching the ocean with gray-white blotches. The ADF needle steadied on Simiutac. I switched to Narssarssuaq; it also homed. The two stations were directly in line, indicating I was coming in on course. I estimated my position as 50 miles from the coast and called Narssarssuaq radio. There was no reply. The undercast was building quickly, so I decided to let down to 9,000 feet, hoping to be below the cloud at that level.

I reduced power and retrimmed the aircraft for letdown. The cloud came up to meet me, and, at 12,000, I punched into its slanting face. Gray streams of vapor enveloped the aircraft. Beads of water formed on the windshield and turned to light rime ice. I took off my sunglasses and switched over to instrument flying, holding a steady rate of descent, 300 feet per minute, wings level, Simiutac dead ahead. At 9,000, I was still in the clouds, so I continued down. The coastal mountains topped at 6,000 feet, but Simiutac came well before them. If I was not out of the clouds by the beacon, I would turn 180 degrees and complete the descent away from the mountains.

The descent was like falling into the earth. As each thousand feet unwound from the altimeter, the clouds seemed to thicken. The gray world darkened, became murky. At 6,000 feet, I was still blanketed, so I continued down below the tops of the unseen mountains. My speed had picked up to 250 miles per hour, so I eased back on the power and brought the nose up slightly. I passed through 5,000 feet. A few moments later, a gray shape from out the murkiness below caught my eye. I looked out, straining to see the surface through the now shredding clouds, and had a momentary glimpse of a mountainous iceberg afloat on a turbid sea. The cloud changed to mist. Other icebergs swam into view and trailed away. Then, out of the eerie grayness ahead, I saw land: a low island, a black patch of lifeless lava awash in a leaden sea.

The aircraft dropped from the last of the dangling mists. Ahead, spectacularly, stood Greenland, in all her silent nakedness, seeming more like the portals of Pluto than of Earth. Jagged walls of coal-black rock, glistening with a sheen of frozen water, everywhere confronted me; foreboding mountains rose from gray ocean below to gray ocean above, and swirling clouds spilled in static slow motion from the crags. Seaward from the coast lay hundreds of islands like a scattering of rough-hewn slate in a midnight pool, and erratic winds taunted the churning sea.

As the Baron sped across the largest island, the ADF needle swung around and pointed to the tail. Simiutac was behind me. I switched the selector to Narssarssuaq, expecting an instant fix. Instead, the needle swept aimlessly around the dial and refused to home anywhere. The plane had dropped below the mountain barrier that separated me from my destination, and I was flying in a radio shadow, somewhere beyond which lay Narssarssuaq in its tiny cul-de-sac. Directly ahead, where the coastal mountains plummeted to the sea, not one but three fjords opened invitingly.

The ADF needle scanned the three entrances with equal dignity. I switched back to Simiutac, hoping for an accurate tail bearing to use as a reciprocal course, but this, too, played me false and pointed down the rocky promontory that separated the two northern fjords. I tried to conjure up the old photograph from the Scotsman's *Captain's Book*, but nothing in my memory could match the three islands in the faded picture with the three hundred that spread around me. I checked the fuel gauges; there was enough gas to explore for a while if I had to.

I chose the central fjord and pulled back on the throttles. The plane slid away from 4,500 feet and dropped through the throat of the fjord like an oyster being swallowed. The winds were strong, the sea choppy with whitecaps. Giant icebergs, exquisitely sculpted and vividly colored with intense blues and greens, moved in awesome procession toward the open sea. The *Captain's Book* had told of glaciers in Narssarssuaq's fjord, so I was somewhat reassured, but I also had the feeling that every fjord would have its icy fingers and its parade of ancient crystal.

I leveled the aircraft at 1,500 feet and flew further into the rock-ribbed canyon. Ahead to the left stood four black islands, larger than the rest. They might have been the entrance identifiers, but I was not sure. As the second of them passed, I spotted a small fishing trawler in the lee of an iceberg. Beyond it were others. With a nerve tingle that altered nothing, my aloneness dissolved into a flurry of social excitement, much as a mirrored face before the acid-opened eye undergoes a thousand intricate changes without the slightest movement of the flesh.

The air in the fjord was turbulent. The Baron bounced like a car in a cornfield and I rattled to one side, then the other. At times an air pocket would drop the plane out from under me, or ram me from below. There was a strong head wind, and my progress was considerably slowed. The wind surprised me; the frontal system was driving in from the west, but within the fjord the air rushed out to the sea in tunnels beneath the storm. The head wind gave me time to marvel at the stark face nature here assumed, and I enjoyed her rough breath, even as it jostled me with sky dragons at home on their field of abundant desolation.

I circled a large and particularly beautiful iceberg and sang it a song with words plucked from the air. Further on, the fjord split into two forks. My heading took me more to the right, so I turned slightly, and followed that fork. Across the open water was a narrow, sloping coast of black lava on which I dimly made out a cluster of gray buildings. As I drew abeam, the area resolved into a small town hugging its barren strip of land with humanity's indomitableness. I was jubilant and kept looking about for the airstrip that I was sure would be near the town. But nowhere did I see it, and my ADF needle still circled monotonously. I called Narssarssuaq again, but no reply was forthcoming. I had not expected any settlement other than what might be associated with the airfield, and now, having found Greenlanders on both land and sea, I was still lost. I checked my clock. I had passed Simiutac sixteen minutes earlier. Allowing for the adverse wind and the circling I had done, I estimated that I was no more than thirty miles up the fjord. My destination still lay ahead.

Beyond the town the mountains again plunged abruptly to the sea. The air turbulence lessened, and for a few minutes I flew in the calm. Several trawlers were busy on the open water. Miles ahead I could see the end of the fjord as a wall of rock extending into the clouds. A narrow arm branched off to the right. I could not see far up it, but emerging icebergs announced the presence of a glacier. A towering cliff of black rock blocked the view to the left; I hoped it was the dome pictured in the *Captain's Book*. Again I called Narssarssuaq; again there was no response, and a sense of forlornness swept through me. I could almost feel the radio waves as they bounded and rebounded across the constricting canyon of rock and ice, but I was the only one listening.

As I passed the black promontory, the ADF needle moved suddenly to the left and steadied. It pointed into a narrow bay on whose far side I saw the last few hundred feet of an airstrip extending past the base of another vertical wall of rock. I turned into the cul-de-sac. A thousand yards beyond the airstrip, it ended in an amphitheater of mountain and ice. The runway was as steeply sloped as the Scotsman had said. Its far end was at the top of a low volcanic ridge cut by the runoff from the glacier beyond. The glacier itself looked like a vaguely startled snow lion frozen in a pounce on the airstrip.

The water in the bay was calm, but the air turbulence in the entranceway was more severe than any I had yet encountered. I called Narssarssuaq radio, my voice ratchety from the jarring of the aircraft. The response cracked like a bullwhip in the cockpit. I had forgotten to turn down the volume on the receiver, and it nearly blew my head off. I quickly muted it and requested landing instructions. A pleasant voice in precisely articulated English welcomed me to Greenland and cleared me to land, uphill, with a tail wind, into the black face of the mountain smiling with teeth of ice.

I dropped down to a thousand feet and flew into suddenly calm air as though I had slipped into a bubble without breaking its membrane. I circled the lagoon, checking the field and its environs. To the north, a canyon of ice climbed out through the mountains. Looking up it, I saw one patch of blue sky, but it was rapidly filling in with the forward edge of the front I had hoped to pass in mid-ocean. I brought the Baron around a green iceberg to a short final approach. After landing, I taxied another half mile uphill along the runway and then off across a large, deserted concrete parking mat to the base of a very high tower, also concrete, which was in complete disrepair. Its upper windows were broken, and its lower ones boarded up, but the fuel sumps near its foot were still being used, so I was directed to park there.

A jeep drove up as I entered the area, and a man in a thick sweater signaled me to a place by the pump. I shut down the engines and climbed out. The air was cool and crisp, but warmer than it had been at altitude, and except for its freshness had no smell. While the plane was being gassed, I pondered whether to reset the circuit breaker on the cabin heater. I was not familiar with the system. I knew a controlling part was missing, and I had no way of assessing possible overheat damage, so, reluctantly, I decided to leave it inoperative. The flight from Labrador, while decidedly cool, had not been uncomfortable. It was not yet noon. The July sun would be up until well after I reached Reykjavik, and I did not expect the afternoon to be any colder than the morning.

After refueling, we drove halfway down the field to an old wooden building, only partially occupied, in which Narssarssuaq radio, tower, flight planning, and weather bureau existed in the ruddy form of one young man busily engaged in building a large flying model of a 1930's biplane. He was a fine blend of information and informality. The weather forecast for Iceland was unchanged; the winds en route somewhat diminished. I worked out the navigational estimates for the leg to Reykjavik, and he helped me fill out the overseas flight plan, talking all the while of Greenland, fishing, and model airplanes. He said lunch could be had at noon in the dining room of the Arctic Hotel, a bright blue building several hundred yards away.

I walked over. The hotel was distinguished by its color from a covey of other, unused buildings squatting at the base of a lava ridge. So far I had seen two people, little vegetation, and no birds. Other than the hotel and the icebergs on the lagoon, Narssarssuaq was an etching in grays and blacks. The hotel was a square, shingled, barracks-type building, so when I stepped through the front doors, I was startled by what confronted me. Within was a large, windowless, well-appointed room, so dim that it took my eyes a few moments to adjust. When they did, I realized I was standing in the entrance of a beautiful dining room. On the floor was a thick, richly hued carpet, the walls were polished wood, the furniture Danish modern. The tables were covered with fine linen, and in the middle of each was a bouquet of fresh flowers. There was not another person about.

In the center of the room was a rectangular arrangement of tables laden with an exquisite array of food. Ten platters of cheese vied with as many of fish and exotic meats in a superb culinary mandala. Chilled bowls of shrimp, clams, and oysters abutted steaming casseroles and plates of hors d'oeuvres. All manner of vegetable dishes, sauces, and fondues were bathed in warm water on large steam plates, and four or five cauldrons of soup burbled on their warmers. A dozen salads were complemented by as many dressings, and at the end of the tables were large bowls of fruit and a tray of luscious Danish pastries, each more mouth-watering than the last.

I strolled slowly around the tables, arms behind my back, sniffing like a maître d', then made for a door on the far side of the room, thinking it might be the kitchen. Instead, it was a small, pleasant bar with windows along the far wall opening out to bleak Narssarssuaq. A bartender was washing glasses. Behind him, excellent whiskeys and liquors lined a richly grained, hardwood wall. He said hello, and something else in Danish. I apologized for being unable to understand him, so he switched without hesitation to slightly accented English, asking if I had brought the small plane in. I said yes and inquired about the wonderful display of food in the other room. He said it was lunch and would be served in fifteen minutes, so I ordered a cold Tuborg and carried it outside to wait. I was very spaced out and just stood looking at what humans had done with the end of a fjord halfway to Iceland.

I tried to remember what I knew of Greenland, this place with the strangely contradictory name, and almost drew a blank. I knew that several hundred years ago it had been much greener, but then the Arctic had reasserted its prerogatives and driven most of the settlers back. Long ago, the ancient Greeks had spoken of a temperate land lying to the north of Europe. They called it Hyperborea, said it was a birthplace of gods, and invested it with mysterious legends. On the other side of the world, the old Taoists of China spoke similarly of a northern paradise that existed in the times of their prehistoric Immortals. I recalled my morning's vision of a gigantic meteorite, of the storms it had unleashed toward here, and wondered what human remnants might lay beneath the snows of this forbidding place.

Shortly after noon, I went back to the dining room. It was like stepping into San Francisco. The hall was warmly lighted and filled with people. They had arrived early that morning from Copenhagen, and had been given rooms until shuttle boats would arrive to take them to Narsagg, the settlement I had passed on the way in, and Julianhaab, a larger town in the next fjord to the south. The smorgasbord was for them, but a cosmic gift for me, so I enjoyed a magnificent feast and went back out to the reality of cold winds and lowering clouds with a feeling of instant nostalgia.

I activated my new flight clearance at the radio building and asked some questions about the surrounding terrain. The blue patch of sky was long gone; the front, two hours further to the east. The clouds were swirling through the mountains, but I hoped to fly visually out through the canyon to the north. If that was socked in, I would have to go back down the fjord, climb to altitude over the ocean, and recross Narssarssuaq at 15,000 feet; a delay of at least 45 minutes. The radio operator told me that if I could make it up the first canyon, there was maneuvering room beyond, for Greenland's 11,000-foot peaks were some distance away and I would be at 15,000 before I need worry about them. I hoped to be past the front by then and in the clear for a good look at Greenland's amazing ice cap. The thought of cold did not even occur to me.

The jeep took me to the service building where I paid my gas bill, and then on to the Baron. It looked very small and alone beneath the solitary tower and misting crags. The takeoff was in the opposite direction from which I had landed, downhill, and into a freshening breeze. I wheeled over the lagoon and turned to the north. The canyon I had chosen rose to a pass through which I could see, but the mountains on both sides reached into the overcast. The aircraft entered the canyon, climbing easily in the cold air. The space constricted. Rock walls rose steeply on either side, very close, and utterly black except where sheets of ice exuded from their cracked sides. I glided up between them and sailed through the pass. The walls fell away sharply as though I had been shot from a cannon, and ahead a ghostly perspective opened out.

Beyond the first mountains lay an inland valley of ice and snow, a great white bowl streaked with lava ridges and pockmarked with volcanic domes. All around it, black mountains burst through the snows and vanished into the solid turgidity of cloud. Glaciers were born between them and swam in frozen time to the sea, while storms of blown snow obscured their surfaces. A thin haze of rain streaking the windshield blurred the scene further and gave it the washed quality of a somber finger painting.

The bottom of the overcast was disheveled, torn and blown into pendulous, hanging shapes and gray-white swirling mists. I had hoped to find a clear area to the east after breaking through the pass but of all directions, that now seemed most ominous, for there the encircling walls were closer and hung darkly above my right wing. I turned more to the north. Across the valley, another steeply sloped pass climbed into the cloud between two massive mountains. I eased the plane into a steep, slow climb and noted the heading through the pass on the gyrocompass. To the west, spirals of ice clung to volcanic cliffs, and sailed like a mote past a thousand-foot icicle perpetually dripping to a valley of eternal snows. It dropped behind, and I was swallowed by cloud.

At 11,000 feet, I eased back to normal climb and turned toward the east. The cloud was heavy and rough, the cabin cold. The ADF needle had stopped homing on Narssarssuaq as soon as I lost sight of the field and without a navigational beacon I could only estimate a heading that would bring me back to course. I leveled at 15,000, still in the frontal system. There was moderate turbulence, and the aircraft was picking up ice, but neither condition was serious. I turned on the propeller deicers and cycled the airfoil boots, watching to make sure the rubber tubing along the leading edge of the wings inflated with air pressure. It expanded, cracking away the rime ice that had formed. I turned the system off, and the boots deflated to the contour of the wing. Every minute or so, the system had to be manually actuated. If left on, the rime would build up around the outer perimeter of the inflated boot until it could no longer be broken off because the boot would then swell and contract within an enclosure of hardened ice. Cycling the system was another routine to fit into the sequence of flying on instruments; another sense to attend to while my eyes scanned the array of dials whose compounded information mimicked their sense of sight.

I wrapped a wool scarf around my neck and struggled into my bulky sheepskin coat, hoping that five layers of clothes would be enough until I cleared the front. I expected to be out of it quickly, but the frigid minutes dragged by, and the cloud, if anything, darkened. I tuned my

ADFs to the radio beacons on the eastern coast; Prince Christian to the south, and Big Gun, the SAC departure point from Sondrestrom, far to the north. Occasionally, I heard a garbled, weak identification signal clothed in static, but the needle wandered in a full circle around the dial and homed on nothing.

I was disappointed at being unable to see more of Greenland and its vast plateau of ice, but as I flew further over it, the temperature in the cabin dropped and I wondered at my earlier eagerness. I was like a fly caught in a gigantic refrigerator. I wrapped my legs and feet tighter in the blanket, pulled the wool hat down over my ears, and rubbed my gloved hands on my thighs to warm both. Fidgeting was all I could do. The leaking oxygen was icy on the bridge of my nose and irritated my eyes, so I fiddled constantly with the mask, trying to pinch off the leak. I called Narssarssuaq radio hoping to get cleared to a lower altitude after breaking from the clouds, but static was my only reply. Ahead lay three cold hours of Arctic sky to Iceland.

Forty miles east of Greenland, I broke from the front and was able to look back under the overcast at the bulwark of mountains containing their sea of ice. The air over the ocean was hardly less cold than that of the ice cap. Even the sun was cool, for it was behind me now, and there was little warmth in its low, oblique rays. The sky was pale blue, the air tranquil. The ADFs were homing on the coastal beacons behind, so I laid out a cross fix on my chart. I was still north of course, but compensating at an angle that would put me back on it eighty miles ahead. There was no hurry, nor were there any other airplanes to worry about.

The afternoon was not as clear as the morning. The storm behind and the one still lurking ahead was joined by a thin film of haze that blurred in the distance and reflected the sun's heat back into space. Busyness would have been a blessing, but I had nothing to do but monitor instruments and stamp my feet. In the clouds I had concentrated on flying the aircraft precisely and thus distracted myself from the cold. Now it became a presence whose guest I was. It nibbled at my composure and sent me scurrying through the warehouse of memory for something to offset it. I recalled a meditation utilized by Himalayan ascetics who, when confronted with cold, defeated it with energy marshaled by the breath and transformed into body heat. If one believed the stories about them, my present chilly circumstances might have seemed like an afternoon at the beach, for their practice was to sit naked in a winter blizzard, melting snow from their bodies. The thought held no warmth, but hoping the practice might, I took off my oxygen mask and fell into the varied cadences of the exercise. The technique was not to leave the body, ignore it, or overpower it, but rather to go into it completely, to energize the spine, then confront the pain of cold at the nerve endings where it began, and where it could be alleviated by concentrated energy. I focused my breath as best I could and persisted until the cold diminished. A heightened sense of warmth and renewed vitality tingled through my numbness, but then I wondered if it might be a touch of hypoxia and clamped the mask back on my nose.

Leaking oxygen, moistened with breath, froze on my sunglasses, and rendered them useless. I took them off, and kept a gloved hand over the mask to save my eyes from the same fate. After a few minutes, I took the mask off again, and tried to chant, but my energy was low, and the effort too much to sustain for long. Time passed, and reveries arose. I altered heading at each predetermined position and somewhere past mid-ocean reduced power to compensate for burned fuel.

Wrapped like King Tut, I watched minutes float by like dandelion seeds. Occasionally, I chortled at my predicament. For a while, I quoted Shakespeare to the empty sky and felt like Prospero trapped on his island, waiting for a storm to come by. Far off on the horizon, very indistinctly, I made out the beginnings of the Icelandic Low. My radios were all tuned to stations in Iceland. The ADFs picked up Reykjavik; the needle steadied. One hundred and twenty-five miles from the coast, the OMNI locked on the powerful station at Keflavik. Shortly thereafter, and much to my surprise, I heard Iceland Approach Control calling me. I replied, requesting an immediate descent, and then worked out my estimate for the domestic entry point.

The Icelandic Low had taken shape and towered before the aircraft like a billowing curtain across the theater of sky. Approach Control called with a descent to 5,000 feet, and, with a frozen sigh of relief, I started down into the maw of the storm. Cloud canyons opened out before me. I turned slightly to enter one of these rather than the surrounding cumulus, and, for a few extravagant moments, enjoyed the pure pleasure of gliding through a fantasy world of cloud castles and cathedrals of crystal. With reduced power, the Baron sailed down a gorge of cascading cloud, while off the nose the westward retreating sun cast the aircraft as its dashing shadow. I rounded a cloud corner in a slip to the right, dropping in altitude all the while. Ahead the canyon boxed, and I dove toward the mock solidity of sky-sculpted wall. Upon this screen of cloud, a nimbus (a perfectly circular ring of colors) appeared, surrounding the shadow of the aircraft. I pulled back on the power and dropped the nose. Both shadow and nimbus grew larger, until, at the last moment, directly before me, a life-sized silhouette of the aircraft was encircled with pulsating bands of color. I smashed into it, dead center, doing 300 miles per hour.

The sunlit afternoon disappeared, replaced by another murky, gray world. I turned on the navigational lights and looked out at the wings. The lights diffused through the swirling cloud and gave the wingtips auras of red and green. I cycled the deicers. The icing was heavier than over Greenland, but I knew it would melt and blow away once I dropped below the freezing level. As the plane buffeted through the storm, I was aware of each flick on any of 20 dials, but the strain of the day was telling, and I suddenly felt very tired. Approach Control called with the weather at Reykjavik. It was bad: a variable ceiling between 500 and 1,000 feet with 30 knots of gusty wind and frequent rain squalls that dropped the visibility to zero. Such weather was not unusual for Iceland. In the navy, I had found it a challenge that exercised my nervous system and concentrated my mind. Now I was too tired and busy to reflect on the years that had intervened. I recycled the deicing boots and watched the hoary rime break away from each wing. Approach Control reported radar contact with the Baron and began tracking. From this point onward, the disincarnated voice of the radio guided my actions. I reported level at 5,000 feet and said that I was still picking up ice. The controller told me to continue the descent to 3,500 feet. I complied automatically. A minute or two later, the aircraft dropped below the icing level. The accumulations on the windshield began to break away from the glass in chunks. The slipstream hurled them aft, but they slapped against the fuselage as they went and sounded within like rifle shots.

The explosions took me by surprise, riddled me with exhilaration and blew away the contents of my thinking. A remarkable transformation came over my mind, and I discovered other, more comprehensive resources at my disposal. A portion of my consciousness detached itself and established its dominion in the emptiness about the driving aircraft. It opened out as an expanding sphere until it reached well beyond the storm-lashed coast ahead, including the air above. My brain became an electromagnetic receiver, and I experienced it as a multidimensional radar display containing every relevant aspect of the encompassing situation, for the sky itself was spatial consciousness. I was able to see the cloud-draped city toward which I flew, the beacons that spoke to my radios, the remote radars that tracked me, the airport, and the runway that glistened as my threshold to Iceland. Enmeshed in this creative presentation, I sat at the calm center of activity like a neutron in the hub of a vast and complicated molecule; the strangely self-insistent separateness of my ego reabsorbed for a time in the perfect continuity of a sharply delineated phenomenal universe. I was loosed in an ancient realm of consciousness whose essence was space and whose aspect was eternal freedom.

New maneuvering instructions came in from Approach Control. I complied without disturbing my interior panorama. Over Keflavik OMNI, I was turned to the northeast and led blindly along the coastal mountains, but my blindness was given form and fullness by the new seeing. Two miles from the field, I started a final descent and broke out of the clouds at 800 feet. Directly ahead were the red-tile roofs of Reykjavik, and close off the right wing was the airfield. The patterns in my brain merged with visual reality and vanished. Approach Control switched me to the tower for landing instructions and wished me a pleasant stay in Iceland.

The tower cleared me to circle the field and land from the opposite direction. There was a stiff crosswind and blowing rain. Ripples of water drove laterally across the windshield as I taxied to the parking area, but a lighter layer of cloud was pushing in rapidly behind the storm, and the rain was only a splattering when I climbed from the aircraft. I was no longer cold, so I shed two layers of clothes and went to customs.

The closest lodging was at the International Hotel, a conspicuous concrete high rise no more than fifty yards from where I had parked the aircraft. After clearing with the airport authorities, I walked to the hotel and checked in. The room was elegant. It was on the seventh floor and had a wall of glass facing the nearby mountains that were aswirl with gray mists and black clouds. The rolling land between was pastured with exuberantly green grass. The room had a large, comfortable chair before the window, so I sat for a while caught in the rugged perspective and let everything relax. I was still high from the flight and strove to maintain the quiet, almost tentative quality of mind that had alternated with my periods of activity during the day. Forty-five minutes later, I showered, dressed casually, and took a cab into town.

Reykjavik is a little city of fine old buildings and narrow streets that, in Iceland's strange evening light, looked like Flemish oil paintings. Shafts of bright orange sunlight punctuated the clouds and washed everything with a golden haze. The cab let me off downtown, and I wandered the city without purpose. There were empty streets full of closed shops, and little parks full of statues. I walked by the docks where large ships were tethered against the tide, then back two blocks when rain began to sprinkle. The splatterings presaged a squall, so I ducked into a sweetshop for hot chocolate and watched the water pour down. Soon the sun came out again, low in the southwest, shining red orange beneath the clouds that still tumbled above the city.

It was after ten o'clock, but still light when I got back to the hotel. The restaurant had a band, three bars, and a rollicking crowd of Friday night stompers who were obliterating the evening with merriment. Their choice of drug was alcohol, and they chose frequently. Everything was going full tilt, and everyone was drunk. Even the maître d' had been tasting. He found me a table, but not a waiter, and hurried off singing to himself as two old ladies staggered across the dance floor. They were holding each other up and giggling uproariously, but nobody else seemed to notice. I collared a waiter on his way by and eventually had a bottle of wine and an appetizer. I toasted the evening and was soon transported back to my navy days when the martini was mistress to a generation of warriors. As though to outdo me, the band played Glen Miller, and I had dinner with candlelight and memories.

I woke about nine to a wet, windy day. I was stiff and my eyes were puffy and sore. I took my time getting down to breakfast and lingered over coffee, hoping the storm might break, but the heavy rain continued to fall. Flight planning was located in the tower on top of the airport administration building, conveniently near the hotel. During a lull in the storm, I hurried over. It was Saturday morning and all offices were closed except the weather station. An air traffic controller in the tower supplied me with the navigational information I needed and filed my clearance. I was heading for Prestwick in southern Scotland, 750 miles and five hours away. The first leg of the journey cut diagonally across southwestern Iceland to the island of Heimaey, 20 miles off the coast, whose beacon at Vestmannaeyjar was the departure point for traffic heading to Europe. I would enter Scottish control off Stornoway in the Hebrides, and thereafter fly airways to Prestwick. The Icelandic Low had moved south, so I would pass through it again. I chose to fly at 7,000 feet where the temperature would be in the reasonable twenties and oxygen unnecessary.

I taxied to the runway in a heavy drizzle and took off into the storm. By the time I was swallowed at 600 feet, I was already on the radar screens at Departure Control. A controller monitored my climb and gave me vectors across the mountains. The clouds hid the volcanic beauty of Iceland and glazed the Baron with ice as it tunneled through the opaque sky. Air turbulence decreased after I crossed the coast, but picked up again over Heimaey. I reported the Vestmannaeyjar beacon to Departure Control and shortly thereafter disappeared from his screen.

South of Heimaey, the icing grew worse. It caked out four inches from the propeller hubs and engine nacelles. The windshield was a solid layer, and I knew ice also covered my antennas, airscoop, and vertical stabilizer, adding significantly to the aircraft's weight. I increased power on both engines, but the buildups continued until the Baron became sluggish and unwieldy. Airspeed slowed, and I had to lift the nose to maintain altitude, but then ice coated the underside of the wings and fuselage, compounding the problem. I slowly lost altitude, letting the added weight pull me down. The aircraft settled to 6,200 feet before the load stabilized and I ploughed on, 40 miles per hour slower than planned.

An hour past Heimaey, the last of the ice melted, and I was again level at 7,000 feet. Though I had burned considerably more fuel than expected, I was running well behind my flight plan. I calculated my remaining range and reduced power to optimum cruise settings. I estimated I had enough gas to reach Prestwick, but Stornoway was 175 miles closer if needed.

Another half hour of turgid cloud swept by before the storm eased. The Baron, like a butterfly, emerged from its gray cocoon into a truly magical sky space. The air at 7,000 feet was clear and calm, but the aircraft was enclosed between layers of rippling cloud like a fly in a cream cheese sandwich. Puffs of cumulus burst from an opalescent blanket several hundred feet below, while stalactites of vapor hung from above and sifted silver from the downward filtering light. I was encapsulated in a mother-of-pearl sky where glowing mists and gardens of milk twisted reality into celestial landscapes like those of oriental scrolls, but here everything moved to the myriad rhythms of a hundred shifting winds.

I flew among marshmallow domes and wisps of dream-stuff. My body, like a vacant powerhouse, rumbled with the accustomed activities of its motorized existence, while I, immersed in the surrounding wonder, slipped beyond myself. I reverberated with freshening consciousness and awoke as an unasked question on the verge of astonishment. Freed, then reabsorbed within this clearly void space, I smiled at the existential catastrophe implied by the realization that my ego was nothing but a focal point in a mirage, my body but a snowflake in life's furnace, and my mind but an emptiness wherein the universe continually created itself. Dispassionately, I watched these three fuse into an illusory self, which, seeing itself watching, vanished, leaving the emptied airplane to course the sky alone.

Too soon the clouds began to tatter and peel away. Here and there, blue ocean winked through the mist, and holes appeared in the overcast. Sunbeams poured down in a thousand spokes that burnished the Baron in passing. I took off my sheepskin coat and loosened the blanket around my legs. The ADF was tuned to the beacon at Stornoway. The needle had not yet steadied on a reliable bearing, but was hunting to the right, indicating I was east of my course. I did some rough calculations. I had been in the clouds longer than forecast at Reykjavik. Apparently, the Icelandic Low had not moved as far to the east as expected and had given me more crosswind than I had allowed for. This also meant I was further behind schedule, so I reduced power for the second time and computed another range estimate.

The clouds broke up rapidly as the baron left the last of the low-pressure system behind. The afternoon was clear: a heavy sea shimmered in the wind, and a sapphire sky masked its invisibility with clarity. Soon, far to the left and low on the horizon, I made out the Orkney Islands and the headlands of northern Scotland. The land was reassuring, but I was far east of course and approaching Stornoway more from the north than the northwest.

Like a mythic land in the dream space of consciousness, the golden hills of Scotland grew larger. While I spaced out on their beauty, Scottish Airways contacted me on the VHF. I reported being east of course and behind schedule, but how far off I was not sure. The controller said the weather over all of western Scotland was clear and I could stop at Stornoway for fuel if necessary. I made out the Hebrides ahead and once more estimated my gasoline reserves. I could make it through to Prestwick, but again reduced power as a precaution or, perhaps, because I was in no hurry to be anywhere else at all.

The northernmost islands drifted beneath me. Stornoway appeared as a small enclave of buildings and an airstrip. I continued south along the inland sea between the Hebrides and the mainland. The high, rolling Scottish hills looked much like those of central California, except that lochs lay behind them and accentuated their contours. I overtook a coastal steamer feathering the water with its wake and a covey of fishing boats at work on the open sea. Thirty miles from the airport, Scottish Airways switched me to Approach Control. I was given a long, straight approach across Prestwick's calm bay and landed on the same runway I remembered leaving years earlier on a snow-swept night in late December.

The airport had changed. A large terminal with service buildings and parking lots replaced what had been a cow pasture on the far side of the field. I taxied to customs and filled out entry papers for the Baron and myself; then, happy at having made my deadline, took a cab into town.

Prestwick is a sea resort with fine old hotels and guesthouses lining a wide, gray beach. It was the height of the season, but I was fortunate and chanced upon a canceled reservation at a Victorian inn. The room was small and fastidious. The bathroom was down the hall and immaculate. I went directly to it and enjoyed a long, hot bath in a greatly oversized English tub that stood in porcelain dignity on lion's feet atop a pedestal of tile. A five-course dinner followed. After coffee and brandy, I ambled along the beach and sat for a while beneath the star-flecked sky to watch the Atlantic roll in from its opposite direction. Lovers strolled by, idling the night with their expectancy, and three gentlemen in knickers passed within earshot, discussing the chess match in Iceland. I had not thought of the contest since Goose Bay, but realized that it must have been the talk of the town in Reykjavik, well concealed by the Icelandic of my hosts. Like a creature of the sky, I had passed through history without noticing.

I slept late and woke with my eyes glued shut. I had developed conjunctivitis and was glad the day's flight was short and uncomplicated. I spent the morning on the beach, below the boardwalk where the Sunday people acted out the age-old ritual of walking the promenade while their kids, dressed for church, eyed the water longingly and built sand castles in their heads. After lunch I returned to the airport, filed for London, and took off into a lazy afternoon. The flight across summering Albion took an hour and fifty minutes and was quite remarkable in that I had never seen England clear before. I skirted London to the west and landed at Gatwick Airport, my final destination. When the formalities were completed, I called BOAC for a reservation on their Monday morning flight to San Francisco via the polar route, nonstop. This left me fifteen hours to squander in London; sufficient time to see an old friend, meet a new one, and flow with the night games of the Empress City.

I had barely slept when I found myself in a cab threading its way through morning traffic to Heathrow Airport. The return to San Francisco was by much the same route I had flown. Flight time: ten hours. London was wrapped in morning fog when we took off, but we shed it in a few moments. Scotland came up quickly, soft and yellow, much flatter from 35,000 feet. Iceland was still socked in, but the storm was below us, and we sailed across like a silver swan on a sea of cream.

Beyond Iceland, I spent a half hour talking with the aircraft's third officer, one of whose functions was flight navigation. I was a lover of the old art and was amazed at the technological revolution that had solved all its problems and made it a science. For transoceanic flights in DC-6s, we had relied primarily on the techniques of celestial navigation, using star fixes obtained with a periscopic bubble sextant poked through the top of the fuselage. We had worked continuously to obtain two fixes an hour; an accuracy of ten miles was considered good, but was only obtained under optimum conditions. It was different now with the BOAC's 707. It carried a self-contained Doppler navigational system utilizing radar pulses reflected from the ground. A computer analyzed the echoes, calculated the aircraft's motion, and told the autopilot how to remain on the optimum trajectory. The only function of the navigator was to tell the computer the latitude and longitude of the departure and destination airports. The margin of error on the ten-hour flight to San Francisco was no more than a quarter mile from the end of the landing runway. The only problem I could detect was that the navigator admitted to knowing nothing about navigation. Science, in its efficient majesty, had weeded a lot of ancient knowledge from the living brains of humanity's storehouse. For my part, I felt like a fossil.

The black mountains of Greenland rose from the distance. It was a sparkling day on the ice cap, so I put on my sunglasses and squinted down. Beyond the eastern mountains, snow glistened endlessly, with only an occasional ridge or solitary peak to relieve the expanse of white. I watched a snow devil dance on the empty stage and wondered again if this lifeless desert of eternal ice was the crystal dome of Hyperborea. The Davis Straits were speckled with icebergs that I watched to the accompaniment of Beethoven and Bach. We penetrated North American airspace at Baffin Island and sailed inland over Foxe Basin. I remembered my visionary meteorite, but saw no scars other than the pockmarks of innumerable blue lakes. These reminded me of a book of my grandfather's that had fascinated me as a child. It was published at the turn of the century and contained a fanciful illustration called *The Classroom of 1950*. The classroom was the gondola of a dirigible from which a schoolmarm taught geography to her students by pointing out the places over which they floated. Aboard the 707, we closed the window shutters and watched a cowboy movie. By the time the good guys had won, we were deep into Saskatchewan and booming toward Idaho and Washington. The Rockies were clothed in green and tipped with white, hauntingly beautiful in the effervescent afternoon. Oregon passed below, and soon we were descending over the valleys of northern California. San Francisco Bay was clear, but the summer fog had already spilled over the hills, and the city was another cloud as we passed. Yellow Bear met me at the airport, so I gave him the postcard from Goose Bay and told him about Greenland.

Gathering Together

A week after my return to San Francisco, I was again on my way, this time to the Brotherhood ranch and San Jacinto Mountains. I was feeling good: my mind was relaxed and my body alive with somatic energies generated by the excitement of the previous few weeks. Consequently, I was primed for tripping and hoped to use my fitness to its fullest. In my pack was a stash of excellent grass from Oaxaca and a fragrant piece of hashish from Afghanistan, while wrapped in my blanket roll as insulation against the pervasive summer heat were a few orange tablets and two large capsules. The tabs were a particularly fine preparation of LSD known as Sunshine, and the caps contained Iboga root purified to an acrid white powder. In my pocket was a single joint, already rolled, of the Oaxaca liberally sprinkled with my fiery friend DMT. During my weekend on the mountain, I planned to use them all.

The drive from San Francisco was less than five hundred miles, and could be done in a day, but I kept to the less-traveled coast and took two steps to my destination. On the afternoon of the second day, I drove out of the lowlands and into the clearer air of the San Jacintos. The temperature in Garner Valley was in the mid-nineties, and I knew that the ranch, tucked in its cul-de-sac of mountains, would be no cooler. The key for the gate was hung on the mailbox post, so I let myself through and started up the five-mile dirt road to the ranch.

The road climbed three ridges and then entered a sloping alluvial plateau with the ranch buildings at its apex. A short distance past the top of the third ridge was a large culvert through which Waterfall Creek, when running, ran. I parked the car in the shade of a solitary pine and walked out on a July-parched ridge to retune myself to the country and review my plans for the next few days. It was Thursday afternoon. On Friday, I would hike to Gooseberry Springs, a well-stocked camp on the far side of Spitler Mountain, and, on Saturday, take the Iboga in the surrounding forest. On Sunday morning, I would walk back toward the ranch but not go all the way. The trail from Gooseberry

Canyon crosses the ridge through the Saddle—an inverted valley atop the mountain that contains mazes of stone, sparkling sand terraces, and gardens of windswept splendor. The place stands as a cup upraised over two worlds: to the west are the ranch, Garner Valley, and Lake Hemet; to the east, the busy desert and distant mountainscape with Palm Springs far below, set out in rectangles. The northern end of the Saddle rises in rounded contours to the pommel of Spitler Peak, while the southern terminates in three groupings of monumental pinnacles. I planned to take LSD at the Saddle and spend the morning wandering its many avenues of mystery. Sometime during the afternoon, I would smoke the DMT atop one of the pinnacles.

I returned to the car refreshed and continued toward the ranch. In the lower pasture, a group of horses huddled in the available shade. They were fenced off from the reservoir that sparkled invitingly in the sun but mostly caught my attention because no one was swimming. The road wound above the tipis in the orchard, an area that also seemed deserted, then curved past the main house. There was no activity in the gardens or barnyard but when I pulled up by the tack room, a couple of people came out of the house and hurried over. They seemed excited and after the usual happy greetings were exchanged, told me why. Word had come through that a long expected police bust was imminent.

The news, though not surprising, pissed me off. Since I had left the navy, I had seen many raids carried out against people who opposed the war in Vietnam, or espoused the new consciousness, or called for fairness in one cause or another. Invariably, the pattern was the same: an organization, or a commune, or a spokesman for change would be set up and busted with a great hullabaloo of publicity, after which the police establishment, touting its success, would demand more guns, more men, and more money to fight the problem it had so neatly concocted. Spineless politicians voted billions to protect themselves from their own children, and the courts turned the Constitution into a bludgeon. At no level did the news sit well with me.

As we walked to the house, I was filled in on what was known. We had reliable information that various police agencies were putting together a raiding party that could strike as early as this weekend. The whole thing was being engineered from Washington. This did not surprise me. We had known for two years that Richard Nixon had personally targeted the Brotherhood for a hit during his 1972 reelection campaign. The president hated hippies, particularly those who had the effrontery to surf at his San Clemente beach and smoke marijuana within sniffing distance of his uptight constituency, so he planned to let his adolescent police state stage a show for the law-and-order vote, after which government by extortion could proceed as usual. The Brotherhood of Eternal Love was an obvious target for his megalomania: long-haired, radical freemen preaching psychedelic consciousness and new age enlightenment—brothers.

We went into the house and down a short hallway to the kitchen. Usually, a few people would be sitting around the counter drinking coffee, shucking peas, or smoking a joint. Now it was deserted. Two of the women were preparing dinner. We embraced away the time since our last parting, and they asked if I had heard about the helicopters. My quizzical look was enough to elicit the story. On three different occasions over the past several days, police helicopters buzzed through the Saddle and low over the ranch, taking photographs. A small airplane circled overhead every afternoon, and the people in town were joking about strangers who hung out in the woods above the Garner Valley gate, watching our comings and goings through binoculars. Somebody said we were the Saigon of south California, and everybody laughed.

I passed my nose ritually over the cooking and asked what they were planning to do. Some had left, some were leaving, and a few were staying to tend the livestock and gardens. The whole ranch was getting a thorough cleaning, every odd corner poked into, every stash emptied. There would be nothing and nobody that could be busted, unless, as usual, the police planted their own drugs so they would have something to show for their effort. I remembered my pack and blanket roll, explained the problem, and excused myself to attend to it. When I returned from burying my stash, the crowd had dispersed, so I went in search of an *I Ching*. The living room was empty, but the late afternoon sun was filtering through its many screened windows, bringing it alive with color. The floors were overlaid with intricately designed, brightly woven rugs from the Orient and Middle East. The wood-paneled walls were hung with Tibetan *thangkas* and psychedelic art, and above the large stone fireplace was a copper sunburst with an anthropomorphic face into which candles were placed at night, giving eyes to the fire. Across the room was a bas-relief of Buddha in meditation, and between the two, affixed to the ceiling, was Dion Wright's epic mandala of evolution. Madras-covered mattresses and colorful pillows lined the walls, and low tables with icons, ashtrays, and many-hued candles were scattered before them.

I found the *I Ching* by a statue of Tara and sat down to get another perspective on what was happening. It was reassuring. The book was not concerned with any immediate danger and advised that I do as planned. The weekend was a gift. As I sat speculating, a car arrived, followed by a covey of kids who burst into the living room demanding to know if I knew what was happening and breathlessly giving me six new versions. I listened spellbound, for children clarify energy, and somewhere in the middle of it all, I caught a glimpse of their young and startled truth.

One of the women came in and began looking under mattresses for stray roaches and seeds. Soon we were all at it, but while we searched, the sun dropped behind the ridge and gradually put an end to out activities. After dinner, with candlelight and incense doing honor to the stately creatures of art that surrounded us, we sat smoking before the empty fireplace late into the night.

I spent Friday morning in the gardens. The barn across from the house had burned down, leaving a cracked cement pedestal on which several tons of hay were stacked. Beside it was the old barnyard, about forty feet square, in which the kitchen garden glowed with a summer luxuriousness that only fifty years of manure could provide. Along the fences, nasturtiums, asters, and string beans grew tall, and beds of marigolds and petunias were scattered among a dozen varieties of vegetables. I pulled weeds until the sprinklers started watering then went to the larger gardens. These were in the upper pasture and were extensive enough to supply fresh food to the Brotherhood co-op in Laguna Beach. The fence was a tangle of flowers, and beyond it were rows of corn, potatoes, onions, and garlic; strawberries were in their second fruiting, squash were the size of softballs, and some of the tomatoes looked like inside-out watermelons. In the center of the corn patch, well within range of the sprinklers, was an open ramada covered with palm fronds and hung with hammocks. On a hot day, it was the coolest place on the ranch and generally tenanted by sharp-eyed, weed-blown farmers. Today it was empty, as were the two geodesic greenhouses whose sultry inner spaces were laid out as living mandalas proclaiming the lushness and fertility of earth—the sanctity of seed.

I picked some vegetables, then labored in the ramada for a while, and, around noon, joined the remaining crew at the reservoir. Those who were going had gone, and the rest of us were somehow cut loose from care by the enigma of the situation. We dallied like children in the sun, playing with rubber tubes and leaky boat. By three o'clock, I was back at the house putting together my pack for the weekend. There was food stored at Gooseberry Springs, but I packed my own. I also included a copy of the *I Ching* because the last people at the camp had been unable to find the old one.

The thermometer was still above ninety when I left the house, but the reservoir had cooled me beyond caring. I stopped for my stash and set off up the mountain. The trail climbed in a zigzag of long grades with switchbacks between. When it entered the Saddle, the ranch dropped from sight, and the rocky side hill with its tangles of scrub and thorn changed to a gentler slope where pine and yucca stood out sharply against the sky. The red soil gave way to white sand, and then the trail forked. The branch to Gooseberry Springs climbed the northwest ridge of the Saddle and continued around the side of Spitler Mountain. Beyond the crest of the ridge, the trail split again, the right fork plunging down a steep draw toward the camp.

It was a long, variable descent. For the most part, the going was easy, but after a while the trail steepened and several sections of it were eroded. The bottom of the draw ended at the upper lip of a still deeper canyon. The trail turned to the left and followed the lip around the ridge into Gooseberry Canyon, which also emptied into the steeper canyon below. The forest ended at the trail, below which jagged, nearly vertical walls fell away. Further down, the narrow bottom of this deeper canyon became a long, rounded backbone of polished granite, aptly named Devil's Slide, which plunged like a streak of silver down the mountainside.

Gooseberry Canyon was a forest of large trees. The way went up among them as steeply as it had gone down the draw, but the camp was only a hundred yards further and its environs were terraced level. The trail, after passing a corral on the side hill, ended at the lower terrace. This was shaped like a dumbbell with a large, pipe-framed storage tent at one end and a kitchen at the other; the two joined by a narrow pathway, almost a ledge built and buttressed of rock. The spring was just outside the entrance to the kitchen. It filled a deep pool in a little grotto, then spilled across the path and drained off down the side hill. The kitchen was a twelve-by-twenty-foot area with a nine-foot-high framework of pipe all around. This could be completely covered with canvas, forming another tent, but for the summer only the top piece was hung. In the center of the kitchen was a big stone fireplace with a cast iron top and a chimney poking through the canvas; across from it was an imposing wooden cabinet, seven feet tall, whose upper front was hinged at the top, opening like a roof over the counter below. Beside it were a table and metal drums full of food.

The camp was buttoned up tight when I arrived, and there were animal tracks in the kitchen. I put my pack on the table and took the water dipper from the cabinet. I drank some, splashed some in my face, and poured two dippers over my head before cooling to the temperature of the forest. I sat on the terrace wall to rest my legs and spaced out on my surroundings. The sun poured through the treetops, dappling the camp. The air was still, laden with smells, and the sound was mostly silence. I complemented my senses with a stream of pleasant recollections, for returning to Gooseberry Springs was almost like coming home.

I had first been here eighteen years earlier with Frank Scovel, the man who, over a period of thirty years, had built the camp and packed in all of its permanent supplies. The kitchen, the storage tent, and an all-weather bin further up the side hill attested to his perseverance, for they were filled with enough gear for a party of ten to outwait a month of blizzards. Frank was the father of Don Scovel, a classmate of mine at the Naval Academy. In 1954, Don and I spent our summer leave skin-diving off La Jolla and climbing the canyons around Gooseberry Springs. During my later years in the navy, I had twice been cycled through San Diego and both times returned to the mountain with Frank. When the Brotherhood acquired the ranch, Frank was already in his seventies and was persuaded to sell his section land as well. The transfer had little effect on Gooseberry Camp, which remained what it had been: a deep mountain retreat.

The sun dropped behind Spitler Mountain, taking sunbeams, like drawbridges, up through the trees. When the highest branches had been burnished to gold, I took a joint and a canteen of water to the far side of Gooseberry Canyon. Beyond the sidewall, the forest gave way to bare stone laced with manzanita and cactus, and a tortuous way led out to a huge boulder perched high above Devil's Slide. From there, the view was magnificent. Miles below, the desert spread out from Palm Springs to Indio, shimmering in the summer heat, and beyond were endless ridges of purple mountains. Behind me, a rough, broken ridge swept in a long arc to the top of Spitler Peak. The Saddle was hidden from view, but I could look past it to a distant ridge with a remarkable formation: a narrow sub-ridge thrust out from an amphitheater of mountain and terminated abruptly in a high tower of dark green rock. Below the tower was Landslide Canyon, so named because of the heavy avalanching that had torn down its sides. Frank had told me stories of Indian caves in that area, but I had never explored beyond the Saddle.

I smoked the joint and remembered my evenings at camp when Frank had talked about the mountains and Indians who had summered here. Traces could still be found: an occasional potsherd or arrowhead, a hand stone or mortar ground into the rock bed near the streams, where women had sat, century after century, grinding seeds and nuts into flour. Atop the boulder on which I sat were two strange indentations, one circular, the other elongated, whose origins were a matter of speculation. It looked as though water might have fallen to the rock and then splashed a hundred feet to Devil's Slide, but there was no place for the water to come from, since the boulder was almost suspended in space.

I could see part of Devil's Slide before the canyon curved and the near wall blocked the view. I had climbed down the slide once, on my first visit, eighteen years before. Below the slide, two canyons met. In the far canyon was an old mining claim with a ten-foot drift in the sidewall. The mine had never showed any gold, but in 1954 uranium fever raged, and Frank thought it wise to check some of the ore. I happily scrambled after rocks and, by the end of a hot, exciting day, returned exhausted with a collection of every different type I could find. There was no uranium in any of the rocks, but just by climbing through the stark and uncertain terrain, I had been able to act out half the fantasies of my childhood.

While lost in these reminiscences, remembering distant scenes with the unusual clarity that marijuana can provide, another perception penetrated my awareness. I heard the faint rumble of an approaching engine, accompanied by the peculiar whoop-whoop-whoop characteristic of helicopters. I spotted the machine, still well below me, climbing toward the Saddle, so I dropped down behind the boulder to watch it pass. It was policemen playing soldiers, but it was too late in the day for a raid. I wondered if it was a last minute reconnaissance for the morning, or merely brass on a boondoggle.

When the reverberations died away, I climbed back on the boulder and sat quietly through evening, watching the mountain shadows crawl across the desert, the sun tinge the far sierra with flame. It was still light when I left for camp, but very dim in the forest. I laid out my mat and blankets on the upper terrace and hung a hammock from the pipe at the far end of the kitchen. Iboga likes an empty stomach, but I was hungry from the hike, so I built a small fire for soup and tea and drank them with cheese and an apple. For dessert, I filled my corncob pipe with hashish and settled into the hammock to float off on a cloud of hemp.

Sometime later, I heard a coyote yodeling far off on the mountain. I returned his call, and he mine. He sounded somewhat nearer, so I tried again, and when he answered, he was still closer. For fifteen minutes, we sounded back and forth, until he was at the edge of camp, warily skirting its perimeter. Something possessed me and I let out a yowl unlike anything a coyote makes. The last I heard of him was a yelp as he crossed the ridge, so I relit the pipe and growled at the shapes in the night.

The first rays of morning sun shone obliquely beneath the trees, flooding the upper terrace with orange light. Insects rose from the forest floor to bask in the beams, and birds arrived to hunt them. I washed in cold spring water and built a fire for tea. A chipmunk joined me in the kitchen. He talked and cavorted until he had attuned me to the mountain's morning rhythms, then dashed off with a cracker to the business of breakfast.

It was a perfect day for a tryst with the Lady Iboga. The *I Ching*, when I checked, concurred. It gave me the hexagram called "Gathering Together". There were no changing lines. I knew this hexagram could be interpreted in either a social or biological sense, and I hoped it was not the former, for Iboga can leave one a quivering, inarticulate protoplasm incapable of social façading. However, since the oracle says that it is favorable to undertake something and foretells both success and good fortune, I assumed it implied interruption and that the gathering together would be on a different level. The book speaks of the religious forces needed to bring the living members of a family together with their ancestors, an allusion that seemed especially appropriate to Iboga, for I knew that the sacrament could put me in touch with my chains of DNA logic, with tribal as well as personal memories, and with archetypes in the collective unconscious. There was also a hint of danger contained in the reading, for the oracle cautions one to renew one's weapons in order to meet the unforeseen.

I had no weapons but the Iboga itself, so I swallowed the two capsules and felt a tingle of excitement course through my stomach, telling my autonomic nervous system that the trip had begun. For the next hour, I wandered through the forest above camp, letting my body exercise while the mind medicine worked its way into my cells. I expected to do very little moving later, since I knew from experience that Iboga would thoroughly discoordinate my body, and indeed, the first effects of the drug were nausea and dizziness. By the time these were intense, I was back at the upper terrace, breathing rapidly, and trying to sit up on the mat; but my legs and head became unbearably heavy and my stomach sagged with pain, so I rolled to my side. I tried to breathe deeply, but doubled up, was unable to do so. My abdomen was swollen and my diaphragm hurt, so I was only able to fill the upper part of my lungs by gulping and swallowing air, mouthful by mouthful. Behind the discomfort of my body, however, I was getting the first of Iboga's exuberant hallucinations. My perceptual space melted to a crystalline liquid where shapes shimmered like stains and vivid, piercing sensations pulsed through as pictures from another dimension. I became a continuum of experience in a galactic swirl whose energy first nullified the pain in my body, then penetrated deeper and dissolved my body as well.

Consciousness awoke to its electromagnetic matrix and bedazzled me with lights. My head, prismed with colors, resolved themselves into eidetic, omni-sensual scenes of long forgotten times. I was ten years old again and running down the railroad tracks near home, off with my boyhood companions into another day of adventures. The tracks became silver cords weaving a Turk's head knot around me, then straightened and became the implacable bars of a crib where I, a diapered baby, howled to be free. The colors turned red, crimson, scarlet, purple; became bright liquids flowing as blood in my sentient tubeways, oozing nourishment through flesh, pulsing with a million aspects of life.

Occasionally, the visionary onslaught would ease for a moment, and I would awaken to my body crumpled on a blanket in a magically unfocusable forest. I managed to sit up several times, hoping to channel the energy more directly along my spine, but could never hold it, and fell over. No sooner was I down than I was off once more, foraging through luxurious strata of psyche, meeting myself in mirrors of mind, abbreviating time to dally with images of yesterday as real in recall as they had been in reality. It was an unending parade, a continuous, extravagant creation, but the flow brooked no impediment. Nothing could be stopped; nothing held for the inquiring mind to examine. Like a volcano, I erupted and bubbled over with marvels, but nowhere could the lava be slowed. The moment of recognition was the moment of transition to a new flux, another bubble to appear, grow, and burst. Often, overawed with beauty, I tried to stop some particularly compelling image, or sought to follow it, but to do so was to court disaster, for the object would quickly decay and molder to ugliness.

Two hours passed before I noticed that I was thirsty. My cheeks were bloated, my mouth gummy, my lips dry. I tried to swallow, but my throat was glued shut. The nearest water was at the spring, a mere thirty feet away, so I got in communication with my muscles and told them what we were up to. I managed to pull my legs under me, rose to my knees, and stood up like a baboon. I toppled over before I got any further, lay for awhile among pinwheels of fire, then tried again, being satisfied this time with knees and elbows. I started toward the spring on all fours, but was unable to coordinate my various parts and tripped over everything, mostly myself. Somewhere along the way, I forgot what I was doing. I tumbled off down the hill into a kaleidoscopic consciousness and got lost in wondering which mirror was me, which end my eye.

I woke on the walkway to the kitchen. I was seeing myself as one of many dynamic focal points in a sentient field of energies randomly ordered by the omniscience of the Tao, but the price of my seeing was physical discombobulation. Again, I tried crawling. It was like rolling through a barrel at the fun house, but my head was clear within the turmoil of movement, and I was soon laughing at the enormous hilarity of my predicament. I fell forward into the runoff from the spring and washed my mouth by opening it. I tried to drink, but the water was like fiery icicles going down, and my queasy stomach rebelled.

I lay with my cheek in the water until a physically lucid interval overtook me. I felt I could walk back to the mat if I could stand up, so I crawled to the edge of the kitchen and pulled myself up on the pipes. I had to wait for the spinning world to stop, but by the time it did, I had gone through yet another metamorphosis and hung as a spider in its web. Flies glistened in a nearby sunbeam, and I, the waiting predator, watched, until the eye that saw them became their eyes seeing me. A thousand-faceted jewel opened out, and I simultaneously saw the forest from every possible perspective. Each was intensely real and brilliantly highlighted, but I could not focus on any single view, for to do so was to destroy the whole. A bird swam through my ocean of vision, leaving a transparent wake in the air. I saw her from above and below, from behind as well as in front, and even from within her where her seeing reflected my own.

I slid down the pipes and half staggered, half crawled back to the upper terrace. I was exhausted by the effort, panting, my heart pounding as I curled on the mat, but the visionary deluge continued without respite. Another hour passed before I was able to sit up again. I propped myself against a tree and stared at the forest. Sun patterns crystallized in my brain and arranged themselves into phantasmagoria in which inside and outside were obliterated in the totality of being. Often I woke to some incredible vision but could not tell if my eyes were open or closed and destroyed what I gazed at by finding out.

By late morning, I was stabilized in my role as actor, audience, stage, and production company for the wonders of neural chemistry, but I also had the feeling that I was not alone in the endeavor. A recurring motif had developed in the unending flow of encyclopedic images: a series of very beautiful, visionary people grew from my mind and moved rhythmically through my seeing. They were lovely to look at. Their bodies were exquisitely formed; their features highly refined. Dark eyes and black hair accentuated burnished skins, and they were strangely alive, though they appeared to be neither awake nor asleep. Their eyes were open, but they seemed not to see, and though they breathed, they made no disturbance. The space through which they moved was sea green, utterly transparent, and as still as the tomb of a pharoah. Figures and faces materialized from the depths, moving effortlessly on unseen currents. Each was unique, each appeared at a different point in my visual sphere, moved toward me, and attained a peak of aesthetic perfection just as it confronted me from the tiniest distance away. Then it dissolved into light as another, equally beautiful, came into being elsewhere. They were a people suspended in time, adrift in a mind-warp through which I could not reach but clearly saw, for when I stared into the forest, the visionary faces were superimposed on whatever I looked at, and when I withdrew within by closing my eyes, my brain space became a theater of many dimensions in which my phantom tribe appeared, peered, and passed in wondrous procession.

Sunbeams shifted through the trees, casting new shapes on the forest floor, whispering of meridian passage and the birth of afternoon. A few islands of normal consciousness appeared in the river of visionary awareness. For twenty or thirty seconds, trees would be trees, and my body real, before the cornucopia would again pour over me. During one moment of ego lucidity, I became aware of a desire to climb down to Devil's Slide and walk the steep canyon below. I found the notion humorous since I could not move, and dismissed it. But it continued to come back and soon was almost insistent. Once, in a strangely dramatic way, I even encountered my self of eighteen years earlier as a phantom setting out for the same climb. The specter walked off into the forest, and I, left bemused behind, felt a longing to follow.

Instead, I went back to the spring. It was like tightrope walking across Niagara Falls on a whip. I needed a solid perspective, but my mind could not provide it. It grabbed indiscriminately at tumbling facets of gravitational reality, and my body reeled in its wake. The world was askew, then upside down. It spun like the wheels of a slot machine, with me helplessly aboard, hoping for the jackpot of stability among the lemons of illusion. At one point, my foot missed the ground altogether, and I fell on my face like a rubber clown.

I collapsed at the spring, washed my face and drank, and then pushed on toward the hammock, hoping its pendulum motion might order my chaos. Getting into the contraption was a major victory, but its motion, instead of helping, spun me out completely. My canteen, half filled from the night before, was hanging on the pipe above me. I tried to focus on it as a stable reference, but it began to twirl, trapping me in its image. I felt an urge to put it on and again experienced the compulsion, stronger than before, to climb down to Devil's Slide.

For a few minutes I swung like a moth in a cocoon, but my stomach did not accommodate to the motion, so I rolled out onto the ground. My spinning continued and became a mandala whose center opened as the entrance to a tunnel. The tunnel was a tube of fiber optics, an octopus arm with an eye at the far end that slithered through the forest. I recognized what I saw. The tentacle was probing the top of Devil's Slide and sending back reports urging that I come. Suddenly, it became apparent to me that I was really going to go, that somehow or other I was going to get my body into the deep canyons to whatever down there was acting as a magnet to my mind.

I was still an hour from going anywhere, so I sat propped against the fireplace, confronting the unending river of creation so richly bestowed by my African lover, Iboga. My ghostly tribe returned, more animated now, each dancing in extreme slow motion to a momentary confrontation with my eyes, then bowing in graceful exit, to let another appear.

I woke, longing to join them, and pulled myself up the pipes after the canteen. I filled it at the spring, took the biggest drink I could, and stumbled off into the forest. I went down the side hill as though one leg was six inches shorter than the other and had a spring attached to it. I gyrated ridiculously, bounced off a tree or two, and had to rest frequently. My body was a ton of tepid mud only loosely associated with any directional signals I initiated, and my heart beat a wild staccato to every misstep. Each time I collapsed, the great river washed me away, and I came back newly confused, dislocated in the ice cube of time-space until I remembered what I was doing and then realized, more or less, where I was.

At the edge of the forest, I was blinded by the sun and sat in the last bit of shade, studying the series of steep, narrow ledges that led down into the canyon. They made no sense whatsoever. Sometimes they seemed to lead up, sometimes off to the side. At one point, they dissolved into sparkles, and the far end seemed closer than the near. It took me an hour to get to the bottom. At the first ledge, my body was quivering so badly that I huddled against the wall for fear of shaking off into space, then had to restrain myself from following a mysterious something that chased a vermilion vapor across the field of sight. Similar things happened at each ledge. I crumpled into a secure position and was carried off by the river, to return later, lost, adrift in wonder, basking in the sun, bedazzled. Once when I opened my eyes everything was upside down and the white edge of the distant desert shimmered like a mirage above my head. The canyon floor was large piles of broken rock choked with dry, thorny vegetation. At the top of the left wall, I could see the protruding edge of the boulder where I had spent the previous evening. The right wall was completely shattered. Its former face was what I stood on, and over it I continued in the same discontinuous manner. I moved five feet then sat five minutes awash in the ongoing, all-pervading flow. Fire etched secrets on gold, and old trees grew through my brain, counting seconds as centuries. I met a clone of myself, balanced on my forehead, looking down as I looked up, each of us seeing into a magical mirror that reflected me perfectly, without distortion, in a glass where eternity was compressed to a micron by the river of time. The mirror rippled like clear water bestirred by a raindrop and resolved into a vision of distant times out of which my phantom people walked, to lead me further down the gorge.

The vision spilled over and toyed with reality. The dry vegetation grew lush with flowers, and ethereal water flowed along the parched streambed, collected in pools, and slipped down the spillways toward Devil's Slide. The ghostly tribe filled me with their images. In rapid succession, which seemed measured and slow, face after face appeared directly before my own, each moving from behind and out of the former. Occasionally, the hint of a smile would ripple a lip, or the eyes staring into mine would sparkle with a flash of recognition. When I again started, unsteadily, to walk, some of the visionary people were playing about me in the canyon, running beneath an imposing wall, and splashing at the top of the slide. I moved as a spastic among them, realizing that I was seeing the way the mountain had been in some remote time, when a heavenly people, receptor-expressers of divine energy, had lived as the crowning consciousness of a true fantasy world on earth.

The going was easier down the water-polished granite of Devil's Slide. In the center, a channel lined with brittle brown moss looked like a huge snake gliding to the bottom. The canyon was narrower along the slide; the shattered right wall loomed above, while the debris had washed down and filled the wider canyon below. Halfway down, the slide had been broken by an earthquake and thereafter plunged more steeply. I rested at the break and became fascinated with the geometries displayed on the towering canyon wall. Straight-line fractures, faults, ledges, veins, all created a complex of shapes, infinitely varied, confronting my mind with theorems to solve and resolve into chaos. Perfection appeared on the edge of profusion, but could not sustain itself and fell apart into the indescribably cold and abstract. The wall glittered in the sun. It radiated something akin to pain, as though its old wounds were new, still raw. I was intimidated by it and stumbled off down the slide as best I could, wary of its overhanging presence, and anxious to be away from its dominance.

At the bottom of the slide, the canyon opened out and was again plugged with debris and brambles. A few small trees increased the tangle along the watercourse, so I went by the side hill. I soon sat down in a piece of shade, took a mouthful of water, and lay back to swirl it around. Somewhere in the liquid, I encountered my visionary people again. They floated into my perceptual space entombed in blocks of glowing crystal whose vibrant transparency magnified their features. The vision was Neptunian, the space itself like an undersea grotto. Crystal on crystal appeared, some tumbling, some spinning slowly, each encasing one of the mysterious, palpably alive people. Déjà vu dallied with time, enfolding me in magic beyond the clouds of personal remembrance. I knew that these people had lived here, that this was their paradise, and that now, though gone, they still slept securely in the memory of the mountain.

I continued along the side hill and passed the junction of the second canyon. Nothing reminded me of the old gold mine, so it passed unnoticed, but further on I found mortars ground into the boulders by the streambed. Behind these, enmeshed in vine and thorn, was a slab covered with the hieroglyphs I had become familiar with at the Waterfall. I sat by the mortars, staring at the strange symbols, while Iboga, priestess of the arcanum, dissolved the wall on which Plato's shadows played and led me to the portal of secret recollections. The rock face dilated and contracted, emphasizing first one section, then another, until the slab became a section of lip, speaking. The mountain talked. I listened and was lifted up to see the canyon from the air as it had been before the avalanche tore down its sides. Water flowed, broadleaf plants and flowering shrubs gave a tropical air, and people were playing again, sliding down Devil's Slide to the clear pool below, laughing among the glades. I turned to look up, to see the mountain above, but a nearby birdcall, like a little hammer shattered the vision, and I was back on the rock, dry as drought, with none but an old Indian woman translucently at my side, grinding seed.

I left the woman to her ghostly labors and went down to where the canyon was dammed by huge boulders, wedged between the two walls. The approach was silted and choked with stickers. The watercourse disappeared into the tangle and emerged at the bottom on the far side in a high, narrow cave. I climbed to where I could see the entrance to the cave from above. It appeared perfectly rectangular, as though made of chiseled stones, and for a moment I pictured the whole canyon as an ancient artifact. The boulder on which I lay and the one at my elbow were covered with hieroglyphs, but I hardly noticed them so entrancing was the totality of the experience.

I had gone no further than this eighteen years earlier, so when the urge to move once more woke me, I decided to head back to camp. The sun was fast falling toward Spitler Mountain, and here and there the canyon bottom was melting into shadow. I decided to climb the sloping wall below the avalanche to cross the rockslide from above. My movements were considerably steadier than before, but my body was heavy and sluggish. The climb was hot and hard. Eventually, though, I was on the broad ledges above the fallen-away face, with Devil's Slide far below. Here the going was relatively easy, but the energy had become incredibly oppressive. My perceptual field was riddled with a chaos of geometries, and my heart was weighted with forebodings. I became too dizzy to stand and crouched down exhausted. Polyhedrons spun through my head, and when I again looked about I was nothing but an abstraction of flat planes. At my side was a rectangular trough that went off into space and pointed at the large, protruding boulder across the canyon. There seemed to be a machine on the boulder. I tried to make it out, but could not, until in a flash of recognition, I saw it as a cannon. In the same moment, I knew that the canyon wall on which I sat had been demolished for some unknown purpose. After a few minutes, the extreme ominousness of the encounter passed. I had been erased and recalibrated for the thousandth time that afternoon and left to reintegrate as best I could. My first move was to escape from the inhospitable ledges and push on to camp. I came out of the canyon not far from the Gooseberry trail and was back at the spring so quickly as to seem a miracle. I drank then fell out on the mat. My body drained away, taking my mind with it. Thinking emptied of content and left me in a midnight void, but an intuition of catastrophe worried my stillness, for I knew that devastation had marked the history of the mountain.

Sometime after dark, I took food and hashish to the hammock. I nibbled at dinner and rocked with the night. Periodically, another visionary onslaught would interrupt my chewing. The visions were as vivid as before, but less frequent. For the most part, I lay relaxed and contented, though when I smoked the hashish, I was swept up again and deposited elsewhere. Reality dissolved with my ego, the motions of my mind and those of the hammock merged, and a new river of color, form, and meaning poured through.

The waning moon mounted a distant ridge and called me forth to fly its magic through the night. Treetops slipped beneath, and I floated the silver sky above the mountain. My being was less tenuous than the air on which it rode and neither excitement nor anticipation disturbed its vacuity. The mountain was a formidable presence clothed in shadow. I drifted past it to hover above the ranch. A dim light from kerosene lamps shone through the windows, and a tipi glowed white. A car approached from Garner Valley, its headlights digging into the ground on the down hills and stabbing erratically at the sky on the up. The driver got out and went into the house. Soon all lights were extinguished and half-sleeping children were carried to cars. Three vehicles left. I followed them to the county road. When they were safely off, my eyes involuted, swept back across the sleeping mountain, and returned to my head, still swinging in a hammock on the far side of the ridge.

The night had become cool. I took a sweater from my pack and sat on a blanket, wrapped in another blanket. Night sounds played with my mind. I was tired, but knew I would not sleep, for this Iboga does not allow. So, wide-awake, I lapsed into dream states and let the night tiptoe through my awareness. In the early morning hours, moonlit mists swirled through the treetops. A night cloud brushed the mountain, and fog, like a damp cloth, settled on Gooseberry Canyon. I went to bed, still not sleepy though wearied from the endless profusions of the day, and stared up through the misty lacework of branches. Change patterned itself on reality and dissolved to the first drops of rain dripping from the canopy of forest. They fell like the beads of an abacus counting the permutations of life and called up the musty, organic smell of humus. They splattered on my face, flushing me out and off to the storage tent where I lay with my head in the doorway, watching drops like diamonds plummet out of the cloud.

The shower was soon over, but water continued to drip from the trees. Somewhere between drops and dreams, the sky lightened and the forest became rosy. I had little desire to move, so I waited until the sun cleared the ridge before gingerly reoccupying the far reaches of my body. It was limp, tired, wobbly, and still subject to periodic takeover by upsurging energies. I shuffled to the spring and washed; then, in an only partially successful effort to revive my drained organism, flushed my system with tea and took a handful of vitamins.

The *I Ching* was aware of my dilapidated condition. I used it to interrogate my energy levels, to find out what another day of tripping was likely to entail. The first hexagram was "Conflict". The judgment said I was being obstructed, that a cautious halt halfway brings good fortune, while going on to the end brings misfortune. I assumed it could mean either to stop now, halfway through the weekend, or continue and back off later in the day, perhaps cancel on the DMT. The first changing line magnified the ambiguity. It says that one cannot engage in conflict, that one has to give way. I agreed, but I was not planning to fight anything anyway. I hoped to find a nice, breezy place in the Saddle and enjoy the day sitting under a tree. If my interior landscapes became troubled, I knew how to back off. The line also contains a strange reference to the people of my town, three hundred households, and calls them guiltless. I took it to refer to my visionary tribe and hoped it was hinting at further contacts during the day.

The second changing line involved ambiguity of a different kind. It speaks of a person who has carried conflict to the bitter end and triumphed, but who then has the ensuing decoration snatched away three times. The line betokens repeated conflict, but I was not dissuaded from tripping because the second hexagram to which it led was, as on the day before, "Gathering Together". Any hesitation I might have felt was overridden by the desire to probe the ancestral consciousness of the mountain more deeply and perhaps solve the mystery of its phantom people.

It was still cool when I left Gooseberry Springs and crossed above Devil's Slide. The long climb up the draw was drudgery, and I was exhausted by the time I reached the top. The view was disappointing, for the day, though cloudless, was hazy. I could see the nearby desert and the tops of the mountains beyond, but everything was indistinct, and the blue of the morning sky was dulling toward gray. When I had rested, I broke out my stash of LSD. Originally, I had planned to take a very large dose, but now I felt unequal to it and, instead, took only two tablets (600 micrograms) of Sunshine.

As I walked to the Saddle, the first tingles of neural electricity flashed behind my eyes, reawakening the Lady Iboga. She worked her magic on the pinnacles ahead, changing them into monuments. Veins of stone high on the cliff faces drew heroic figures, and the whole façade appeared as a wall of stelae from an ancient ruin. The trail stayed some distance below them and passed around the side of the ridge. I had been planning to go off to the terraces below the Monuments, but the air was still, and the Saddle very hot. The trail continued up the ridge in the direction of the high tower of green rock, swathed in forest three ridges away. I hoped it would be cooler in the trees and pushed on, but as I labored up the dusty trail, my body rebelled. I felt as though a large rubber band was attached to the center of my back and the further I walked, the tighter it stretched. I was finally unable to take another step and fell down by the trail. There was no breeze to cool me, no shade to block the blazing sun, so I lay like a leaden soldier until a spurt of vitality enabled me to stumble back down to the Saddle.

I went off into the terraces as soon as I could. They descended for several hundred feet then abruptly dropped away into a great canyon leading down to the desert. Far below, this canyon was joined by Gooseberry Canyon from the left and Landslide Canyon from the right, making the whole a gigantic enclosure of cascading mountainscape. The terraces formed a multilevel labyrinth of gravel and sand, a mazeway where huge boulders, clumps of manzanita, and twisted rows of oak made avenues among little glades and sloping meadows. Here and there stood large pine and fir, and many fallen trees, long dead from fire, were scattered about and sculpted by time into fantastic shapes. Some burned snags still stood taller than the trees replacing them, jutting up from the greenery like black fingers reaching for the sky.

I found a spot under a piñon pine and dropped my pack. The place was an oven. I stripped down to a film of perspiration and sagged sunken-eyed into the sand. Time evaporated in the furnace of eternity, and the pores of my mind, like those of my body, opened, washing me out for moments of lucid freedom. Beyond the emerald edge of the universe lies the diamond of consciousness . . . no sound is heard, for no communication is lacking; nothing is perceived, nothing unknown . . . a haunted stillness reigns; silence revolves endlessly, ghosted by infinities . . . nothing is brought back from the ocean of being; the fisherman catches nothing in his net, the hunter is hareless, for there is nothing here for the human utilitarian to appropriate . . . a pretonal recollection, glimpsed over a reconstructing shoulder fashions the baby brain with wonder; the essence of unconditioned life resonates to new thoughts, in a new consciousness, in the old, aching body propped against a tree in July's sultry air . . .

I came out of my reverie with my mind hovering at the tailing edge of an intuition that had eluded it once again, and I marveled that I could no longer recall what had just happened to me, even though my body still quivered with the intensity of the experience.

I whiled away the hours of midday heat, occasionally wafting off to mysterious, hidden places in the deep space of the stoned forebrain, or to walled cities of the heart where heaven waited, much like a cat. Early in the afternoon, the breeze picked up, and a few wisps of cloud darted overhead. I felt an urge to move again, to wander the terraces and bask in their energy fields. As I set out, I noticed a nearby boulder covered with a beautiful set of hieroglyphs. I brushed past it and climbed out on ramparts of stone similarly enlivened with arcane symbols.

The freshening breeze had swept the desert clean, and the afternoon was sparkling. For the first time since taking the Iboga, I felt coordinated and at ease in my body. I climbed castellated piles of rock and walked curveways of glistening sand. Wind-shaped trees, both alive and dead, whispered as I passed, and high overhead, two hawks circled, watching. I was soon lost in the maze, vaguely aware of my predicament, but not caring, for I was lost in the ruin of an ancient city where everything was positioned to a purpose.

I moved from one piece of shade to another, from a place to gaze down on the desert, to another for surveying the mountain. Eventually, I came back to my clothes and pack. I was enjoying a psychic second wind and felt ready to smoke the DMT. I dressed and broke out the joint. My intention was to smoke on top of the highest pinnacle, so I set off in that direction and made my way up through the labyrinth. The way took me near the base of the cliffs on which I had seen figures that morning. The larger designs were formed by rust-colored veins in the rock, which now showed through a background of the hieroglyphic script. They radiated magic and stopped me as I passed. I remembered the morning's *I Ching* saying that a cautious halt halfway brings good fortune and realized that I should go no further, that I should smoke the DMT here, at the lower rather than the upper cliffs.

A chasm separated the cliffs from where I stood, so that two-thirds of their height towered above and the rest sank below. Part of the abyss was filled with tumbled boulders; the remainder was open. To my left, an old pine, mostly snag with a few vigorous branches, stood slightly elevated in a circular enclosure of boulders. To my right, facing the cliffs across the deepest portion of the chasm, was a peculiar formation that stood like a pedestal thrust into the air. It was a broken pyramid of boulders, slabs, and hardened sediment, which rose thirty feet above me. Part of it had fallen into the abyss, but the opposite side was sloped and not difficult to climb.

I scrambled to the top of the Pedestal and found the place I was looking for. The apex was a sunken enclosure shaped like a broken cup. What remained was a half-moon ledge three feet below rounded lips of sandstone. I dropped to the ledge and leaned back, half-sitting, on the lip. The place was much like the cockpit of an aircraft, for the sandstone was covered with glyphs that might well have been instruments, and the view was what I would have had flying through the Saddle. To the north, I looked over desert and distant mountains; to the south, the ranch's sloping plateau and Garner Valley. Directly before me, even more monumental now that they towered above, were the sculpted cliffs. In a moment of acid euphoria, I felt like a conductor surrounded by an orchestra of megaliths. I conducted them with waving arms, then turned to bow to the audience, and saw Spitler Mountain looking down. It was so massive it blotted out the whole range of the San Jacintos beyond, yet its contour was gentle, rising to the sky in a medley of ridges and rounded sub-peaks.

The breeze was blowing more strongly. Twenty-knot gusts snapped my hair and felt unbelievably good. The DMT joint was stuck precariously behind my ear, so I put it under a rock on the ledge where someone had built a small stupa of milk-white quartz. Hawks glided above, playing the thermals of the ridge against the down draft over the Saddle, and clouds were building in the distance beyond Spitler Peak. I sat immersed in the place like salt in water. Several times, I thought to light the joint, but the wind dissuaded me, and blew me off elsewhere. Finally, I decided to wait no longer and crouched on the ledge to light a match, but the wind slipped through my tightly cupped hands and pinched off the flame as soon as the phosphorus had sizzled. I waited for momentary calms, then spaced out and missed them when they happened, until with a bit of luck the corner of the joint caught and began to smolder as I puffed.

With the first, full lungful of smoke, I knew what I always rediscovered at that point: that I had completely forgotten what consciousness compounded by the LSDMT synergy was like, so different was it from any other reality. I took more smoke, and held it as long as possible. The kinesthetic structure of my body fell away and the unsupported mind dissolved. After the third inhalation, I stood up involuntarily, my mouth agape in wonder. A preternatural light radiated from everywhere and pulsated with transcendent brilliance. I eased back into the half-sitting position and was overwhelmed by the sculpted Monuments. Above and below, to either, everywhere my eyes fell, was an exquisite mosaic vibrant with a tangible, intelligent presence.

I was wonderstruck, and only a spark falling into my cupped hands reminded me to smoke again. I pulled on the joint, and, as I did so, turned my head to the left. My eyes swept the desert and purple mountains beyond. Both radiated a voluptuous magical presence, and guided my head so it continued to turn until I was looking over my shoulder at Spitler Mountain. But what I gazed at was eternity.

My breath was suspended. I was bathed in a new spectrum of radiance to which the outer reality joyfully conformed, and within which my body sat stunned. I no longer confronted a mineral mountain slumbering beneath a torpid sun, but one transformed and utterly resplendent, for the whole of Spitler Mountain was the reclining figure of a mystically beautiful woman, heavy with child. She lay as though resting in labor, her head turned to gaze down her left arm, eternally, at the desert. Her hair swept out from under her cheek and billowed down the arm, which was the long ridge above Gooseberry Springs, and her hair was the forests of Spitler's northern face. The mountain's three sub-peaks were her breasts and belly. The breasts were full; her belly, ripe to the time of delivery. Her legs came down as ridges that bent at the knees and crossed out of sight below the far side of the Saddle. She was clothed in mystic patterns woven from the vegetation and bare rock of her contours, arranged by the geomantic currents of earth. From her breasts came fountains of water, which fell into pools and ran off as nectar. I saw entranceways to her interior colonnaded in lustrous stone, with porticos of flowering vine and carpetings of moss. Exuding serenity, she reached across the gulf of time to smile in my mind, giving substance to intuition, certainty to seeing. I knew this Mountain Lady was a living, sentient presence, a transhuman creature of earth cosmically attuned to the wonder of creation.

I sat astonished, still staring behind my own back. The clarity of the vision increased. I saw people playing on the Lady's belly and about the pools of water. Some were sitting, seeming to stare back, and I wondered what they saw. In an instant I knew, for another, invisible layer of mind peeled away and I apprehended the mountain more completely. Many of its marvels were simultaneously present in an arabesque of self-shining images: the Waterfall, Devil's Slide, the Monuments beneath which I sat, the distant tower of green rock, and constantly present, within and behind the others, the superabundant figure of the reclining Lady, eternally bringing forth children, but dozing now for a moment on the lap of aeons.

I hovered in amazement in the space before my eyes. A storm cloud, carved like white jade, tumbled behind the Lady and provided a new pillow for her radiance. Again my eyes swept the desert. It was like a receptacle of all the world's treasures. They offered themselves for acceptance, but a spark of light from the Lady's belly flashed in the corner of my eye, distracting me, so I turned my head to see what it was. It was a bolt of lightning, or so it seemed to me who was struck by it. Even as my head turned, I knew the truth of utter finality, of doom, of absolute inevitability, for I felt myself turning into death, stepping off into hypertime from where I sensed a projectile screaming toward me with such precision and speed that it would strike before I could twitch. And in the act of pivoting, even as these ultrafast thoughts created themselves, I was struck full on by what they portended.

My body exploded in an incredible clap of thunder. I was spun around in the air and thrown to the rock, my eyes ripping out through the back of my head. Smithereens of skull bone riddled my brain tissue, and severed a psychic master nerve so that no impulse of will could trigger a single somatic response. I was thrown down like dregs from a glass, and from hypertime knew I was far beyond sanity or insanity, that not one of my realities had substance, for if death was a reality, I was dead.

Speed froze to epochal cadences. I plummeted through space, but the wind controlled my falling. It left me spread-eagled on the ledge, my face pressed into the gravel. My body was incandescent: a torrent of energy blasted through, and I howled with the white pain of its intensity.

Consciousness compressed to a molten center and quenched me in burning oil. I became aware of my screaming and pushed convulsively to my hands and knees. Pebbles fell away from my face, and I screamed the louder for having more room to breathe. But behind the agony, within it, and at the center to which I had been compressed, another awareness rested. It was an awareness of something, someone else: a profound Presence breathing peace through the inferno of my being.

I gulped air and continued to scream. In the presence of this Presence, the existential dialectic between heaven and hell arced the gap between the lobes of my brain, and an ancient memory blazed into consciousness. It was the memory of destruction, of the devastation of this mountain kingdom temple city, at this place, long ago. I was the theater of this memory, wherein the serene countenance of the Mountain Lady exploded into the sky, casting debris, like ash, across the highlands. Boulders showered down. The back of Devil's Slide broke, the tower snapped. The mountain shuddered, and canyons fell in on themselves. The gardens and grottoes, the ancient written rocks, the temples and deep chambers, all were smitten, and avalanches filled the tumult with a great uproar.

The memory of the catastrophe revitalized itself, again and yet again, until the enormity of the destruction weighed down on my being. Nowhere in history did I know of a comparable place to this, which crashed upon me. But the Presence, in whose stillness I was held as in a fist of iron, infused the cataclysm with cogency, and I knew that the disaster had been consummated in league with the creative force of the universe. Kali transcendent sacrificed at the shrine of Shiva, and an epoch crumbled from existence.

I was buffeted like a mote in a turbulent sunbeam. The Presence smiled through my agony, and from its timelessness, I remembered the ancient covenant, the cosmic mystery preceding DNA, that nothing of truth is lost, that everything in God's universe is perfect. The catastrophic destruction of the mountain had served to balance the planet. In a moment of sizzling finale, the old world encoded its secrets in the depths of the mountain and yielded its powers back to earth, so the epochs of time would unfold in orderly sequence.

I continued to scream, but now an ocean of realization burst through me and dispersed my pain like fragments of phosphorus. I knew that the consciousness which once reigned here would return; that its beneficence would be reestablished and its gateways to infinity reopened.

The mountain quieted, and my screaming trailed off into sobs. Suddenly, the number 536 appeared in my mind, etched in fires that blazed behind my eyes until 536 was branded on my forebrain. When the smoke cleared, I found myself walking the charred mountain as an Indian, one of a silent people from forgotten times, who passed through, sifting the debris, but left neither story nor song of their findings. And yet, it was because of them that legends of the Seven Cities of Gold grew back into human memory.

Soon my DNA reasserted its prerogatives, and the Indian gave way to a conqueror, arrogant and bold, frightfully clever, and murderously intent. Waves of compassion eroded the distinction, and fire again engulfed me, to rage unhindered over the devastated mountain and cool to cinders in the backs of my eyes.

When my sobbing subsided, I pulled myself up to the sandstone lip above the ledge. Tears blurred the world, and I stared at the mountain as though through rain-splattered glass, but my body seemed submerged in a pool of soothing liquid permeated by the Presence.

For a long while I sagged exhausted, then a fit of screaming recurred, during which I struggled into the half-sitting posture from which I had fallen. I yelled with the intensity of uncontainable energy, but behind it, I felt utterly alive and aglow with the Presence. I took control of my screaming and changed it into the primal sound: AUM. The wind joined my song, and the mountain opened to our call. It pulsed with rhythms of tangible wisdom, its rocks sang their riddles, and space became a medley of songs orchestrated by sunlight. The Mountain Lady, alight in her mystic presence.

I sat cross-legged. The circle was in the lee of the Pedestal, and the wind was above me. It roared through the Monuments and sang with the trees, but where I sat it was so still that I seemed enclosed in a crystalline chalice. The match flared into life; the joint rekindled. I took a long hit of acrid smoke and pressed it in my lungs.

A bubble burst to leave a drop of chatoyant water, like a diamond, on my head. It pulsed with memories of other times, of recollections and reflections, of spectral scenes and ancient understandings. Backward and forward, wave on wave rolled from it, and everything that appeared did so in transcendent beauty. Loveliness, like ripples in a bath of scented oil, stilled to a vision of the Mountain Lady's face, rapt in eternity, gazing at the heavens.

I took another lungful of smoke and the world and my flesh commingled. What before had shone with great Presence from behind the appearance of the mind-spectacle, now became the appearance, and everything was charged with its essence. Perfection was everywhere displayed, alight with creation, and eternal. The demiurge walked on the mountain, and the numen shone from the sky . . .

Again my hand presented me with the joint. The self-radiant realm of time-space disappeared, and with it my astonishment. My nervous system became an organic superconductor, and my interior landscape became that of the sun. As I plunged into incandescence, my every thought, every capability, every memory, every dream, every abstraction, every perception, and every sensation were simultaneously present, bathed in every emotion, every shade of feeling, and every desire. For an instant, the balance was perfect; Libra, the air cardinal, triumphant. Then this, too, fell away, and reality was not different from itself.

Twice more during the next half hour, I relit the DMT. Sometime later, I awoke to myself, looking at the remnant of charred paper in my hand and at the hand itself, so strangely shimmering, so alien and mysterious, so fully alive. I sat transfixed as other parts of my being reconstituted themselves: the feeling tones of the body, a knowledge of seeing, a persona with its protuberant ego, all repackaged and sitting in a circle of rocks beneath a mountain, with an old snag tree for companion.

The sun dropped toward Spitler Peak and threw new shadows on the Mountain Lady. I sat for a while longer filled with what had happened and alight with new, unthought possibilities. When the hawks left, I knew it was time to go, so I shouldered my pack and went out through the labyrinth. At the edge of the Saddle, I looked back at the monumental cliffs, but I had no words to say.

On the way down the trail, the Presence remerged with the present, and the reality of the contemporary world came down like a prismatic latticework of ego-related ideas. I could see the ranch buildings. They seemed very quiet, and I felt no threat emanating from them, so I lost myself in the ecstasy of walking and all too soon arrived at the house. It was almost deserted. Everyone had left the night before, when word came that the police raid was set for this morning. The raid had not materialized, and one woman had come back with her family to tend the animals.

There was little danger of a raid this late in the day, so I showered and stayed for dinner. First, however, I took my *I Ching* back out to the side hill, to sit under an old oak and ponder the events of the weekend. I was curious to see how the *I Ching* would explain what had happened, and I hoped to discover, if I could, what it all meant, and where it was pointing.

"Peace" said the book, and "Break-Through":

> Heaven is on earth, and their powers unite in deep harmony.
> Flutter down, without boasting,
> But resolutely make the matter known at the court of the king.
> Gathering is followed by dispersion

Part II
CLOUD

Conceptual Interlude

The experiences that accompany the use of psychedelic substances demand an explanation or life soon becomes frozen in an apparent contradiction between the ordinary and the profound. Fortunately, high consciousness has a long history of careful study, and the methods by which it may be apprehended are well tested. Each level of our awareness is more comprehensive than that which flows from it, but its expression is more fundamental. The level we are generally constrained to use is that of conceptual understanding, whose intelligible pattern is verbal. Unfortunately, this is a precarious place to take a stand, for even the best ideas are but fingers pointing at one's half-hidden face in the mirror of reality.

The only truth worth specifying is misleading when spoken, in that it gives rise to the many ways of erroneous thinking. We, and everything else, and all we do, are one consciousness, itself not separately existing, wherein we perceive ourselves as what we are. This consciousness needs no elucidation. It presents what is, and enjoys it. Its intrinsic expression is identity with every level of creation and all the patterns of being. Consciousness, creation, and being are not different, but our failure to see this constitutes our bondage and creates, in turn, the necessity of words.

Within the patternings of the Tao, lightning flashes, and ways of access linger like luminescence. To see them is to blow out the candle of ego within the lantern of thinking, for it is a commonplace of psychology that to eliminate one set of stimuli is to sharpen the perception of other sets. Such a task is often difficult. We too easily identify with being a body among bodies and craftily set out to get what we want, forgetting for the moment that that which thus sets out is but another facet of the one consciousness, which, like a planetarium, projects a universe of stars on its own black dome. This consciousness is not aided in its expression by our usually vain attempts to register and catalogue everything within it as ego-relevant concepts. It needs them no more than an eye needs an eyelash to see, but since we are usually sleepy-headed dreamers anyway, the knowledge of perfection is lost amid a compendium of myths, a cast of millions, and the fascinating props of our eternally spinning stage.

In the spectrum of creation, we are organic beings patterned by energies that issue from the fundamental character of the universe. From out an apparent emptiness, existence appears. It precedes life, and includes it. The relationship between them is like that between electromagnetism and chemistry. The latter, as science has demonstrated, is but one aspect of the former, and all chemical phenomena are completely explainable in terms of electromagnetic theory. Similarly, our humanness is an electromagnetic pattern that, in its chemical expression, gives rise to dual-brained bipeds capable of functioning in a planetary milieu. We exist because a unified field of consciousness radiates its designs as the pulsations and mutations of energy that, in creating the universe, support the appearance of the physical and its manifold forms of life.

This ontology is taken from modern physics, but it also expresses the epistemological imperative that has long been the foundation of metaphysics. A structural trinity is involved: first, the undifferentiated field; second, its energy transformations as time, space, and the substrata of things; and third, the precipitation therein of individualized beings such as ourselves. In Christianity, a discipline of the heart, the three are referred to as the Holy Trinity and depicted as persons. In Buddhism, a discipline of the mind, they are called the Triple Jewel, and are described as the three aspects of our own enlightenment. In the Buddhist tradition, they are named Dharmakaya, Sambhogakaya, and Nirmanakaya, but it is emphasized that these are but heuristic distinctions within the sublime perfection that is them all.

The Dharmakaya is the unified field. Since it precedes all that exists, it cannot be placed in the categories of existence. Thus it is characterized as the void, or as nothingness, and is not vulnerable to further conceptual incursion. Its existential metaphors are the nonexistence of space and the unreality of time, for both time and space are coterminous within it. Eternal in scope, instantaneous in action, it is the conscious substance of the universe, wherein it moves as the ecstatic flow of energies and resides as the infinity of bodies.

The creative expression of the Dharmakaya is the Tao whose appearance is the Sambhogakaya. The Sambhogakaya is creation in all of its splendor, and the whole of it glitters with the speed of thought. It is the fundamental category of phenomena wherefrom all things arise with equal dignity. Among its plenitude of aspects, the nearest and most constant is our planet Earth, whose biosphere and noosphere provide us with bodies and minds. The Sambhogakaya is the living consciousness of this marvelously complex world, the comprehension of all its sentient beings in all of their modes and relationships. Thus it is also our species consciousness, or collective unconscious, and the wisdom of our cells. It is so vast that we must ignore it as such in order to exist as separate, and so we do, and so it is, and so also exists the peculiar fact that we then confront what we are with what we are not, and give the nearest illusion our name.

The Nirmanakaya is that which perceives itself as separately existing. It is what each of us knows we are, for its attribute is individuality. It is a distinction within the Sambhogakaya, much like the sparkle of a diamond. And just as a sparkle, were it to think, might mistake its glitter for the substance of the stone, so too, the Nirmanakaya may grasp its illusion as reality and see itself as an ego. This impasse persists as long as the Nirmanakaya suppresses its innate sense of universal identity by asserting its own, for its own is but a fragment of the universal slowed to the speed of an organic mechanism.

As independent entities with self-cognizing energy systems, we confuse ourselves with our chemical modes of transformation and perceive the world in terms of its compatibility with our bodies. The Nirmanakaya becomes trapped in its ego-object's reflection of the world as other objects, which it then seek to control or adapt to more perfectly. But in the Sambhogakaya, where the form we have is not different from those we perceive, the ego strives in vain, for it is, at best, an ungainly creature frozen in time, reacting no faster than an eye can wink and seeing its source only as a hypothetical superconsciousness, or an alien, pre-civilized unconscious.

The Sambhogakaya manifests as the radiations of our neurological circuitry. It is our electromagnetic nature, and only its statistical effects can be perceived in terms of our Nirmanakayaic chemistry. But this is no loss, for though the Sambhogakaya appears to us a supervening phenomenon, it is the controlling agency of our being and may be experienced in its own right. In Buddhism, the science of this experience and the arts used to obtain it make up the philosophy and practice of tantra. Consequently, a tantric adept is one capable of living in the electromagnetic mode of consciousness.

According to tantra, the human mechanism is both constructed and controlled through six chakras, or energy centers. These are located in relation to the spinal column and brain, but are not specifically identified with any organs. Their exact locations are indeterminate because changeable, for they are six foci in the energy field that arises by virtue of our electromagnetic essence. Each chakra controls a primary sector of our being and establishes one of the separate facets that, in toto, enshrine our human nature. Thus the chakra system constitutes our primary awareness, and even though physically nonexistent, its experiential reality is spectacularly more vital than that of our chemical sensors.

The chakras can be designated by the areas in the body where they manifest, and so are called the root, sex, stomach, heart, throat, and ajna—the last being the third, or middle, eye in the forehead. Each has autonomous controls over a full range of human functions, but all are interdependent and harmoniously related.

The root chakra provides us with our grounding in the physical, for it is consciousness as things and their relationships. We experience it not only as the kinesthetic awareness of the body, but also as our territorial instincts and our penchant for possessions. Thus it is the dungeon of the miser within us, but it is also the root of the tree of life, the promised land of biblical expectation, and the seat of human perfection.

The sex chakra activates the physical. We know it as the libido and experience it as the serpent, power. It is that which infuses the body with dynamic stability, adding function to structure. It is the ego as a composite physical awareness, the force that propels us through the world, seemingly free to do as we please.

We are, however, path-following animals, and the energies that move our bodies do so in accord with the programs of the stomach chakra. Here are found the blueprints of the body, the index to its library of actions. The stomach chakra is the accountant of the body's needs and the distributor of its food; the warehouse of habit patterns and skills that manifest as temporal instructions to guide our doings.

The heart chakra is the seat of the human mind, the home of our emotive nature. It selects what we dwell on and constructs our worlds through magnetic principle of attraction and repulsion, thereby underlying everything we are capable of knowing. This principle manifests organically as love and aversion and, when rightly understood is a reliable guide, and delightful companion, among the pitfalls of life.

The throat chakra sits astride the heart like a horse and thinks to use the mind to *its* purposes. It is the ruler within, the place from which the head is turned and the eyes directed, the energy source that unleashes the tongue and sets the arms, with their competent hands and delicate fingers, to weaving patterns with the prosaic world. It is the throne of human destiny, set beneath the crystalline aperture of ajna.

The ajna chakra validates life. It is the portal for that which comes into existence and for that which departs. Poised intangibly between the lobes of the brain, afloat in a pool of fire-liquid, it sprinkles intimations of eternity, like dewdrops, below. Without trifling with the world, it stands as its mentor, for it is the specific nonexistence of everything that is just about to be, the cornucopia of time through which life is enticed to earth by the fragrances of the Tao.

Such is the teleological analogy which tantra provides. It accords with our fundamental nature as human beings and with that of the universe within which we find ourselves. The ancient Chinese experienced our electromagnetic nature in a very similar fashion. They accepted their existential insight as the Tao of our species and from it constructed a completely comprehensive paradigm of human life. With their penchant for binary perception, they took the operational modes of the chakras as being either positive or negative, firm or yielding, and thus effectively encoded us as the hexagrams of the *I Ching*. The commentaries on the hexagrams metaphorically describe the 64 behavioral configurations that are physiologically possible for us; and the changing lines, in their various combinations, depict the 4,096 different ways we have of switching masks instantaneously. The wisdom of the book teaches dexterity in the process.

The *I Ching* antedates Buddhism by two thousand years, but it is unsurpassed as a tantric text. It describes the functional relationships that exist among the chakras and the dynamics that relate them. Each hexagram is made up of two trigrams, one on top of the other. These are considered the essential structures of mind and body, for the trigram is the Chinese expression for the Triple Jewel.

The lower three charkas, the root, sex, and stomach, comprise a single register that is said to be within, or behind. Similarly, the heart, throat, and ajna chakras form a unit described as without, or ahead. The two trigrams are structurally analogous, for the three lines, from bottom to top, represent the Sambhogakaya, Nirmanakaya, and Dharmakaya. The integral correspondence expressed by the hexagram links the root with the heart, the sex with the throat, and the stomach with the ajna. Thus the heart chakra is to the mind what the root chakra is to the body—the quintessence of its structure. Together they make up the Sambhogakayaic correspondence, which provides embodiment for the laws of our being. The Nirmanakayaic correspondence is between the sex and throat chakras, the second and fifth lines of the hexagram. This is our motility nexus, the master of the powers that move our bodies through space, our lives through time. The upper correspondence is between the stomach and ajna chakras, and reflects the Dharmakaya. It programs us with the cosmically pre-existing authority of order and thereby establishes us in life amid the patternings of existence.

In our electromagnetic nature, we exist as hierarchies of attunement in which each chakra is a responsible and independent entity in a democracy of unequals. The principle of relatedness is yielding dominance because the upper chakras must, of necessity, give precedence to the demands of the lower chakras. Were it not so, even the Dharmakaya would not deign to exist, and the Creative would be unmasked in its essence. In reality, however, each chakra nourishes those below, sees itself as some sort of ultimate, and intuits the existence of those above.

Although there are six chakras, only the lower five control phenomena that can be said to be existent. In the *I Ching*, the sixth line, that of the ajna chakra, is characterized as the place of heaven, whose human analogue is the sage. The sage abandons the world's fashions for its reality. The fifth line is that of the son of heaven, the ruler who rules what the sage abandons. The progression of analogues continues through the heart chakra, which is the place of the minister, to the stomach chakra where the official resides, to the sex chakra where the general exercises delegated powers to maintain the physical integrity of the whole. The lowest line is reserved for assistants and is characterized as the place of the masses, for it sees us as straw dogs and deals with us as statistics rather than persons.

In yielding to its lower expressions, consciousness gives rise to a universe of utter uniqueness wherein the nature of its own existence is expressed as forbearance. Our habit of perceiving ourselves as personalized bodies indicates that we habitually assume awareness in the lower chakras, and assign primary reality to their phenomena, for consciousness gives way to its lowest common denominator and directs itself through the felt imperatives at each level of its expression. Thus, though the dynamism of the sex chakra is the perfection of the body, it will, if called on, yield to the body's desire for security and harden into defenses. Similarly, the vast, archetypical realm of the heart chakra will yield to the stomach chakra's demands for primacy and shrink to the size of a body.

These dysfunctions are an unnecessary tragedy, for to remain in the body chakras is to accept wretched conditions for life. When we are unable to free consciousness from the imperatives of the root chakra, we become hoarders and money grubbers; caught in the sex chakra, we are sadists, masochists, and power junkies; enmeshed in the stomach chakra, we bicker endlessly as control freaks and spend life building social pyramids with ourselves, conveniently, at the top.

The tantric way is to reverse this value sense and undertake the epochal walk upward, chakra by chakra, through the magical, transorganic domains where ontogeny recapitulates theogony. In this ascent, the dominant patterns of ego-centered consciousness are shattered by advancing into the heart chakra, where the Sambhogakaya dwells as our collective nature. From here, emerging again as a unique individual, one stands on the shore of infinity, alight in the brilliance of ajna, and conjoined to reality by the stillness within.

Dispersion

The people of a nation founded in revolution are blessed in having a fundamental right to question the motives of those who shroud themselves in the authority of government and presume thereby to speak for the nation. This critical function is the hallmark of democracy, but when office is confused with authority, and inferior people use the one to impose the other, criticism is called conspiracy, and the government wages war on its citizens. Such is the impasse to which the victors of Vietnam have brought us, and even more ominous than the current chaos are the specters that hover over our future as a consequence of their policies and pretensions of leadership.

A nation, like an individual, is a physical and ideational projection of the Sambhogakaya. It, too, pulsates with the Tao, and changes. As with our bodies which continuously recreate their substance, a nation brings forth generations who alter the country in accordance with their understandings. This alteration is the history that Nirmanakayaic man writes into the earth and that the earth reflects as our physical and psychological environments. This reflection is called karma: the manifestation of our destiny.

Karma means we reap what we sow. It is a true ethical proposition, generally overlooked by those who think to violate it and by those for whom ignorance is a form of false security. It applies as surely to nations as it does to individuals. Not only the love and kindnesses, but also the violence and devastations we have wrought on others must return to us, for such is the law upon which our laws are based—the law of justice, the principle of karma.

In Southeast Asia, our brand of violence was termed impersonal. Brutality was statistical, euphemistically denied. Death was by poisoned defoliants and skyloads of sanitizing bombs, delivered by the most ponderous military complex known to history. At home, the same consciousness manifested as another set of interrelated bureaucracies, many of them newly formed: a macro-bureaucracy of federal and state police agencies, replete with contingents of spies, informers, burglars, and assassins, all computerized by the FBI into a spider web of political control. Thus has our national karma expressed itself. Our leaders have succeeded in harnessing us with that which Asia has contemptuously rejected. Now they wage helicopter wars in Mexico and poison marijuana fields as they once did Vietnamese rice paddies. But this time, they poison their own children.

In the history of nations, violence is often conjoined with incompetence in the affairs of state, and inferior men establish police networks to keep themselves in power. During such times, the norm of established government becomes conformity rather than conscience, and the foundations of the state wobble on the brink of an ethical void. Such is happening in the United States. Our cynical, prerogative-encrusted leaders place armed men at every crack in their crumbling citadel and institute reigns of legal terror, arguing that a tyranny of laws is the fulfillment of democracy and the promise of rational government.

Tyrants tell us what to believe, laws tell us to suspend belief in deference to words. So, except in the capriciousness of what is forbidden, a tyranny of laws is no different than a tyranny of men, and we distinguish the two into categories of good and evil only at our own peril. We are told a great deal about people everywhere, and their plight under totalitarianism, conditions of which we have little direct knowledge and over which we have no control, while at home, a national pogrom against the new consciousness goes unchecked and virtually unnoticed. We are righteously horrified by the Gulag Archipelago, yet unable to see that our own prisons are operated as exercises in degradation by the minions of a punitive government.

We are in the midst of a classical inquisition, but most of us ignore it in deference to official deceit, and the destruction of our constitutional liberties by predatory bureaucracies is accepted as a necessary burden on both the national treasury and the nation's conscience. Since 9/11 the government has been able to solidify opposition to those they call terrorists, and gradually use that opposition to oppose any political enemy they care to. Political empires are being carved out of our freedoms and administered by fiat by people whose profession is to control our thought and direct our lives. The actions carried out against the Brotherhood of Eternal Love illustrate the threat posed to our values and principles by the new, self-concocted and self-serving, punitive establishment of America.

The long-expected raid on the Brotherhood ranch came before dawn on the Saturday following my weekend of tripping on the mountain. It was, however, but one arm of a federal police octopus simultaneously striking in three states and overseas. Agents of thirteen police forces were involved, including the Federal Bureau of Investigation, the Bureau of Narcotics and Dangerous Drugs (BNDD), the Central Intelligence Agency, the Internal Revenue Service, the Bureau of Customs, and the Orange County, California, District Attorney's Office. The Orange County District Attorney was ostensibly in charge of the operation so it would look less like a Washington bulldozer. He was chosen for his malleable grand jury that, a few days before the raids, issued ninety secret indictments for people the BNDD claimed were members of the Brotherhood of Eternal Love and therefore involved in a conspiracy to undermine the government of the United States by heightening the consciousness of its citizenry. With these indictments as their paper foundation, task forces struck throughout the United States. It was an official crime wave, timed to make the Sunday newspapers as well as the November election, and it was carried out with the imperial legerdemain of a corrupt, jealous, and graft-ridden police empire.

In the summer of 1972, the raids represented the climax of a neatly orchestrated dramatic fiction, a scenario the Bureau of Narcotics and Dangerous Drugs had created to justify its existence and greatly expand its operations. At the critical point, however, the juggernaut faltered, for none of the raids uncovered any evidence on which its prosecutors could base their contentions. Nevertheless, more than fifty people were arrested, and bails totaling nearly seven million dollars were set. The BNDD was steamrolling to political significance, and neither truth nor justice was to be an impediment. It had only to cover up its blunderings and dominate the media with the mendacious.

At the mountain the operation was a caricature of Vietnam. The raiding party, in a caravan of cars, vans, and trucks, broke through the county road gate an hour before dawn and descended on the sleeping ranch. The few who had stayed were routed from bed; wives were separated from their husbands, children from their parents. During the day all, including the kids, were repeatedly interrogated while the ranch property was systematically taken apart by search parties. Nothing, except for a small bag of marijuana in the truck of a visiting couple, was found, and yet six people were arrested on spurious charges and their bails were set at more than a quarter of a million dollars. Sometime after midnight, the tentacle for the ranch was set in motion. At 2:00 am, a justice of the peace in the small town of Hemet was gotten out of bed to sign a warrant that had been prepared in conjunction with the Orange County indictments. The full company then assembled at the Anza house, and the final go-ahead was received by telephone from Washington.

The raiding party, in a caravan of cars, vans, and trucks arrived at the county road gate an hour before dawn. They had been given a key by the forest service, but chose not to use it, and battered down the gate with sledgehammers. They proceeded up the six-mile dirt road in a predetermined formation, for they had aerial photographs from which to work, and each building and tipi on the property was separately targeted. The first house was that of the ranch foreman. It was a hundred yards back from the road, half a mile from the main cluster of buildings. The last vehicle from the convoy detached itself and pulled a short way into the drive. Officers and agents slipped out and took positions around the house. Then, under the Hitleresque no-knock provision of the Nixon-Mitchell Crime Control Act, three of them burst through the front door and, a moment later, into the bedroom of the house. The foreman and his wife were in bed, their children asleep in the corner of the room. They woke to find themselves surrounded by guns and blinded by bright spotlights. The first words they heard were the classic shout of American goon squads: "Don't move, you bastards, or we'll blow your heads off!"

Spotlights swept the room. More agents came in through the back of the house, kicking in the door as they did so. Soon, all the agents surrounded the bed, pointing an arsenal of pistols, automatic weapons, and shotguns at the couple. The commotion woke the children, both less than five years old, who terrified, began to scream. A narcotics agent ordered the foreman and his wife to get up and lean against the wall, hands above their heads, for searching. They were not clothed, so the foreman told his wife to stay where she was. The agent reached down and ripped the covers from the bed. Two others grabbed the foreman and dragged him to the floor, where the first agent kicked him, straddled him, and cocked his pistol. He put the muzzle between the foreman's eyes and told him that if he did not do what he was told his brains would be all over the bedroom. The foreman froze. His wife, followed by spotlights, went to the children and tried to quiet them, for they were screaming uncontrollably. But they could not be comforted, and for the next few days stayed in shock.

The remainder of the police convoy stopped short of the ranch house, leaving vehicles strung out along the road above the orchard. The raiding party split into small groups: some for the tipis, some for the outlying buildings, and the rest for the main house. The main group, weapons ready, moved stealthily along the side of the ranch house toward the two doors in front. Unbeknownst to them, they crept past the toilet where Silvertongue, a veteran of previous encounters with police bureaucracy who was wanted elsewhere for the crime of providing enjoyment for others, was sitting. He had arrived the day before and would have left immediately except for a nasty case of Montezuma's revenge. Now, enthroned as he was, he could do little except deposit his ID beneath him and reflect ruefully on the vicissitudes of fate.

At the front of the house, the raiders divided into two groups, one for each door, both of which led into the same room. At a signal, they burst through the doors with a great cry, but the room was dim and deserted and, in the confusion, the two groups ran into each other, guns to the fore. As they sorted themselves out, there was a brief silence into which Silvertongue boomed from the toilet that they should cool it, women and children were sleeping, and no one was armed.

His call brought the spearhead of the raiding party to his door. It was kicked open, and two agents rushed in, only to back out again, even more quickly. His condition made him relatively immune to further intimidation, so Silvertongue told them to shut the door, he'd be out when he could. They did.

The raiding party routed through the rest of the house and came up with one couple and child. They were taken to the living room where they were soon joined by others pulled from a tipi and a small house on the far side of the barnyard. As soon as the preliminary search of the house was completed, the adults were separated and put into different rooms.

Sometime after dawn, the police vehicles were brought down to the house. Among them was a mobile crime laboratory. An interrogation and mugging facility was set up under the oaks, and the technical phase of the operation began. Police technicians examined, photographed, and fingerprinted everything in sight. Art and equipment was confiscated as evidence, and a mountain of irrelevant information: farming records, letters, calendars, recipes, schoolbooks, was taken to support the contention of yet another conspiracy against the government. In the process, several small shrines and the central shrine in the house were destroyed and a number of shrine pieces pocketed.

Later in the morning, the prisoners were taken, one by one, for interrogation before a triumvirate of special agents. The agents alternately intimidated, threatened, and cajoled them, but got nothing for their efforts except homilies on love, ranching, and the rights of free men. Afterward, each of the prisoners was mugged. One of the mothers objected to her infant being fingerprinted, but she was held back while it was done and told to tell her grievances to the Supreme Court. Silvertongue avoided the whole process by pleading diarrhea at the appropriate moment and, later, when the night of no sleep had taken its toll and policemen of every sort stretched out snoozing in the shade, he was forgotten.

The dismantling of the ranch continued through the heat of the day. The house was turned inside out, the tack room and tool house were emptied, and every vehicle was taken apart. The result of the effort was less than an ounce of marijuana found in the camper of a couple who had come that week to visit. Early in the afternoon, some political types arrived from the city and went about having their pictures taken. After that, the show was over, and those arrested were put in the paddy wagon. The foreman was arrested for resisting arrest, the man in the main house for a dubious ID. The couple with the camper was arrested for possession of marijuana, and the couple in the small house for possession of controlled substances, which later turned out to be vitamin pills and an herbal douche. (The bail for the six was set at more than a quarter of a million dollars.) Silvertongue was left behind. He posed as an itinerant hitchhiker who had lost his wallet in New Mexico, and, since his sleeping bag and pack were in the back of a truck, his story was credible. They told him to stay at the ranch and help the remaining two women with the chores.

Similar raids were conducted elsewhere, all before dawn, all without warning. The results were also similar, for virtually no drugs were found: altogether, a little grass, a personal stash of mescaline, and some sacramental LSD. By Saturday evening, the Bureau of Narcotics and Dangerous Drugs came out with a press release, the truth had been altered to fit the political aspirations of its mutilators. The truth was that the raids were committed as an exercise in tyranny; people were arrested without cause, jailed without reason, and publicly punished for their religion. But this is hardly what the federal policemen were going to say about themselves.

The nature of the government's fraud became evident on the following morning when the police version of what had happened was released as the Sunday news. It was aimed at a national audience. The county newspaper (the Riverside *Press-Enterprise*) carried a short article on page three, but both the *New York Times* and the *Los Angeles Times* featured the story on page one. The New York story began:

> Fifty-seven persons connected with Timothy Leary's sex and drug sect, the Brotherhood of Eternal Love, were arrested or indicted and large quantities of LSD, hashish, hashish oil, cocaine, mescaline and marijuana were seized in dawn raids in California, Oregon and Hawaii today, the Bureau of Narcotics and Dangerous Drugs announced.

The *Press-Enterprise* was more specific, for it had direct access to the man who was nominally the head of the nationwide operation:

> Orange County District Attorney Cecil Hicks said an estimated $7.9 million in hallucinogenic drugs had been confiscated . . . He said 1.5 million LSD tablets, 30 gallons of hashish oil and 2½ tons of hashish were netted during the raids.

These charges were malicious fabrications of self-serving men, speaking with the authority and under the sanction of the United States. With them, Vietnam had come home to roost, and the official prevarication was established as surrogate social truth. The amount of proscribed substances taken in the raids was miniscule compared to the claims of the police. A month later, the district attorney was forced to retract his statement. He said he had been misquoted, and that the quantities he mentioned were not from the raids, but rather were the total of all psychedelic drug seizures that year. This information hardly made the newspapers.

More insidious than the outright lie, however, was the simultaneous slander and vilification unleashed by the strategists at the Bureau of Narcotics and Dangerous Drugs against the Brotherhood, for this was the United States government openly attacking a bona fide American religion and using despicable tactics to do so. The Brotherhood of Eternal Love was a small religion with less than a hundred members. It was incorporated in the State of California during the halcyon days of the mystical sixties. Its members used, and taught their children to use, psychedelic sacraments for their religious celebration, communion, and growth. Timothy Leary became associated with the Brotherhood some time after its founding, when his League for Spiritual Discovery (a similarly oriented, psychedelic religion in New York) was destroyed in a police action that was a prototype of the one launched later against the Brotherhood. Dr. Leary's association with the Brotherhood was short-lived, for, less than a year after his arrival in California, he was arrested for a half-joint of marijuana, reportedly planted in his car by police under orders to halt his campaign for governor of the state. Thereafter, he was either in prison or self-imposed exile following his escape. As the country's prime political boogieman, he was excellent copy, and anything said about him was fervently believed by the government's captive audience. He was linked to the Brotherhood by a scurrilous charge of "ideologic trafficking", and both were paraded before the nation as degenerates.

The Bureau of Narcotics and Dangerous Drugs' news release called the Brotherhood "a clandestine cult founded by Dr. Timothy Leary . . . a profit-oriented criminal enterprise ceremoniously practicing group sexual freedom in connection with cult beliefs and the use of drugs." Dr. Leary was called the "high priest of hippydom," and the Brotherhood was castigated as a corrupt form of the psychedelic-religious subculture. The newspapers printed the only side of the story they were allowed to hear, and the country was once again pap-fed on sensationalism.

Concurrent with the denigration of a religion by the police functionaries of our government was an economic assault against both the individuals who were arrested in the raids and the Brotherhood as a legal entity. Implicit in any conspiracy charge is the enormous cost of legal defense, for it is an arduous and expensive process to disprove governmental calumny. Consequently, the charge of conspiracy is itself an economically punitive weapon and a political tank for overrunning opposition. As the opening move in their assault, the government prosecutors demanded, and got, record-setting bails, averaging over $100,000 each, placed on those arrested. Such sums were previously reserved only for the worst of criminal offenders, and bails of this sort levied against members of the Brotherhood can only be understood as an assault on public opinion, imputing guilt by treating innocent people with contempt and displaying them as though they were highly dangerous felons.

The actions taken against the Brotherhood as a legal entity were on a similar scale. The ranch property constituted the physical assets of the Brotherhood, and the machinery of government was set into motion to confiscate it. A tax lien of $76 million was laid on the property, which was then taken in lieu of payment. The precedent established here is interesting, for it could also be used by organized and militantly democratic citizens of a city like Detroit to take General Motors for themselves. In the case of the Brotherhood, the action could not even be contested without the risk of arrest, for many unused and secret indictments were still being held by the district attorney. Against this background of official slander and coerced silence, the hullabaloo of deceit rode triumphant, and an American religion was effectively proscribed.

The lies and preposterous claims were dry ice thrown in the waters of public trust by governmental authorities. The $7.9 million in confiscated psychedelics, the $6.8 million in punitive bails, and the $76 million in hypothetical taxes, all had the single purpose of dramatizing the police action in terms of money. The Bureau of Narcotics and Dangerous Drugs needed to justify the outrageous sums they had spent in creating the Brotherhood as a formidable national threat, and, as was soon evident, they wanted much, much more. Over two hundred agents were used in the campaign against the Brotherhood, a church whose membership, even according to the exaggerations of the BNDD, was itself no more than two hundred, including children. Preparations for the raids alone had taken well over a year, and uncounted thousands of hours had gone into them. Consequently, only a dramatic fiction of gargantuan dimensions could cover so vain and presumptuous an expenditure of national energy.

The Bureau's demand for more money from Congress rode on the success of this deception, for if a tiny subculture like the Brotherhood was as rich as the Rockefellers, as far-flung as the CIA, and as devious as the devil, it would go without congressional question that hundreds of millions of dollars would be needed to defend the country against it. Within a month of the raids, President Nixon requested a tenfold increase in funding for national anti-drug agencies and called for the creation of a new macro-bureaucracy, the Drug Enforcement Administration, composed of all of them and controlled by him. Congress gave unstintingly. A year later, in testimony before the Senate, agents of the new bureaucracy multiplied their old BNDD estimate of the Brotherhood's membership to three thousand, a fifteen-fold increase designed to keep their delusions forever before Congress.

If, in a climate of deception, it is illegal to demur, it is perhaps permissible to examine the logic of the lie that oppresses, and hope therein to find the real problems with drugged America. The lien of $76 million dollars levied against the ranch represented the aggregate tax the government claimed was owed them by the Brotherhood. This figure was calculated as seven percent of the profit the Brotherhood was supposed to have earned as a capitalistic enterprise during the five years of its existence. In short, the government contended that the Brotherhood made well over a billion dollars during this period. At the same time, it was alleged that these same people were spaced out behind orgiastic hallucinations, and carried out their activities under the influence of dangerous, debilitating, and dispiriting substances.

There would seem to be a contradiction here that, if analyzed, might yield a rational culprit. It is evident that psychedelics have not been outlawed because of any danger to their users, for the officially presented picture of the Brotherhood is one of astounding success. It would rather appear that it is this success itself that the government seeks to outlaw, for any increase in the psychic effectiveness of the people is viewed as a threat by inferior men who use the offices of government to undermine and control our lives.

It was not always so. In their political wisdom, the founders of the United States placed God before the nation, but their successors put policemen before God, and ambitious politicians now pass judgment on the religious convictions of the people. With leaders such as these, democracy founders, for when our freedom to believe is subverted, all other values collapse. Today that catastrophe has overtaken us. We have forgotten that when the ethical consciousness of a nation is openly attacked by it government, when citizens are spied on and arrested, imprisoned, driven into hiding or exile, kidnapped, or officially murdered for upholding their beliefs, the political illness is terminal, for no nation can long survive the moral corruption of its leadership.

Four decades after these prognostic events, the situation has deteriorated. The BNDD was superseded by the Drug Enforcement Agency and became bigger; a political plum with huge amount of money and support for many who, one way or another, stuff their pockets with monies that should be spent in far better ways. Instead, as our surrogates, we arm and pay the Mexicans and Columbians to fight huge, multi-billion dollar drug cartels. The problem, as everyone well knows, is with demand. People want drugs, use them, and cherish them. There will always be a market to sustain them, so the War on Drugs is not only a stupid but an endless war, draining resources into the dubious hands of new agencies staffed with yet more men with guns.

Washington, it seems, is a washed up city. The buildings sparkle; the politicians do not. They are hopelessly grounded on deceit, being unable to understand the difference between a good drug and a bad drug. Prohibiting all recreational drugs translates to money in the pockets of political con men, for if drugs were legal they would make many people richer, but not authorities who would be only allowed to tax the lawful sale of such substances, The riches they garner, either willingly or subconsciously, from so useless a war proves how well they pay themselves to continue approving our national idiocy.

Part III

MOUNTAIN

Historical Interlude

These are biblical times. Our home is a nuclear/space age in which the possibility of utter annihilation is a shared consciousness, and mythic archetypes fashion the beginnings of the new epoch. The unreconstructed present confronts the irreducible now directly. Energy overwhelms life. We have eliminated cities in a single flash and put our finger on the moon, but in so doing we have stepped beyond history, for in the face of massive discontinuity and catastrophe, the orderly sequences of historical civilization lose their relevance, and the collective unconscious of our species mind grows restless before time. A man sweeping toward Niagara is unconcerned with the tributaries of the river. He is freed from speculation by the reality he faces and from which he must extricate himself. Under such compulsion, consciousness slips into biblical gear, while history, like an abandoned boat, sweeps on.

Death is an illusion, and the superior man bows his head in order to see with perfect clarity. The autumn of 1972 progressed as a paid political charade. In Washington, Tiberius M. Nixon and his Prussian circus barnstormed to righteousness, and in Orange County, the district attorney did likewise. I watched from a distance and devoted myself to other interests. Among these was a study I pursued whenever I passed a library or found a museum of antiquities in which to while away an afternoon. I sought to discover the meaning of the visions I had experienced above the ranch, hoping to find historical corroboration for my still smoldering memory of a great temple city and a mountain carved like a woman.

In the weeks following my trip, I was on the move and had little time for reflection, but often as I drifted to sleep, remembrances of the mountain arose, swimming like luminescent fish through the depths of my mind and off into the dream state. Veiled images slipped through shadows and disappeared in the spotlight of my noticing them. I swirled as mists brushing the cheek of the Mountain Lady and raged as a whirlwind through the epic destruction that terminated her existence as a human artifact, then woke with a myoclonic jerk, suddenly adrift and alone as in the aftermath of a shipwreck when all that remains is a bit of flotsam and an iridescent slick of oil.

At times while awake, driving perhaps, or rummaging through a newspaper, I would almost remember something. Then, as I sought to grasp it, obscure pieces on some multidimensional gameboard would disappear into their accustomed places. Nothing made sense, yet nothing dissuaded me from the reality of what I had seen. I tried to rationalize the events in psychological terms, as a random juxtaposition of internal states and forgotten perceptions, but the intensity of the experience allowed no such equivocation. Unable to outflank myself, I finally left off where I had begun, accepting a psychedelic vision as historical reality.

I had very little to go on; no background to probe for relevance and no guide save a set of deeply etched memories. I tried to place the event in historical time. My only clue was the number 536 branded on my brain at the time of the vision. The most obvious explanation was the number of individual years since the catastrophe, but the effacement of the mountain was too complete to have been the work of so brief a period. I knew the world was speckled with ancient ruins of far greater antiquity than the fifteenth century of our own era; many of them were in harsher climates than that of the mountain, and yet they were far better preserved. Consequently, I dismissed the idea that a superbly gifted society, completely unknown to us, antedated our coming by less than a century.

I still felt that 536 was some kind of time reckoning, but had no idea if it referred to a specific time interval, or if it was a different order of temporal expression. I calculated various periods. Assuming the unit to be decades put the event more than 5,000 years in the past, centuries pushed it back more than 50,000, and millennia over half a million. All were beyond the edge of historical certainty, and yet none seemed implausible. I knew that Buddhists spoke of Dipamkara Buddha who lived two million years ago, and that paleontologists currently dated the emergence of our species at upward of three million years. Moreover, I knew that consciousness is not limited by time, though it expresses itself as such, and that the abstruse patterning we call intelligence is a function of the universe itself, not merely of its derivative protoplasm. Consequently, I realized that what might appear as a deep thrust into the illusion of past time to an egoistic or sociocentric reference, might well be no more than a pinprick to our phylogenetic ancestry, and would be nothing at all to eternity. With this in mind, I opted for more perspective and sought to banish my ego and its cultural biases. I accepted the premise that my DNA contained a memory trace of a severely traumatic species event that had been reactivated under the proper stimulus. This gave birth to a universe of speculative freedom into which, with curiosity as my navigator, I embarked on a search for the distant past.

I began with the mountain and the people who lived there when the Spanish arrived in the sixteenth century. These were the Cahuilla Indians, inhabiting the northeastern watershed of the San Jacintos, the San Gorgonio Pass below, and the stretch of Coachella Desert along the base of the mountains from Palm Springs to Indio. Their life was simple. They lived in thatched mud houses, made earthenware pottery, and wove baskets of grasses and rushes. They did not farm, for they believed that to do so wounded the Earth Mother whose land was as abundant with food as it was alive with spirits. The staple was pinole, a flour ground in stone mortars from mesquite seed. They gathered wild plums and elderberries along the watercourses, and yucca, agave, and manzanita from the steep mountain slopes. In the high valleys, pine and juniper cones were roasted to extract the nuts, and at the lower elevations, desert cactus provided fruit and seed oil. Their visionary intoxicant was tolache, what we refer to as jimson weed or datura, a dangerous preparation used sparingly, with proper ceremony, ritual, and caution.

The religion of the Cahuilla, like the life it reflected, was simple and thoroughly adequate. They believed that the Earth was the first and exemplary mother. Beyond her, a great spirit presided over the creation and destruction of the universe through a pantheon of cosmic and terrestrial forces. These were always personified, frequently encountered, and never ignored. The historical memory of the Cahuilla extends back to the time of the Deluge, but they remember nothing of what came before that climactic event. Unlike peoples with antediluvian legends, they say that man himself first came forth with the waters, so it is clear that their tribal memory came into being some time after the Flood. I presumed them descended from survivors of the event, and, since their genealogies chronicle no catastrophe other than the arrival of Europeans, I assumed the devastation of the mountain to have preceded them, and perhaps to have been associated with the Deluge itself.

If the Cahuilla were the silent people of my vision, they represented a break in chronology, a primitive interlude in history. Such a break is not unusual, for histories in every part of the world are cyclical, and periods of splendor are separated by ages of darkness. Great cultural transformations are more frequently discrete than evolutionary, and the gaps are bridged only by myth and legend. Between peaks of successive civilizations stands the recurrent void into which history falls, to emerge some time later as the dawn of a new era. Long before Moses led the Jews out of Egypt, the Great Pyramid of Cheops stood vacant and untenanted, its purpose lost in the blur of time and becoming. So, too, it was with Babylon and Stonehenge, and with the cosmologic temples of America. I was reminded of the Seven Cities of Gold, which unlike these others, have never been found, and I toyed with the idea that the mountain was one of them, unnoticed because its grandeur is different from what we expect. Since it lies so close to the western ocean, I assumed it would have been the seventh city and that six more like it lay scattered across the land. If this were the case, memories of the times in which they flourished might still be accessible elsewhere.

To the east of the mountain, in the mesa lands of the Great American Desert, other Indian nations such as the Navajo, Zuni, and Hopi preserve their ancient lore with painstaking care. As I read through their chronicles, it became apparent that much of their data deals with antediluvian times. They consider themselves chosen people, which I took to mean that they had survived the Deluge with their tribal memories more or less intact. These memories are virtually ineradicable as long as the nation exists, for they are encoded throughout the tribal life of the people. They manifest in the wisdom of the elders, in the epic tales of storytellers, in the magic of shamans, in the patterned art of hereditary craftsmen, and in the great ceremonies where meticulously perfected chants, dances, and rituals reenact the pageantry of ancestral knowledge.

The tribal memory of the Hopi reaches to the beginnings of human time. Their creation and emergence myths are a whirling mandala of spiritual forces spinning threads of terrestrial existence through the epochal cycles of macro-history, from the foundation of the world to the present. Their story is one of cultural devolution, from paradise to the current order of machine empires dedicated to annihilating each other.

The elders say that before the beginning there was only Taiowa: the vast, fathomless void, utterly alone. In his mind, which was endless space, Taiowa conceived Sotuknang, the creative force of the universe. The relationship between was that of uncle and nephew—not a direct connection, but partial identity, and a feeling of temporal succession. Following Taiowa's plan, which was the essence of his being, Sotuknang brought forth visible creation. With forces of physics and mantras of magic, from primal chaos to galaxies of order, Sotuknang created until he brought forth a sacred beauty called Kokyangwuti, or Spider Woman, who was the receptive, productive intelligence of Earth. The Hopi tell of her birth:

> When she awoke to life and received her name, she asked, "Why am I here?"
>
> "Look about you," answered Sotuknang. "Here is this earth we have created. It has shape and substance, direction and time, a beginning and an end. But there is no life upon it. We see no joyful movement. We hear no joyful sound. What is life without sound and movement? So you have been given the power to help us create this life. You have been given the knowledge, wisdom, and love to bless all the beings you create. That is why you are here." (Waters 1963)

During those days the earth was a ball of insentient matter, coagulating in space about a small yellow star and cooling to contours through geological time. When Sotuknang told Spider Woman to engender life, she responded by fashioning two forces: one to stabilize the planet and the other to charge it with the dynamism for independent activities. Among the Hopi, these forces are revered as supra-intelligent entities who protect and nourish earthly life. They are called the twins, Poqanghoya and Palongawhoya, and their initial work of preparing the planet laid the groundwork for all of our future expressions:

Poqanghoya, traveling throughout the earth, solidified the higher reaches into great mountains. The lower reaches he made firm but still pliable enough to be used by those beings to be placed upon it and who would call it their mother. Palongawhoya, traveling throughout the earth, sounded out his call as he was bidden. All the vibratory centers along the earth's axis from pole to pole resounded his call; the whole earth trembles, the universe quivered in tune. Thus he made the whole world an instrument of sound, and sound an instrument for carrying messages, resounding praise to the Creator of all.

"This is your voice, Uncle," Sotuknang said to Taiowa. "Everything is tuned to your sound."

"It is very good," said Taiowa. (Waters 1963)

When their work was completed, Spider Woman stationed the twins at both poles of the earth, Poqanghoya north, and Palongawhoya south, to keep watch over the delicate balances they had established. Ages passed and the earth prospered. Spider Woman molded its environments, and, in the fullness of time, brought forth four races of people: red, yellow, black, and white, all of whom knew her as the Great Mother. For each race, she conceived an archetypical man in the image of Sotuknang, and for each of these, a consort in her own likeness.

When the first people appeared on earth, they were in every way perfect and suited to their environments. Sotuknang, who in those days talked with people, gave them but one commandment: to respect their Creator at all times. This was not the ego of a jealous god speaking, but a simple expression about the meaning of life, for it was this respect that kept the Hopi fully alive and attuned to the earth, and through her to the cosmos. This attunement was an expression of their electromagnetic nature, for the Hopi understanding of life is based on their physiological knowledge. Like the tantric sages of Asia, they describe experience in terms of the chakra system. They deal only with the upper four chakras, considering the functions of the lower two to be included in the third. This understanding, and the upper chakra commitment to life which it implies, is what makes them hopi or human beings. They say that when the chakra system functions properly, the doors on the top of the head are opened, and a person, guided by inner wisdom, is in communion with earth. The spine is aligned with the earth's axis, and the chakras resonate with similar vibratory centers in the planet controlled by the twins, for Poqanghoya is the spirit of the earth's dynamics and Palongawhoya is the spirit of her magnetics.

The first World into which our ancestors emerged was a Garden of Eden, but during the long epochs of history, it was destined to be destroyed, not once, but several times; and each subsequent period, according to the elders, was a marked degeneration of what had been before.

The Second World was less perfect than the First; the Third even more distorted; and the Fourth, upon whose nether edge we linger, the least desirable of all. To the Hopi, the Fall of Man was not an event, but a continuing process.

The First World of the Hopi was destroyed by fire, the Second when Sotuknang ordered the twins to abandon their posts, and the Third by the Deluge. When the waters receded, the Hopi embarked on a great migration, first by sea, then by land. Following their inner wisdom, they crossed the Pacific Ocean and came eventually to North America. Here they wandered for many years until they were led to their present, inhospitable homeland, where, Christ-like, they accept a humble portion.

The arrival on this continent of a people such as the Hopi describe themselves to have been is well marked in the archeological history of Mexico. Human habitation in the Mexican highlands has been traced back for twenty thousand years. During this period, there was a very gradual transition from a nomadic to a settled way of life, from hunting to farming. Culture remained primitive until about 1500 BCE when a very advanced civilization suddenly appeared in its fully developed form. We do not know where they came from, or what they called themselves, but we refer to them as the Olmec and know that the society they founded was profoundly religious in nature. They were a sacred people. They arrived, won over the natives without conquest, instructed them in arts and sciences, built magnificent temples and pyramids, and then departed as mysteriously as they had come, leaving behind monumental works of art and engineering, and stone altars incised with strange figures and graphic rites. Their legacy was a series of civilizations that continued to blossom for the next two thousand years, and, although each was less accomplished than those that had come before, they were still flowering as the Aztec, Maya, and Zapotec when the booty-minded Spanish arrived with Cortez.

The Hopi claim kinship with the Aztecs, and the Aztecs were the cultural descendants of the Olmec, so I broadened the scope of my study and was soon immersed in the massive enigmas of pre-Columbian Mexico. I confronted history in terms of millennia rather than centuries and found an America far more mature and remarkable than I had ever been taught or dared imagine. I paged through books of drawings and photographs revealing abandoned cities where towering pyramids, crumbled temples, and fallen halls lay mute in the embrace of nature. Great stone sculptures, boldly, delicately done, peered through creepers, and brilliantly colored paintings weathered back to stone. Cities and buildings, as well as the art within them, were fashioned into the flowing forms of deities, mythological beasts, men and women, animals, and elemental forces. Gods were depicted in their chakra bodies, shown incarnated as the whole range of human types, as zoomorphs and sacred plants, and as teratoids of any of these in elegant combinations. Inscribed on temple walls, on stelae and staircases, on friezes, facades, altars, and shrines were sacred symbols, narrative motifs in now forgotten languages, and the stylized glyphs of cosmological speculation. Often I was struck by the similarity between these and what I remembered seeing on the mountain, and the pictures, like a hit of good grass, startled my memory.

I was tantalized and delved deeper, reading as history the archeological reconstructions of successive empires. Relics and ruins abounded, but multiple book burnings and centuries of anarchy had erased what was known of former times, and only deserted cities remained to tell of the consciousness that had inhabited them. The epic of Mesoamerica from the Olmec to the Spanish is a tale of strange appearances and disappearances, of sudden violence and periodic upheavals. There are splendors and there are horrors, for both are reflections of the epochal peoples who saw themselves standing in defiance of fate. Scattered in the debris of more than 3,000 stone cities are the reminders of a majestic effort to contain or elude destiny, for their religions were built on the knowledge that their future was predetermined, implacable, and catastrophic. Traditions from every age and every part of the country spoke of multiple world destructions. People lived always in the expectation of the next, prophesied cataclysm, and fashioned their civilizations to encompass this condition as well as those of their physical and social environments.

The Aztecs were obsessed with an acquired knowledge of the world's degeneration. In the center of their massive Calendar Stone is an anthropomorphic representation of the sun with his tongue stuck out—a tongue in the form of their sacrificial obsidian knife, which they used with great frequency and ceremony to cut the living hearts out of human sacrifices. In the first mandalic tier of the stone, symmetrically arranged about the sun, are two clawed fists grasping hearts, and four squares, each of which contains a representation of one of the last four planetary destructions. The first concerns a time before humanity. The second depicts cataclysm by horrendous, planetwide storms; the third, by fire raining from heaven; and the fourth, again, by the Deluge. The Aztecs anticipated the next catastrophe. They knew it would take them with it, and, as though to add irony to the iron of fate, Cortez and his cannon arrived on the day their savior god was prophesied to return.

My readings in Mesoamerican history struck a resonant chord in my genetic memory and led me back across the oceans. I found strange similarities between the Old and New Worlds, for many civilizations have woven the same, enigmatic pattern into the human tapestry. The Olmecs were late on the postdiluvian stage, contemporaneous with the sage-kings of Vedic India; a period, according to Hindu legends, when lesser gods danced on earth, monsters roamed, and titanic battles rent the portals of heaven. Hindus today think much like the Hopi. They say that humanity is immeasurably old, but now degenerate and immersed in time like ocean fish in a muddy stream. They call our era the Kali Yuga, or Fourth World, an age of iron and epoch of darkness. Nor are the Indians of two continents alone in their sobering appraisal of modern man, for traditional cultures, in every part of the world, view life on the surface of this planet as a precarious frequently disrupted phenomenon wherein humanity is left successively less attuned to its earthly environment.

In anthropology, accounts of the Deluge are ecumenical phenomena. The Deluge was a planetary disaster that few survived, and those who did in homeless, hopelessly altered, and alien environments. Social tribulations and wanderings followed, and only slowly were people able to reestablish their lives and retune themselves to the new rhythms of earth. For uncounted generations, life everywhere was primitive. Then, quite suddenly, in the centuries clustered around 3000 BCE, the great civilizations of antiquity sprang forth and bedazzled the world with their marvelous feats. First in Sumer, then Egypt and China, in a simultaneity of cultural consciousness exploding into time, wise rulers appeared and united the energies of their peoples into magnificent enterprises. They constructed cosmically attuned empires of stone, taught the fundaments of culture, and established their works as the model for all subsequent human civilization. Then, as the Olmecs were to do fifteen hundred years later, they disappeared into the mystery of history. By 2150 BCE, they were all gone, chaos and dark ages intervened, and the societies that later emerged, though mighty, strove vainly to recapture what had been.

The evidence for macro-historic devolution is impressive. Throughout the Pacific Ocean, scattered on islands from Indonesia to Tahiti, are gigantic stone ruins of pyramids and temples built by people whose abilities were manifestly superior to those of their successors. Later peoples invariably refer to these ancestors as gods, or ones who came from the sky, bearing gifts. Even the practical Chinese, the only people in the world who still speak a language from these remote times, precede their historical knowledge with stories of the Deluge and tales from the times of the Immortals. In the Middle East, clay tablets from Iraq, dated by archeologists at 1900 BCE, refer to kings who reigned 240,000 years before the Flood; and the postdiluvian civilizations of Mesopotamia, Sumer, Babylon, and Assyria display a markedly degenerative progression. So, too, with Egypt, where the pyramid age attained its perfection 2,500 years before Christ and was abandoned a thousand before Solomon. In relation to these seminal cultures, Mesoamerica is like the echo of an explosion returning to earth after 700 years and resounding as a new world.

The degeneration of the planetary milieu was acknowledged at the beginnings of European civilization. One of the most elegant descriptions of the process comes from Plato, the ancient master in whose image we are still taught to think. In *Timaeus*, a later dialogue set in post-Democratic Athens 400 years before Christ, he presents Socrates engaged in a discussion with Critias concerning the actual existence of an ideal state. Critias was Plato's maternal great-grandfather.

In the Dialogue he is a very old man. He tells Socrates that his own great-grandfather was a friend and kinsman of Solon, the Athenian lawgiver who was called the wisest of the Seven Wise Men of Greece. Solon had studied in the temples of Egypt and there had inquired about the antiquity of his own country, a time that was, even in the seventh century BCE, a period of myth and vague genealogies among the Greeks. An elder among the Egyptian priests responded to his questioning:

> "O Solon, Solon, you Hellenes are never anything but children, and there is not an old man among you."
>
> Solon in return asked him what he meant.
>
> "I mean to say," he replied, "that in mind you are all young; there is no old opinion handed down among you by ancient tradition, nor any science which is hoary with age. And I will tell you why. There have been, and will be again, many destructions of mankind arising out of many causes; the greatest have been brought about by the agencies of fire and water, and other lesser ones by innumerable other causes. There is a story, which even you have preserved, that once upon a time Phaethon, the son of Helios, having yoked the steeds in his father's chariot, because he was not able to drive them in the path of his father, burnt up all that was upon the earth, and was himself destroyed by a thunderbolt. Now this has the form of a myth, but really signifies a declination of the bodies moving in the heavens around the earth, and a great conflagration of things upon the earth, which recurs after long intervals; at such times those who live upon the mountains and in dry and lofty places are more liable to destruction than those who dwell by rivers or on the seashore. And from this calamity the Nile, who is our never-failing savior, delivers and preserves us. When, on the other hand, the gods purge the earth with a deluge of water, the survivors in your country are herdsmen and shepherds, who dwell on the mountains, but those who, like you, live in cities are carried by the rivers into the sea. Whereas in this land, neither then nor at any other time, does the water come down from above on the fields, having

always a tendency to come up from below; for which reason the traditions preserved here are the most ancient. The fact is, that wherever the extremity of winter frost or of summer sun does not prevent, mankind exist, sometimes in greater, sometimes in lesser numbers. And whatever happened either in your country or in ours or in any other region of which we are informed. If there were any actions noble or great or in any other way remarkable, they have all been written down by us of old, and are preserved in our temples. Whereas just when you and other nations are beginning to be provided with letters, the stream from heaven, like a pestilence, comes pouring down and leaves only those of you who are destitute of letters and education; and so you have to begin all over again like children, and know nothing of what happened in ancient times, either among us or among yourselves.

"As I or those genealogies of yours which you just now recounted to us, Solon, they are no better than the tales of children. In the first place you remember a single deluge only, but there were many previous ones; in the next place, you do not know that there formerly dwelt in your land the fairest and noblest race of men which ever lived, and that you and your whole city are descended from a small seed or remnant of them which survived. And this was unknown to you, because, for many generations, the survivors of that destruction died, leaving no written word. For there was a time, Solon, before the great deluge . . ." (Plato)

Writers of classical antiquity approached the antediluvian world with something akin to amazement. Beginning with Homer, tales of a paradisical past were a common theme among poets and dramatists. Plato devoted two Dialogues to Atlantis, while the historian Herodotus, the poet Pindar, and many others spoke of Hyperborea, the place-behind-the-north-wind, where Apollo's grandfather was born and Perseus cut off the Gorgon's head. Nor were such stories confined to the Mediterranean world. The Sumerian tales of Engidu and Uttu, dating from the end of the third millennium before Christ, tell of the earthly paradise that preceded those times, while the epic of Gilgamesh details the Fall of Man. In China, too, such tales were frequent. That they were believed is attested to by the first emperor of the Chhin dynasty who, in 219 BCE, sent an expedition in search of the Isles of the Blest where genii were said to live, drinking secret elixirs that conferred immortal life. Even earlier than this, Taoist tales are replete with accounts of former paradises and often refer to a northern country similar to Hyperborea. The *Lieh-Tzü*, or *Book of the Master Lieh*, a compendium of traditional wisdom written eight centuries before Christ, contains this story:

> After Yu the Great had set the waters and the land in order, he lost his way and came to a country which lay on the north shore of the northern ocean. I can't say how many hundreds of thousands of miles it was from the State of Chhi It was called "Northendland" and we don't know what lay on its boundaries. There was neither wind nor rain there, neither frost nor dew. It did not produce the birds, animals, insects, fishes, plants and trees of the same species as ours. All round it seemed to rise into the sky. In the midst of it there was a mountain called "Amphora", shaped like a vase at the top of which there was an opening in the form of a round ring, called "Hydraulica" because streams of water came out of it continually. This was called the "Divine Spring". The perfume of the water was more delicious than that of orchids or pepper, and its taste was better than that of wine or ale. The spring divided into four rivers, which flowed down from the mountain and watered the whole land. The *chi* of the earth was mild, there were no poisonous emanations causing sickness. The people were gentle, following Nature without wrangling and strife; their hearts were soft and their bodies delicate; arrogance and envy were far from them. Old and young lived pleasantly together, and there were no princes, nor lords. Men and women wandered freely about in company; marriage-plans and betrothals were unknown. Living on the banks of the rivers, they neither ploughed nor harvested, and since the *chi* of the earth was warm, they had no need of woven stuffs with which to clothe themselves. Not till the age of a hundred did they die, and disease and premature death

were unknown. Thus they lived in joy and bliss, having no private property; in goodness and happiness, having no decay and old age, no sadness or bitterness. Particularly they loved music. Taking each other by the hand, they danced and sang in chorus, and even at night the singing ended not. When they felt hungry or tired, they drank of the water in the rivers, and found their strength and vitality restored. If they drank too much, they were overcome as if drunk, and might sleep for ten days before awaking. They bathes and swam in the waters, and on coming out their skins were smooth and well-complexioned, with a perfume which remained perceptible for ten days afterwards.

King Mu of Chou, when he was on his journey to the north, also found this country, and forgot his kingdom entirely for three years. After he had returned home, he yearned for that country with such a yearning that he lost all consciousness of his surroundings. He too no interest in wine or meat, and would have nothing to do with his concubines and servitors. It took him months to recover himself.

The magical Mount Amphora of Master Lieh was not an isolated vision, but stood in excellent company, for sacred mountains are a recurring motif in ancient accounts of antediluvian times. Postdiluvian peoples continued to venerate them even to the extent, as with the Egyptians, Sumerians, and Mesoamericans, of building their own. The Greeks, who worshipped Mount Olympus, put the throne of Zeus on its highest peak and reserved the lower crags for the lesser gods. In the Old Testament, the prophet Ezekiel speaks of the King of Tyre as a god living in paradise atop an earthly mountain, and so it was everywhere with our primitive and not so primitive ancestors, for there were hundreds of sacred mountains around the world. In Palestine were Mounts Tabor and Sinai, in Persia, Haraberezaiti. India was famed for Mount Meru; Japan for Fuji. Nor was the New World less well endowed, with Machu Picchu in Peru, Popocatepetl in Mexico, Boboquivari in Arizona, Shasta in California. All were sacred, and all were regarded in remarkably similar ways. Each was an axis of the world, an entrance to heaven, and a center of the cosmos, for each attuned humanity to the creative forces of the universe.

In historical times, the lineal descendants of sacred mountains continued to embody these functions. The ziggurats, or stepped pyramids of Sumer, were gigantic, mathematically precise structures. They were symbolic reductions of the cosmos to four tiers, which represented the underworld, the primal waters, the earth rising therefrom, and the heavens above. A godhouse, or sanctum, was placed on the summit of each. The Sumerians called them Cosmic Mountains and said they were the modality by which people entered into communication with the gods. Thus they were also known as Bonds Between Heaven and Earth and Mountains of God. It was only much later in history that the Jews, who had little cause to honor the Babylonians, referred to them as Towers of Babel. In the fifth century BCE, Herodotus, the itinerant Greek chronicler known to us as the father of history, reported from Mesopotamia that the fairest virgin of the realm was housed in the sanctum, there to attend to the god who nightly descended. Mythologies from those times speak frequently of intercourse between gods and men, attributing to their union the birth of both heroes and monsters.

Recent evidence suggests that the ziggurats were primarily scientific institutions in which cosmic forces were harmonized with spiritual principles. The major gods of the Sumerians were the trinity of Anu, Enki, and Enlil: heaven, earth, and the great mountain. Enlil was also called the father of the gods and was depicted as a mountain with a human form arising from it. Anu, although generally used as a comprehensive reference to the skies as sentient heaven, was given a more specific definition in Babylonian astronomical treatises, where it was the name for the pole of the ecliptic. The ecliptic is the plane of the earth's orbit around the sun and is traced on our sky through the band of constellations comprising the zodiac. It is canted at an angle of 23½ degrees to the celestial equator, whose pole is an extension of the north pole of earth. This point the Babylonians called Bil, but they did not accord it the prestige of Anu, for while Bil controlled the dynamics of earth, Anu established the earth's orientation to the sun, and with the sun, to the galaxy.

The line from Enki to Mu was the meditational axis of earth. It was focused by Enlil into communicational channels open to people. This belief is similar to the Hopi description of planetary vibratory centers resonating with their own chakras and is still accepted as a cosmological fact in Buddhism. The Tibetan Buddhist Lama and Germanic scholar Anagarika Govinda envisions this identity as the Way of the White Clouds and, in describing it, offers a salutation to Mount Kailas, aloft in the towering recesses of the Himalayas:

> Thus it is that above all the sacred mountains of the world the fame of Kailas has spread and inspired human beings since times immemorial. There is no other mountain comparable to Kailas, because it forms the hub of the two most important ancient civilizations of the world, whose traditions remained intact for thousands of years: India and China. To Hindus and Buddhists alike Kailas is the centre of the universe. It Is called Meru or Sumeru, according to the oldest Sanskrit traditions, and is regarded as not only the physical but the metaphysical centre of the world . . . And as our psycho-physical organism is a microcosmic replica of the universe, Meru is represented by the spinal cord in our nervous system; and just as the various centres (Sanskrit: *cakra*) of consciousness are supported by and connected with the spinal cord (Sanskrit: *meru-danda),* from which they branch out like many-petalled lotus-blossoms, in the same way Mount Meru forms the axis of the various planes of supramundane worlds. And as the psycho-physical microcosm of man is crowned by the highest center of consciousness, the thousand-petalled lotus of the mind (Sanskrit: *sahasrara cakra*), so Meru or Kailas is surmounted by the invisible temple of the highest transcendental powers, which to each devotee appears in the form that symbolizes to him the highest reality. Thus to Hindus Kailas is the seat of Shiva, while to Buddhists it represents a gigantic Mandala of Dhyani-Buddhas and Bodhisattvas, as described in the famous Demchog Trantra: the "Mandala of Highest Bliss".
> (Govinda 1966)

The meditational axis connecting man and earth to the cosmos was also honored by the ancient Chinese, who developed their understanding of it into the science of geomancy. The pre-dynastic sage-rulers, looking within themselves, realized that humans responded to the vibratory fields of the earth and that to mold one was to mold the other. Thus a primary objective of their governance was to recreate the physical environment of their nation in ways that brought it into harmony with the physiological structure of humanity. As a result, they effectively pre-patterned their social history by sculpting the forces of nature. Under the beauty-seeking eyes of the Tao-divining geomancers, China was transformed into a flowery kingdom in which every temple, building, tomb, and wayside shrine was positioned with reference to the local earth currents and constructed to conform to their energies. Superior currents were sought; excellent ones accentuated. Where discordant, noxious, or hostile currents were discovered, they were broken up and their negativity grounded. Mountains were altered and rivers were rerouted. Hills were built where none existed before. Swamps were drained and lakes molded into the countryside, until a grand matrix was constructed within which temple towns and cities, the roads and canals that connected them, and the forests and farmlands that sustained their lives, were all positioned according to geomantic principles. Gradually, the postdiluvian world was harmonized, and its energies were focused as civilization. The Chinese referred to the exquisite result as the Middle Kingdom, the enchanted Realm Between Heaven and Earth.

The extent of the Middle Kingdom was geomantically determined. Its boundaries were established by the relationships that existed among five sacred mountains. These were the focal points of the country. Geographically, they were positioned like a cross controlling the six directions, with one mountain near the terminus of each cardinal axis, and the fifth, in the middle, ruling up and down. They were cultural and religious centers, objects of worship and pilgrimage, and storehouses of spiritual power, for they, too, were congruent with the meditational axis of the earth and were geomantically adorned with gardens, grottoes, temples, and monasteries to aid in the accomplishment of their purposes.

The mountain of the east, Tai Shan, was considered the most sacred, for it daily welcomed the sun from the sea. It was called Mother of the Five Peaks, Gateway to Heaven, and Mount Genesis. Hidden in its mysterious depths were spirit chambers and peacock galleries, sacred pools and magical caverns. Shrines clung to its crags, and hermitages nestled in its valleys. Pagodas, growing from rock spires, tuned the wind. And long tortuous stairways led to promontories where glories wove garlands from the prismatics of heaven. The haunting, ofttimes miraculous reverberations of these places found secondary expression in the nuances of Chinese calligraphy, but only rarely could they be explained by the words that described them. A weathered inscription on a bare cliff called the Mirror of the Mountain whispers of the magic contained within, but only hints at the cosmological significance behind it:

> May I mount on Tat Shan
> Find myself with the Immortals
> Eat the purest jade,
> Drink the ambrosial spring,
> Yoke up the hornless dragon
> Thence across the floating clouds,
> Drawn by the white tiger
> And go straight to heaven.

The aesthetic Chinese have always enjoyed expressing their scientific ideas poetically. The hornless dragon and the white tiger are geomantic concepts. The dragon is the movement of celestial power. Its appearance implies the action of heaven manifesting as the male principle of creation. The white tiger is the female principle. Together, they construct reality as currents of energy coursing through fields of force. The study of this flow, specifically in its manifestations as earth energy, was the province of geomancy, a science the poetic sages named *feng-shui,* or winds and water, for these were the elements associated with the dragon and tiger.

Wind was the earthly archetype of invincible but intangible energy. Its prototype was the "hard wind" of space, a concept in ancient Chinese astronomy similar to that of solar and galactic winds in astrophysics today. The natural habitat of the dragon was the great vault of space, and it was here that the Chinese sought him. The earliest postdiluvian temples were precursors of sophisticated astronomical observatories. Originally, the temples were small thatched huts set on islands within circular moats of water. Nothing is known of the rituals and practices connected with them, but their name evokes an image of men involved in the enlightened contemplation of the cosmos. The temples were called *Ming T'ang*: *t'ang* meaning hall or dwelling, and *ming*, whose ideogram is a combination of those for both the sun and moon, denoting great brightness. Thus the *Ming T'ang* were known as Halls of Light, but the same term was also the Chinese name for the ajna chakra, so they were Halls of illumination as well, and the interplay between the two meanings was identical to that between the macrocosms and microcosms of those who understood them. Over the years, however, the clarity of this identity dimmed, meditational energy dwindled, and the emphasis shifted to the physical expression of the temple. In dynastic times it grew into an extensive cosmological palace in which the emperor, as the Son of Heaven, lived and carried out the great ceremonies of the Chinese year. As the temple-palace expanded, pagodas and pavilions were added, and the simple hut became a tower surmounted by a celestial observatory in which huge astrolabs, water clocks, and gnomons traced the track of the heavenly dragon. Thus, in the Chinese experience of macro-historic devolution, the *Ming T'ang*, which began as an entrance to heaven, became a house of many windows gazing out upon it, and the dragon was ensnared by the laws of motion.

The white tiger embraced the earth much as clouds do mountains. The Chinese felt this embrace as the earth's magnetic field, which like cat's fur, could spark with electricity. They were fascinated with geomagnetic phenomena and were astute observers of their own interactions with the magnetics of their many environments. They studied the magnetic properties of lodestone and carved delicate spoons, called "south-pointers," out of fine magnetite. These were designed to balance on their bowls so that their handles would align toward magnetic south, thereby indicating the lateral component of the local earth field. No examples of the spoons remain, only pictures of them in profile, but we can assume that the liquid in the bowl provided an additional reading of the magnetic dip, thereby indexing the vertical component of the field. The Chinese were so impressed by the power expressed through the spoon that they honored south as the imperial direction, and for all state ceremonies oriented the emperor's throne to face in that direction. Eventually, the spoon evolved into the magnetic compass. This development is considered a major advance in Chinese science, but, as with the elaboration of the *Ming T'ang*, it was not so in terms of the subtleties involved, for the spoon as an interrogator of a three-dimensional field was replaced by a needle that would swing only in two, and men who were never lost were followed by those who could find their way.

With their wonderful spoon, the old Chinese conversed with the earth, and from the *Ming T'ang*, learned of her place in the celestial vault. For the purposes of geomancy, data from both of these sciences were integrated on a small, portable computer called a geomancer's board that was programmed in the field by both man and nature. The board had three parts. The base plate was square and made of hard, polished wood. It represented the earth. A circular heaven plate of metal, pivoted in the center and left free to rotate, was mounted on the wood, and a lodestone spoon was placed on top. The stars of Ursa Major, the Big Dipper, were engraved on the heaven plate and joined by thin straight lines. In Chinese astronomy, this constellation was the key to a system of celestial coordinates, and it was used to locate every point in the heavens. On the geomancer's board, it could be positioned with respect to three sets of data inscribed around the periphery of the earth plate. These were the twenty-four compass directions; the twenty-eight "lunar mansions," or divisions of the Chinese sky; and the eight primary trigrams of the *I Ching*. We no longer know how this information was correlated, or how the board was set to function. Neither do we know what data emerged as readout, or what principle guided the geomancers in transforming it into the beauty of China. The picture left, however, is suggestive, for here we have the coursing heavens supported by earth, and a magnetic spoon, stabilized in the cosmic wind, whispering secrets somehow connected with the *Book of Changes*.

Chinese history has been edited by the Tao, which, like a master of suspense, tells irrelevant stories sprinkled with clues. The *I Ching* is one of these clues, perhaps the oldest and most persistent, and is ubiquitous in Chinese culture. Under the gentle prodding of geomancy, I found myself once more invited to inquire into its mysteries, to investigate it in entirely new ways. Rather than as oracle or system of philosophy, I approached it as a historical document and as a treatise in the science of geomancy.

The development of the *I Ching* over millennia reflects the vicissitudes of the Chinese nation and provides a periodic report on the nature of epochal orientations among our species. The version of the book that has come down to us was compiled toward the end of the strongly patriarchal Chou dynasty, sometime around the third century before Christ. It is a composite of many symbols, texts, and commentaries, and the sixty-four hexagrams are ordered with "Ch'ien" (heaven, the male principle) as the first in the book. There were, however, two earlier books, now both lost, which were the parent and grandparent of the *I Ching*. The younger of these was the *Kuei Ts'ang*, a title provocatively translated as *Flow and Return to Womb and Tomb* that hints, perhaps, at the recurrent continuity of our species history. The *Kuei Ts'ang* was written a thousand years before the *I Ching*, during the matriarchal Shang dynasty, and one of the few things known about it is that it began with the hexagram "K'un" (earth, the female principle). A thousand years before this, however, the first in this series of classics appeared: the *Lien Shan*, or *Manifestation of Change in the Mountains*, a work from the egalitarian Hsin kingdom when sages were said to have ruled on earth. The *Lien Shan* began with the hexagram "Kuan / Contemplation" whose image is the sacred mountain. I assumed the Hsin sages placed it first for reasons associated with their use of the book, and I probed the *I Ching* for an answer. There, the sacred mountain is called the representative of heaven on earth, an intermediary between celestial powers and man, so I surmised that the *I Ching's* grandparent might have been used to converse with this dignitary. If so, the *Lien Shan* acted as an interpreter for man, speaking with the voice of the mountain and telling of heaven.

The structural foundation for all three books is the eight primary trigrams. They antedate the *Lien Shan* by at least 500 years. They and the system they symbolize are attributed to Fu Hsi, the legendary first sovereign of China, whose reign began in 2852 BCE. The pictograph, which is the earliest written form of Fu Hsi's name, shows a mountain with a garlanded human head emerging from it, and in a surviving commentary the contemplative mode of his awareness is emphasized:

> When in early antiquity Fu Hsi ruled the world, he looked upward and contemplated the images in the heavens; he looked downward and contemplated the patterns on earth.

He contemplated the markings of birds and beasts and the adaptations to the regions. He proceeded directly from himself and indirectly from objects. Thus he invented the eight trigrams in order to enter into connection with the virtues of the light of the gods and to regulate the conditions of all beings.

The fundamental pattern, which Fu Hsi uncovered was the eternal trinity: the universe, the worlds within its withoutness, and the particularized things that arose therefrom. The trigrams related the three as they appeared in humanity's macro-reality, with man between heaven and earth, wherein the ever-shifting polarities of the lines repeated themselves indefinitely as the flux of life. Congruently, each human as a microcosm incorporated the three, but Fu Hsi saw, too, that humans were self-conscious and could look at themselves as though in a mirror. All saw with their minds and objectified their beings. Consequently, Fu Hsi doubled the trigrams in order to show humans to themselves as reflective entities, as the beings they were in their electromagnetic nature. Fu Hsi's archetypal person was a creature of six perceptual spheres held in a complex identity by the mysterious magnetics of consciousness. These magnetics are the delicate aura of the human organism, but in essence they are no different than those of the earth or the universe beyond, for human beings, like other things, are but shifting nodes in an ambient field.

In Chinese art, Fu Hsi is often depicted with his consort Nu Wa. They are commonly shown against a background of sky as serpent-tailed, human-headed teratoids with their tails entwined. Legends associate them with the Deluge. The stories that have come down to us have been filtered through many a dark age, and are mythological in form, but the information they preserve is suggestive. The tales of Nu Wa, for example, say that she not only soaked up the waters of the Flood with the ashes of burnt reeds, but also that she mended a hole in the sky with stones of five colors and replaced heaven upon its four pillars. The stories lend credence to the idea that the Deluge was both a flood and a sky-borne catastrophe, and I soon found other tales that added to this fragmentary picture.

In the legends of Chuan Hsu, another sovereign of dynastic China, the rebellion of Kung-Kung is recounted. Kung-Kung was defeated, but not before he had bent the heavens by running his head against Mount Pu Chou. The same story is found in Chinese astronomical literature as a statement of cosmological fact. In the *Huai Nan Tzu,* a first century BCE compendium of natural history, it is given as an explanation of how the earth's axis was tilted:

> In ancient times Kung-Kung strove with Chuan Hsu for the
> Empire
> Angered, he smote the Unrotating Mountain
> Heaven's pillars broke, the bonds with earth were ruptured,
> Heaven leaned over to the north-west
> Hence the sun, moon, stars and planets were shifted
> And earth became empty in the south-east. (Morgan 1933)

A similar idea is contained in the legends of the Hopi whose Third World was destroyed by the Deluge. The Hopi survived because Spider Woman, forewarned of the disaster by Sotuknang, sealed each of them in reeds and set them afloat.

> Then Sotuknang loosed the waters upon the earth. Waves higher than mountains rolled in upon the land. Continents broke asunder and sank beneath the seas. And still the rain fell, and the waves rolled in. The people sealed up in their hollow reeds heard the mighty rushing of the waters. They felt themselves tossed high in the air and dropping back to the water. Then all was quiet, and they knew they were floating. (Waters 1963)

The throwing of the Hopi into the air can be taken as the result of a sizable impact elsewhere on the planet. Since it seemed improbable that nothing but myth remained to tell of so epic and recent an event, I turned to science, hoping to find corroboration among its records.

The earth is a ball of molten iron, cooling toward the surface, and like a cracked egg, crusted with a thin shell composed of about twenty contiguous plates. Upon these plates the oceans float, and the lighter continents are pushed up like cork. The interactions among the plates give rise to such phenomena as continental drift, the upward thrust of great mountain ranges, and earthquakes. I tried to imagine what would happen if an extraterrestrial body with enough momentum to even slightly shift the earth's precessional axis would strike. I presumed that the plate upon which it hit would be devastated. The abrupt lateral movement of the plate and the shock wave attendant on the concussion would obliterate the larger forms of animal life even at a great distance from the impact site. The plate would react like a cymbal struck with a hammer, but for the other plates the devastation might not be so severe. The earth would absorb the blow in her liquid heart, and only a shudder would shake the rest. Like water in a jiggled pan, the oceans would spill out over the land and wash away an epoch, but survivors would stagger to their feet and begin anew.

This line of speculation agreed with the visionary experiences I had had both on the flight to Greenland and on the mountain; in the first I had seen a cause; in the second, an effect: the gigantic meteorite, striking Hudson Bay, destroyed the distant Mountain Lady and unleashed the Deluge. Other bits of information, such as anomalies from modern geology and paleontology, added to my store of knowledge and finally convinced me that the story was essentially true.

The earth's crust is thinner than eggshell. Primal material from the interior wells up between its plates as magma crystallizing to metamorphic rock, which thereafter spreads out as the underside of the crust or is pushed up as mountains. On the North American plate there are three large areas where this material is not buried but forms the surface of the continent. The first two are the mountainous areas of our eastern and western coasts, and the third is a broad, circular area around Hudson Bay. The presence of primal metamorphic rock in the Appalachian and Rocky Mountains can be explained by crustal and orogenic forces, but the ring around Hudson Bay is a scientific enigma. I wondered, therefore, if it might be the eroded rim of a magma mountain that arose with the death of the epoch that preceded our own.

Plato states that the destruction of Atlantis occurred 9,000 years before his time, placing the event about 11,500 years ago. At that time, a good portion of North America was still beneath the ice cap of the last glacial period. The ice cap reached its greatest southward extension about 25,000 years ago and then began to retreat; at first slowly, later more quickly. The alluvium from the melt washed down the Mississippi drainage system and collected in the Gulf of Mexico as sediment. Recently, cores of this sediment have been subjected to Paleoclimatological and isotopic analyses, providing a life history of the alluvium. Approximately 11,600 years ago, a short period of very rapid ice melting occurred. A vast amount of water rushed down to the Gulf, causing a dramatic rise in the sea level. This could have been caused by a meteorite melting a hole in the heart of Canada.

A startling piece of evidence from the fossil record of North American animals supports both this conclusion and the date assigned to it. According to paleontologists, as recently as 12,000 years ago, the lands south of the ice cap were alive with fabulous creatures. There were mammoths and mastodons, armor-plated glyptodons, giant beavers, huge peccaries, and lumbering tapirs. Horses and camels of many species shared the savannahs with great oxen, antelopes, and giant sloths, as well as two species of saber-toothed tigers, and another of dire-wolves, to hunt them. Sometime between 11,000 and 12,000 years ago, two-thirds of all large animals on the North American plate, altogether more than a hundred species disappeared, leaving only their bones to remind us of the discrete character of history.

Having dated the Deluge to my own satisfaction, I was left with a chronological anomaly. According to the world's most ancient traditions, the antediluvian epoch was one of very advanced civilizations. Then came the Flood, followed by virtual silence from humanity, for there is a 6,000 year hiatus between the fall of the great meteorite and the rise of the first pyramid. During this interval man became primitive and everywhere fell into patterns of subsistence living. We were effectively turned off. Our adaptations to the earth were damaged, and much of our noosphere neural circuits was shorted out. For uncounted millennia, the earth had spun in a stabilized orbit. The many motions of her celestial mechanics were built into us and balanced as stillness. When she was jarred into a different cosmic orientation, new movements were added to the complex pattern she already wove with space. Our Nirmanakayaic attunement to her electromagnetic and gravitational grid-works was shattered, and ancient, instinctive alignments within our DNA became virtually useless. We responded with suffering and blocked our perceptual systems in order to banish the pain.

The earth moves. To break its motion into components is to destroy its uniqueness, but to see it as simple is to miss its meaning. Not only does the planet's orbital plane slip and wobble but the planet itself is subjected to many erratic motions. We have long known that its precessional axis takes about 26,000 years to complete a single circuit, but recent satellite observations have shown that it does so in filigree, for every 14 months it describes an irregular circle on its track. The magnetic pole is even more eccentric. It is a careless wanderer that has staggered more than 8,800 miles around northern Canada, Greenland, and the Arctic Ocean since the time of Christ, and scientists tell us that it can flip polarity at any moment. In music, where a pure note is the product of a steady vibration, the instrument earth would be thought of as badly out of tune. Survivors of the catastrophe that accomplished this found themselves, not only on a physically devastated world, but one with which they were no longer physiologically resonant, a kinesthetically foreign place, and subsequent generations were unable to maintain either the energy or the knowledge of the previous cosmic order.

If the earth was detuned, so too would be her sacred mountains and the creatures who inhabited them. The Hopi legends, like those of the Old Testament, demonstrate this point. After the Deluge, when the Hopi had floated for a long period, Spider Woman took them from their reeds and placed them on the summit of their highest mountain, which was then an island. Following her instructions, they made boats from the reeds and set out on their long migration across the ocean In search of the Fourth World. Spider Woman guided them for a short time, then, claiming she had accomplished what she was commanded to do, departed, and the earth no longer spoke to people.

The Hopi continued to the east, finally reaching the shores of America. Here they had their last, direct contact with Sotuknang. He told them that thereafter they would have to rely on their own inner wisdom to carry them through the Fourth World and foretold that living in it would become more difficult as time went on. Then he, too, disappeared, and the Hopi, like the rest of us, were left alone in an alien world. During the millennia since, like a many-faceted crystal swinging in the sun, the earth has reflected cosmic energy as flashes of short-lived civilizations. Six thousand years after the Deluge, the first glimmer of purpose reappeared, bursting forth as Sumer, Egypt, and China: great astronomical civilizations that strove to reorient the earth among its old galactic reference points and that may have succeeded far better than we know.

Prologue

Winter passed. The war in Vietnam, for ourselves, was finally over, but those who had so ineptly led us through it remained. Spring came, and the politics of Watergate warmed up. My life flowed with the patterns of the *I Ching,* moving me from place to place with random regularity. In the beginning of May, through a combination of circumstances that at first seemed unfortunate, my plans for the near future crumbled, leaving me with a few weeks to do with as I pleased. During the months since the ranch had been busted, I had often toyed with the idea of going back to the mountain and probing its secrets more deeply. Now that tenuous hope became a possibility and my readings in prehistory welled up to fill me with excitement. I was convinced that the mountain was a pre-Deluge temple, destroyed by the shattering impact of the Hudson Bay meteorite, but beyond this I did not venture to speculate. The answers to its ancient mysteries lay with the mountain itself, and with the psychedelic substances that tuned me into its incredible store of remembrances.

A trip to the mountain also posed a set of more contemporary problems because the ranch was restricted, and no one was now allowed to live there. It had been seized by the government; tied up in judicial red tape, and left to perish from neglect. I heard that it had been ripped apart and stripped by both police and vandals, but more ominous for me was the added report that it was still under surveillance. The narcs apparently thought that some sort of treasure was buried there, and, since they had been unable to find it, feared it might be spirited off in the night. Consequently, they were keeping tabs on their pipe dream. If I went, I would have to carry everything I needed with me and disappear into the backcountry. I was familiar with the terrain and could eat sparingly, so the hardships were minimal, and I knew that the excitement of insecurity would add its own energy to the trip.

It was an ideal situation to discuss with the *I Ching.* I took the book and a pipe of hashish, walked into an Arizona canyon, and settled by a waterfall to ponder the aleatoric universe. I had a choice of joining some of my brothers immediately or first going to the mountain, so I decided to make two inquiries, one for each alternative. I began by asking about the mountain. The coins fell at my feet in the sand and constructed a figure of six broken lines. It was the second hexagram of the *I Ching,* "K'un / The Receptive, Earth", standing alone and in her majesty. As an oracle, it implies guidance that, if followed, would lead to good fortune and success. The emphasis is on following, a technique of yielding to the subtle promptings of the environment, for the controlling factors in the situation are beyond the manipulations of the ego. "K'un" symbolizes the Sambhogakayaic mind of earth, the vast receptacle of our lives. It is both the mirror in which "Ch'ien", the Dharmakayaic mind of heaven, reflects itself, and the stage on which the sixty-two succeeding hexagrams display themselves as composite states of the Nirmanakaya. "K'un", by herself, is never a summons, but I took the oracle as an invitation from earth to visit her mountain and bothered the book no more with alternatives. Instead, I set about putting together the things I would need for the trip. I began by borrowing a goose down sleeping bag and a large backpack. Unfortunately, both were bright red-orange, so I included a camouflaged nylon tarpaulin to cover them. Within a few days, the pack was bulging with clothes, food, and utensils. I hoped there would be extra food still stored at Gooseberry Springs, but I did not bank on it and included a book on the edible flora of southern California. I added a gasoline stove and fuel to give me smokeless fires, and two canteens and a plastic bottle for water. For companions, I brought the *I Ching,* three small statues, and a large black notebook hungry for words, sketches, and measurements.

As a one-man expedition, I gave some thought to dealing in a systematic manner with what I might find, and brought minimal equipment for the purpose. I took a magnetic compass for bearings and alignments, a saw to clear underbrush from rock faces or cave entrances, and a tape measure and plumb line to gauge them. I also borrowed a pair of binoculars and a 35-mm camera. For the latter, I got three kinds of film: daylight color, and both color and black-and-white infrared. I had never used either of the infrared films, so I included reading material about them and the special filters they required. Finally, I brought a varied stash of psychedelics, including two types of

LSD, a few dried psilocybin mushrooms, three DMT joints, and two large capsules of Iboga. I was low on marijuana, but had a fine piece of primo Afghani hashish and my favorite pipe to smoke it in. Thus armed, I set out to be conquered by the mountain.

Less than a week after consulting the *I Ching,* I found myself on the highway driving west from Arizona, mildly amazed at this abrupt intermezzo in my life, and deeply excited. Under the tranquil prodding of the endless desert, I discovered I also carried another, weightless piece of baggage with me, an antisoporific in the form of a Zen koan lodged in the back of my head. A koan is a statement from high consciousness that appears paradoxical or nonsensical at lower levels of analysis. By cogitating on it, one may be catapulted to a solution; to a place where the koan makes sense, and become transformed into the overview that contains it.

The particular koan that had taken up residence in me was from the Heart Sutra, where the Buddha says with utmost seriousness that all form is emptiness, and emptiness, form. Translated into the modern idiom of our binary brain world, the Enlightened One is saying that 1=0 and 0=1, an obvious absurdity to the logical frame of reference, and a starting point for nowhere at all.

West of the Colorado River, the freeway climbed gradually to Chiriaco Summit and then dropped more steeply to the Coachella Desert at Indio. During miles of descending road, the San Jacinto Mountains were directly ahead, forming a massive barrier from horizon to horizon. The ridges rose up from the southwest like the back of a colossal lion, while Mount San Jacinto towered as his head. Spitler Peak was above the haunches, and Palm Springs was below, tucked in his side. The day was clear. The mountains were snow peaked and cragged with towering black cliffs that gave texture to the lion's mane. Miles below, I rolled into the hot desert. Sections of it were below sea level. The highest peaks were more than 10,000 feet above. The transition between them was abrupt, the escarpment imposing, its eminence inescapable.

I followed the freeway to San Gorgonio Pass. The road went like a concrete arrow through the center of the desert, bypassing towns that hugged the mountains and hid in their shade. A railroad paralleled the freeway, and both were shielded from the ever-shifting dunes by tangled lines of tamarisk trees which blocked my view of the towns and made the desert a chunk of moonscape with eight lanes of deserted freeway rolling down the middle. I stopped for a few pounds of fresh dates and raisins and then drove into the mountains from the northwest on the road from Banning to Idyllwild. The blacktop wound up the steep mountainside and slipped into the forest above 4,000 feet. The lower slopes of San Jacinto were fields of shattered rock: great boulders lay tumbled about, and old avalanche rubble was cut through by new streams. My predisposed eyes saw everything as evidence of catastrophe. I continued deeper into the mountains past Idyllwild, where Garner Valley lay nestled among its peaks. At the mouth of the valley, a few miles short of the ranch gate, I pulled off the main road and drove to the home of some old friends. I had telephoned the evening before to ask if I could leave my car with them while backpacking in the mountains. They had agreed, so my trip began with a reunion.

At dinner I discovered that my hosts were moving to the city on the first of June. I would have to reclaim my car no later than that. This gave me twenty days on the mountain, long enough to discover if there was substance to my vision, and about as much time as my food supply would allow. After dark we drove to a place a few hundred yards from the ranch gate, where I slipped into the night. The evening was cool, and the still air was remarkably clear. The moon was three-quarters full and cast a silver light over the mountains. I hooked my pack over one shoulder and carried the camera, canteens, and binoculars by their straps. At the fence, I hoisted everything over and then followed quickly, doing a delicate barbed wire boogie.

Two cars, their headlights piercing the silvered night with gold, approached from both directions. Feeling conspicuous, I struggled into the bulky and unfamiliar pack. I meant to hurry off as soon as it was roughly positioned on my back, but my arms got twisted in the straps and the bulk of the load was off balance, so when I tried to stand up, I sat down instead. My arms were pinned behind me, and the pack was jammed into the ground, so I could only move by rolling to my side. I went down on my cheek, swiveled to my hands and knees, and came up like an elevator. As I lumbered away from the fence, I was chortling so hard that I stumbled. Twenty yards in, I went down on all fours and stayed there until the cars passed.

I had a half mile of open ground to cross before reaching the sparse pine forest along the edge of the valley. I aimed for a solitary tree thirty yards from where the ranch road started up the ridge. The pack was heavy but finally well balanced. It stuck up above my head, and the sleeping bag and a rolled foam mat hung below. It occurred to me that I must look like a walking stump from the road. The nonsense brought another chuckle. A moment later, I was talking to a gopher hole into which I almost stepped and then singing to the moon. I was warm but not sweating when I reached the tree. I dropped the pack, took off my leather shirt, and sat for a few minutes trying to psyche out the road. I had no idea if anyone was at the ranch, or if the road was used at night. Long sections of it were cut into steep ridge sides, where it would be impossible to get off on either side. I would be vulnerable, but it was the only feasible way up to the level of the Waterfall.

It was a gambler's night, so I called on the Lady as luck and set off in a mellow frame of mind. I chugged up the ridge at a slow but steady pace, my moon shadow tagging along to the side and lurching ahead where the road turned. Thirty minutes later, I was on top of the second rise. The road leveled off for a while, so I speeded up and soon was walking like one possessed, my feet responding with an unaccustomed deftness to the uneven road. By the top of the third rise, I was running with rivers of sweat. My T-shirt was soaked and my skin cold from the night breeze, but inside I was all fire. When I felt sprinted out, I moved off into the chaparral to rest, and immediately discovered the wrong way to get loose from my pack. I squatted straight down to let the rolled mat sit on the ground as I unhooked my arms, but in so doing I went completely through my center of balance and was pulled over backwards. For a moment, I was spread-eagled, belly up, on top of my pile of possessions, which then shifted again and rolled me to the ground. I crawled out amid more laughter and stretched out to the side, still tangled like Gulliver in all my other straps. It was an excellent position from which to kiss the earth and bow to the moon, so I did both.

Soon refreshed, I set out again and followed the road for another forty minutes while it climbed continually. The easiest way to the Waterfall was from above, where the sloping plateau funneled into the canyon, but I left the road early and took to the side hills, hoping to shorten the walk by dead reckoning cross country. The strategy worked. I wound my way through tangled brush, and in another half hour I was at the circle of boulders above the first gorge of the Waterfall. I dropped my burden before a huge yucca, from the center of whose thousand pointed swords a ten-foot stalk of flowers climbed into night.

The place, like magic, had many levels. Large pine trees grew at the bottom of the gorge, and smaller ones grew in terraces among the rocks. I drank from the stream, crossed it, and climbed among the boulders on the far side, talking to the night and chanting to the water sounds. Then I sat and listened, until a hooting owl broke my reverie and called me back to the pack. I dug a sleeping depression in the sand and laid out the mat and mummy bag. At the head of the bag, in a clump of flowers, I set the three small statues with a candle before them. I settled facing them with the *I Ching* and the black notebook in my lap. I left a few pages blank in the beginning of the notebook, then scribbled the details of the first leg of my journey. When finished, I turned my attention to the *I Ching* and tried to quiet my head. I had no question in mind. I was excited, filled with a dozen ideas of what to do first, and merely wanted to see what the book had to say to my exuberance. The coins fell in the sand. They were old, worn, and hard to read, but were still able to fashion the field into two hexagrams: "Duration" and "Pushing Upward".

I read the book by flashlight. "Duration" represents that which always is: a state whose movement is not worn down by hindrances or satiated by manifold experiences. It is union as an enduring condition, as the essence of eternity, and the book points out that if one meditates on what gives duration to a thing, it is possible to understand the nature of heaven and earth. The configuration promised success, but the changing line was very disquieting. It says simply: "No game in the field."

My heart sank. My guide, having brought me here, now dropped me much as the backpack had done. This time there was no laughter, and my lightheadedness clouded over, forcing me to a more serious appraisal of my situation. The commentary says that one who persists in stalking game where there is none may wait forever without finding any, and it concludes that persistence in search is not enough: what is not sought in the right way is not found.

I reviewed my plans and predispositions. My only firm intention was to take an acid trip in the Saddle, four days hence, on the occasion of the full moon in Scorpio. Beyond that, I was flexible, but I discovered as I ruminated on my more fundamental intentions, that I had come to the mountain as a hunter ready to seek out what I expected to find. But if the mountain guarded itself well, and hid its secrets, this approach would only lead me to a new perspective on what I already knew. In some way, I would have to orient my search differently. How, I was not sure, but "Pushing Upward" said emphatically that I had to see the great man. Since this personage is the archetype for the superior man, the prospect of encountering him was exciting, and the book also gives directions for finding him. "Fear not", it says, "departure to the south brings good fortune". Since that was the direction I planned to go in the morning, it eased my mind, and I fell asleep with my cloud of concern somewhat dispelled.

Timothy's Waterfall

I slept well, but woke several times rolling over in the unfamiliar bag. On each occasion, I became alert to the night canyon and turned to stare at the passing moon whose light made lace of the treetops. Each time, too, my thoughts reverted to the depressing line from the *I Ching*, and I returned to sleep brooding on it. I awoke to morning in a rock-walled circle of white and purple flowers, the sun already well risen but shadowed from my face by a large pine. I slid out of the bag and sat naked in the morning cool, enlivened with the sounds of calling birds, croaking frog, and tumbling water.

For a while, the sun-dappled day camouflaged the worries of the night, but when my mind quieted, I found myself again cogitating on the changing line from the I *Ching*. I wondered if the objective world were no more than a pawn for my idiosyncrasies, if my past summer's vision were but a filament of brain tissue rent by a psychedelic wind. There was only one way to find out. I took the book and went in search of a spot to resolve the question, soon settling among the gnarled, rock-grasping roots of a pine tree.

My plan with the *I Ching* was to use it as a guide to the energy patterns of the mountain. As such, I would need to ask no questions, only consult it each morning and then watch how the day fell into its expression. Now, however, I formulated a specific question that reflected my concern. I needed reassurance, and, as though to provide it, a pine cone fell from the tree, hit a stone, and bounced due south, while the sprig of needles it displaced fluttered to my lap. The earth seemed pleased. The space became tranquil. I inquired about the reality of the vision that underlay my return to the mountain and threw the coins. One broken line followed another until "K'un: The Receptive", once more displayed herself. Reading the familiar words activated deep psychic tides, soothing me and promising secret things, but also reminding me that I had not come to the mountain to hunt, but to follow.

I lingered to play by the Waterfall. Grasses grew in the stream, and wild roses along its banks. Tiny spring flowers were out everywhere, and thistles and poppies were budding. The pools were too cold for a plunge, but I washed beneath a spill of iced liquid and carried a jugfull back to the circle. I had a lingering sinus infection, and my eyes were draining a bit, so I rummaged in my pack for medicine. Months earlier, I had been given a homeopathic first aid kit, which then got lost in my gear until I rediscovered it while packing for the mountain. I dug it out. It contained three tubes of salves, one each for burns, sprains, and cuts, and six little bottles of tiny white pills. One of these said *Arsen. Alb. 6* on the label and was good for food poisoning, diarrhea, vomiting, and running colds. I took two with a gram of vitamin C powder dissolved in water. For breakfast, I had a drink of powdered milk, soy protein, and chocolate, savored with half a cup of granola, two dates, and some raisins.

At ten o'clock, I filled a small backpack with camera, binoculars, measuring equipment, notebook, and food. I stowed the large pack and sleeping gear, covered with the camouflaged tarpaulin, under an overhang further up the side hill. My objective for the day was a place called Timothy's Waterfall, a small falls that Tim Leary had found when he was living at the ranch. It lay in one of several canyons emptying into a large amphitheater of forest on the edge of Garner Valley. I remembered it as dropping between very regular, geometrically shaped cliffs and wondered if they might have been fashioned by man. The only way of approach I knew was from below, so I decided to go down Waterfall Canyon to Garner Valley, follow the base of the ridge to the amphitheater, and then go up the other canyon.

The Waterfall gorge descended to Garner Valley in a southerly direction, along a series of sloped levels. The stream meandered along the bottom, collected here and there in deep pools, and dropped euphoniously between levels. Gigantic boulders were strewn about, and the canyon walls were sometimes rock cliffs, sometimes steep side hills. Pine trees arched above, scattering the sunlight and occasionally forming cool tunnels along the nil. Ferns and cactuses drew an invisible ecological line between themselves, and copses of poison oak waved semaphore of battle with their new, shiny red leaves.

The gorge seemed smaller and slightly changed from my memory of it, but no less beautiful. I climbed over several downed snags, evidence of a windy winter, and soon arrived at a place where the canyon narrowed. Here the stream twisted past a house-size boulder to fall to a pool below. Several years earlier, on the summer solstice, I had had one of the most dramatic encounters of my life here when, during the first rush from 1,000 micrograms of LSD, I had jumped across the stream and landed by the nose of a huge rattlesnake. He had flashed up like lightning, and I, utterly startled, had reacted by jumping backwards across the stream. It was as though I had unexpectedly leaped to a trampoline and been summarily returned to my starting point. I landed in a sitting position and remained frozen like a petrified person from Pompeii, while the snake rose to his tail and quivered as though drawing energy from the earth. Our eyes were level as we confronted each other across the ribbon of water; his were like the fires in the center of the earth and watched me with smoldering intensity. I could see his defensive perimeter radiating all about him like a flattened magnetic hemisphere centered on his head. Its boundary was the locus of his fangs. Beyond this, the probing ultrasonics of his vibrating tail penetrated my own flimsy field.

I Aum Tao'd and begged his pardon, for I was clearly the clod in the situation, but his rattling continued, so I changed tactics and chanted AUM in resonance with his rattle. After a few minutes, his rattling ceased while I chanted, but when I stopped for a breath, he began again. We went back and forth a number of times: he silent as I AUM'd, and I quiet as he rattled. During the whole performance, he maintained his astounding upright position with liquid ease, and I, having centered within the energy of the encounter, was stable as the eye of a psychedelic vortex. Eventually, his body retracted to the ground in exquisite slow motion. He lay for a time with only his head raised a few inches and looked across at me with his normal sensors, his defensive shield having shrunk to a glowing cylinder of barely visible radiation six inches around his body.

It was apparent that both of us had been approaching the same passage in the rock. He turned and went back the way he had come. I thought to do likewise, but did not, because I was returning to where I had first seen glyphs on the rocks a month earlier. Under the circumstances, I compromised. I had no desire to preempt the snake by taking what he declined, so I took an alternate route over the huge boulders of the canyon side. As it turned out, I should have heeded the serpent. The lower pools were stagnant after a dry winter, the grasses burned brown by the sun, and the heat of the day was oppressive.

When I reached the rock faces, I was too stoned to move for several hours and was joined by a horde of noxious insects. It was a dreary time from which I found no escape, until I re-crossed the boundary set by the reptile.

Today, though, the stream was full and fresh. I hoped for the snake but found only a lizard on a rock and a towhee in the tree above calling out my presence. I wished them good morning and pushed on to the glyph rocks. These were wreathed in color with flowering bushes all around and were reflected in the pool below. I could see no glyphs, but it hardly mattered. Half buried in the sand, I found the clay bowl from a large Afghani water pipe. It was like a jinni's bottle, and when I sniffed the residue of hashish in the bowl, it filled me with nostalgia, so I sat in the shade and enjoyed my first small pipe of the day. Soon everything brightened. The glyphs remained invisible, but I did not push my sensory systems with the hashish, for the day was meant for moving, for stretching muscles, and acclimating myself to the mountain.

I relaxed for a few minutes before the non-appearing glyphs. Frogs clung to the vertical stone, safe from the small snakes that prowled the stream; and a large black lizard, like a drunken emperor, paraded erratically above them. I remembered my camera. It contained half a roll of color film that I was going to finish during the day. Tomorrow, I would return with infrared film and make duplicate pictures. I hoped that comparison of the two sets would reveal some subtle differences, perhaps the glyphs themselves.

During the early part of the afternoon, I made my haphazard way to the valley floor, stopping now and again to take a picture and mark the spot. The stream disappeared under Garner Valley, leaving me in the sparse forest at its edge. I turned to the southeast and walked among the outermost trees, keeping a wary eye on the ranch gate and occasional traffic on the highway. At one point, I walked far enough into the valley to look over the foothills at distant Spitler Peak, where my reclining Mountain Lady lay in profile. I crossed the ranch road without incident and continued to the amphitheater, going first to the far side to investigate a set of interesting cliffs, but when I got there my legs were too tired to climb them. I moved around the periphery of the amphitheater looking for the canyon that led to Timothy's Waterfall, but my memories were confused, and I no longer knew which to follow.

My search proved futile, and, as the afternoon wore on, I found no water to replenish my supply. I climbed around for a couple of hours, but I was weary and realized that, at least for today, there was no game in the field. I started back to camp thoroughly exhausted, admitting to myself that I was not in as good shape as I had thought. I had planned to return the way I had come, but that was the long way around, and the ranch road was inviting, so I threw caution to the wind and followed my route of the night before.

Somewhere along the way, I got a second wind and made it back to camp in good spirits, albeit hot, dry, and famished. I dunked my head in the water and drank with my eyes open, watching blurred stalks of grass wave in my bubbles. It was too cold to bathe, but I sprinkled some water on my shoulders and chest and carried more back to the boulders for dinner. I needed a feast to revive my energies, so I began with a cup of bouillon and a toasted tortilla, followed by an entrée of freeze-dried chicken and rice, and ended with dessert from a chunk of Swiss cheese that had bloated with the heat of the day and melted like curd in my mouth.

Dusk mutated to moonlight. I smoked an evening pipe, then walked about the gorge feeling the energies that swirled among its shapes and finding eddies in which to sit. Later, I changed film in the camera. The infrared film required complete darkness for loading, so I removed the exposed film by moonlight and ran through the loading procedure a few times. Then, feeling confident, I put the mummy bag in the shadows, covered it with the tarpaulin, and crawled in head first, pushing the camera and film before me. Unfortunately, my practice loading translated into visual rather than tactile images. With the film tangled around my nose, the camera apparently upside down, and my hands as helpful as ham hocks, I decided to remember to be more than observant in the future. I sizzled with frustration several times, but eventually backed out of the bag, soaked with sweat but triumphant, and set for the morning.

Hidden Lines

The night turned cold. I woke several times, first startled, then soothed by the resplendent light of the brightening moon. Shortly after dawn, mosquitoes made me uncomfortably aware of my protruding nose and ears, and the sounds of early morning pulled me into the day. My sinuses were running, my body was sore, and, for some unknown reason, my tongue hurt as well. My head, however, was in fine shape, so I downed a massive dose of vitamin C and climbed about the gorge until my soreness dissolved.

After breakfast I took the *I Ching* and settled in a sloping meadow above the first falls. I had no question and hoped only for correlations between the book, my behavior, and the mountain as the day progressed. The coins tinkled in my hands and fell softly. I built the hexagram of twigs, and, for the third time that week, much to my amazement, "K'un" constructed herself in the ancient coding. This time there was a change: the yielding line in the third place became firm. The commentary on the transformation reiterated much that had already been given but puzzled me. It says:

> Hidden lines.
> One is able to remain persevering.
> If by chance you are in the service of a king,
> Seek not works, but bring to completion.

It seemed to say, don't do anything, but keep at it and don't give up: there are things here that you do not understand. I agreed with the last part, so I explored a different level of interpretation. The third line of the hexagram represented my stomach chakra, which controlled the patterns that enacted me, and those to which I responded. The change indicated that energy was being focused here, and the flip from negative to positive polarity pointed to a time of reaching out, with all of its attendant possibilities for renewed clarity and expansion. I hoped that the hidden lines spoken of would prove to be the glyphs on the rocks, and that the success portended by the hexagram referred to their interpretation.

The second hexagram was "Modesty". It exalts the lowly state and describes it as the fruit of a long effort that has resolved itself and is no longer evident in the result. The image associated with this wisdom is the mountain in its final condition, eroded back into earth. Thus "Modesty" is like the plain that remains when all inequalities have vanished and nothing obstructs the view. The commentary says that our behavior determines whether we open ourselves to the benevolent or to the destructive forces that exist around us and recommends conduct that would empty one of personal hubris. It is the law of fate, says the book, to undermine what is full and to prosper the modest.

I pondered the image of a mountain sunk back into earth and found it appropriate to this ancient place. It was also very promising for the day, so I packed the psilocybin mushrooms with my gear, hoping they would do for my eyes what the infrared film would do for the camera, and somewhere among the interstices of reality reveal the hidden lines. I left camp and was at the place of the serpent's passage by nine-thirty, but it was too early to take the pictures I wanted. Infrared film is sensitive to heat radiation, not light, and the rocks had to warm up before they would become visible to it. The place was still in shadow and the stone cold, so I pushed on to the glyph faces. They were heating in the sun. I lined myself up with my marks, guessed at camera settings, and snapped pictures of the stone's thermal patterns.

On the level below the glyph faces, a gigantic boulder lay like a tower against the side hill. I sat in the sandy wash across from the rock's overhanging base and fixed a pipe. I filled it with a mixture of grass, hashish, and mushrooms crumbled to the same consistency and loosely tapped in the bowl. The smoke had a musty, earthy taste that filled my mouth, like a cave, with paintings. I became absorbed within for a while, then opened my eyes to a shimmering world. An iridescent hummingbird danced a Bolshoi solo among the spines of a many-armed cholla cactus, while his audience, a hawk, circled above. The huge boulder was about forty feet tall, and, although fallen against the steep canyon-side, still mostly stood. I had hoped to see glyphs, but my eyes caught a different perspective, and the stone rippled into focus as a giant figure worn away beneath the knees. His left shoulder was broken off, its hand shattered, but his beckoning right arm was firmly attached to a robust torso. Above, where his head should have been, grew a tangle of low green brush, and beyond this, askew and further up the side hill, lay a smaller boulder, watching me with a time-eroded face.

Many years before, in one of life's preludes, I had memorized the words of Shelley's short poem "Ozymandias." Now, from some hidden recess of my being, they welled up, and I spoke them aloud to the megalith:

> I met a traveler from an antique land
> Who said: Two vast and trunkless legs of stone
> Stand in the desert. Near them, on the sand.
> Half sunk, a shattered visage lies, whose frown,
> And wrinkled lip, and sneer of cold command
> Tell that its sculptor well those passions read
> Which yet survive, stamped on those lifeless things,
> The hand that mocked them, and the heart that fed:
> And on the pedestal these words appear:
> "My name is Ozymandias, king of kings:
> Look on my works, ye Mighty, and despair!"
> Nothing beside remains. Round the decay
> Of that colossal wreck, boundless and bare
> The lone and level sands stretch far away.

I let the magic of the words echo through my being. The rock radiated in response. It then seemed as though the stone itself sang, and I became its echo. A different poem formed in my mind as answer to the humbled pride of Ozymandias, and, deeply lost in listening, I spoke line after line, which disappeared like moisture into dry air. Eventually, a locust interrupted me with the vibrancy of its own sound, and I woke with only a concluding fragment in my consciousness, ending with the words:

> So our more modest expectation
> Was grounded in a kingly nation. (Shelley 1818)

I lingered in the wake of the muse, wondering if this fallen megalith, bearded with lichen and clothed in moss, had culled from me the hidden lines of the *I Ching*, which, now spoken, were gone again.

I bid the colossus good-bye and continued like the stream: flowing, stopping here and there, and playing among the rocks. I forgot about the camera and notebook, but imprinted my sensory surfaces, like magical film, with everything I met. Where the canyon shallowed out into foothills there were acres of granite basin through which the stream, like a serpent, wound. After eating a Spartan's banquet, I recharged with a few tokes of hashish and began wandering among the sculpted pools. Flakes of mica and bits of pyrite sparkled in the sun, and pebbles in the stream looked like jewels. The water was no longer cold to my touch, but chilled like ambrosia to perfection. I slipped into a pool fed by a ten-foot plume of cascading diamonds and rolled face down to watch ripples pattern the bottom with the Tao of dappled light. I dried in the sun, then swam again, further down, at the base of the bedrock, in a circular, sandy pool rimmed with tall grasses and peopled with frogs. In the middle of the pool, I came nose to nose with a brown and yellow garter snake and had a conversation of sorts: I chanted Aum, and he swam off like the sine wave of C-sharp.

I dressed and kept going. In a small clump of trees, I found some large pieces of pine pitch and, happily intoning, "Pine tree, you're a fine tree," collected them for incense and fire-starters. Then, as suddenly as on the previous day, I felt very tired and became aware of a blister forming under the fourth toe of each foot. This was a real blow to my plans, for I thought I had been taking it easy during the day as a prelude to a nighttime trek to the Saddle. I checked my watch (it was nearly four o'clock), and noted unhappily as I did so that some water had leaked in during my swim and condensed inside the crystal. The stem was loose, but I did not tighten it, hoping instead that the sun would evaporate the fluid. I rested while it tried, with my feet up in the breeze and my socks airing on a branch.

I made my way back to camp at a slow but steady pace, walking gingerly. When I reached the circle of boulders, I unrolled my sleeping bag and broke out the first aid kit. Using a cactus needle, I lanced the blisters and applied a salve of marigold and wort. I also checked the little bottles. One of them recommended itself for shock, bruises, injury or accident, physical or mental tiredness, and boils. I took some and stretched out on the bag, completely drained. The evening's walk seemed a dismal, virtually impossible project. The Saddle was twice as far and three times as high as I had already come, so I lowered my sights and hoped only to make it as far as the ranch house.

I was still exhausted when the sun dipped below the ridge. Dinner did nothing to increase my energy, and I set out fatigued as soon as the first stars appeared. The pack was a Titan's torment tied to my back. There was a barbed wire fence to climb, a gorge to crisscross, and a rolling side hill to follow as I came up out of the canyon. The road was a relief, but I continued along it slowly, as though carrying rather than walking the mountain. I stopped frequently, squatting to rest the weight of the pack on the side hill, and nibbled at some grape sugar, pretending it helped. The wind was my friend. It picked up as the night advanced and rolled off the mountain in gusts. The trees shivered, the canyon moaned, and I, buffeted by its cold fingers, was glad for its diversions and thankful for its coolness.

Below the lowest pasture, the road divided; only the right fork was passable to vehicles. I took the left. It was cut with erosion ditches, but followed a more direct and less arduous path to the ranch buildings. It went by the pasture fences along the steep side hill of the draw, whose lower slopes were dotted with large oaks. I kept to the shadows and moved past the tack house. The ranch showed no signs of occupancy, nor did I get the feel of other people. Rather, I had a sense of an alien presence hosting an aura of desolation. Fence posts were pulled down, their rails splayed like broken fingers. A wrecked car sat abandoned in the yard; broken boxes, bottles, and toys lay strewn about; and the doors of the buildings swung on their hinges, occasionally clattering against a wall. The wrathful deities had had their day, dancing for a frenzied moment and lingering as a stench, an oppressiveness that submerged my exhaustion in melancholy and dragged at my feet as I crossed through the old barnyard.

Beyond the house were clumps of big, ancient oak trees. I made for the nearest and dropped everything at the first level spot. The wind was cold, I was sweating, and ice was forming in my shirt. I kept moving until I had scooped out a contoured depression, unrolled the mat and mummy bag, stripped, shivered, and slid in. My hands were swollen from the day's exertions, and my rings were too tight for comfort. I worked them off and stuck out an arm to put them in a pocket of the pack. Clouds, like eyelids, darted across the moon and obscured it. I joined the darkness and slept almost immediately, but fifteen minutes later awoke to a sharp, stinging pain that erupted beneath my right eye. By the time I was awake enough to know what I was doing, I had pulled a tick from the skin and thrown it away from the sleeping bag. I lay for a few minutes with my eye on fire, but I was too tired to go after the first aid kit. I was sure I could hear the tick crawling back, and I fell asleep feeling like a fool. An hour later, he struck again, on the ring finger of my left hand. This time I was more circumspect and held him in my fingers for a moment, contemplating his fate. I felt no compulsion to violence, and remembered that I was not here as a hunter, so I sat up in the howling gale and threw him as hard as I could, while calling on Boreas, the north wind, to take him to Garner Valley.

Birds in the Saddle

It was a night of eerie omens. The ticks bit, the wind howled, and I tossed in the mummy bag on unyielding ground. A door clattered continuously against clapboard, and the outbuildings creaked like old men in rocking chairs. My dreams were gray blotches specked with black, from which I surfaced around five o'clock and pulled myself out into the cold, dark morning. Breakfast was a piece of cheese eaten as I walked to the house, and a protein drink when I got there. I was almost out of water, but knew I could tap into the ranch supply somewhere around the buildings. The water system was elaborate. Huge tanks on the side hills stored the runoff from the surrounding peaks, and the houses and irrigation lines were gravity fed through an interconnecting grid-work of pipes. At the house I discovered that the system was still working well, for the pipes in the pantry had burst with the winter freeze, and a river ran out through the door.

It was black in the house, so I switched on a flashlight. The hallway was ankle deep in debris, and holes were punched through the walls and ceiling. I picked my way into the kitchen amid a litter of beer cans, broken glass, mattress stuffing, pots, silverware; books, magazines, and paper. Leaves had blown through broken windows, and a child's doll, forgotten in a corner, was grotesquely twisted and crushed underfoot. I filled the canteen and made a protein drink, sipping it as I walked through the house. Every room was a wasteland, each closet ripped apart, its contents strewn about. Ceilings were pulled down, and chunks of plasterboard were scattered everywhere. The back room had flooded; it was now growing mold, and the smell of rot and decay followed me out into the gray morning.

The sky was awash with half-light as I started up the mountain, and the wind was gusting about the slopes. I was heading for Gooseberry

Springs to set up a semi-permanent camp, but the hike was a bleak prospect. My feet were sore, my body ached everywhere, and I was anything but cheerful. My right eye had swollen partially closed from the tick bite, and my ring finger was bloated. The ranch repelled me, but I went slowly, like a tortoise caught in brambles. I tried to focus my energy by fitting a mantra to my breath, but the best I could do was huff an occasional word and keep trucking. The jeep trail climbed steadily, zigzagging up the face of the slope and ending where a small stream emptied from one of Spitler's steep canyons. The banks were lush with grasses and flowers, but I was too worn out to be impressed.

I rested a few minutes and soaked my sore finger and eye in the stream. The cold water on my face created its own consciousness and washed several bits of information together. I had three rings: a gold band with a Sanskrit Aum on the right hand; and, for the left, a lapis lazuli set on a silver moon, now in my pocket due to the swollen finger, and a silver rattlesnake curled around the pinky. The Chinese ideogram for the Tao was carved on the side of the lapis ring, and it was in the corresponding place on my finger that the tick had bitten. Juxtaposed, the two bites said: Eye-Tao, which I read as I-Tao and applied to the ticks. I took them as an expression of the mountain's inhospitable side and resolved to let them guide me for the rest of the trip by leaving any place where I found them.

I pushed on to the Saddle. The sun broke over the ridge as I went, and the wind increased. Where the trail forked to Gooseberry Springs, I kept to the right instead and went toward the monumental cliffs with Pedestal and Chalice below. A sloping maze of tangled bush and boulders separated these from the trail, which circled below and continued to the Palm Springs side of the Saddle. I entered the maze, dropped my pack in the first clearing, and continued to the Pedestal. With the weight off my shoulders, I felt like I was bouncing along lightly, but inside I was sore and tired. I had expected to feel elated on reaching this place again, but I felt discouraged instead. I climbed the Pedestal, and was nearly blown from its top by gale-force winds. I crouched on the ledge; behind me, the sculpted cliffs hummed and whistled with the air, and before me, the Mountain Lady lay in tattered desolation. For nine months, I had lived with the vision of her beauty, but now I saw only rock mounds and ridges molded to the provocative shape I remembered, but they were dormant and unanimated by magic. The view of the desert was obscured by smog blowing in from Los Angeles, and Garner Valley was somber with haze. Feeling bedraggled, I climbed from the Pedestal and followed my footprints back through the maze to my pack. I put a sweater on beneath my shirt, then, using the pack as a windbreak, curled up and fell asleep on the sand.

The nap helped immensely. I woke to a fragrance of perfume and opened my eyes to an overhanging manzanita teeming with tiny pink and white flowers. Beyond was the deep blue sky, against which two ravens and an eagle drew swirls and flourishes. It was my second awakening of the day, so I decided to do it differently and broke out the pipe and hashish. The wind was too wicked for matches, but I remembered a sheltered place among the boulders jammed in the cleft between the Pedestal and cliffs. I climbed into the chasm. At first, it was like a venturi tube, but below this the air eddied, and the match flame only wobbled in my cupped hands. The smoke was like new wind, as forceful as that above. It blew through my brain, shredding cobwebs and dissipating fog. The rock before me enlivened and then shone forth as an Indian swastika: the ancient sun sign, and symbol of the sacred mountain.

I climbed from the chasm and felt the inner and outer winds merge, belying the boundaries of my being. The earth-field sparkled with conscious Presence and irradiated the mountains. I stood in the midst of a vast, organic artifact, shattered perhaps, yet still living: a paradise of flowers amid a splendor of rock. Red and yellow sandstone, green-black gabbro, multilayered gneiss flowing in black and white, speckled schist glittering silver, and chunks of milky quartz were scattered on golden sands. The mysterious glyphs pulsed from them all, and the rock of the Pedestal and Monuments was further adorned with strange, free-form figures traced in the stone by two-inch veins of rust. At the base of the Pedestal was a four-foot boulder shaped like an egg, cleaved in half. On its exposed face, I recognized features from a map of the world, but strangely altered, as though geological ages had passed since its engraving.

The wind was now an incomparable companion. On the desert floor, it had driven away the smog, but blown up a dust storm. In the Saddle, it changed shape a thousand times, whipping about, cajoling, singing from creviced cliffs, startling me with momentary lulls, then dashing from behind to flap my hair to the front. It boosted me to the top of the Pedestal and made crystal the air through which the Mountain Lady, supinely asleep, radiated tranquility. She was altogether more beautiful than my memory had been able to contain, and I saw her as virgin, new and fresh, covered with spring, and budding into motherhood.

The ravens glided by on the wind, while far across the Saddle, the eagle hung on a thermal, showing red in the mid-morning light. I turned to the Monuments and let my eyes drift over their convoluted surfaces. Directly across from me, two heroic images stared from the stone: one, the visage of a man; the other, that of an elephant like animal. Both were swathed in glyphs, which I sought to translate with reference to the features on which they were impressed, but I merely bemused myself with pictures. The *I Ching* called through my musings, so I left the Pedestal and renegotiated the maze. I carried the book and statues to the Chalice at the foot of the Monuments, where I had smoked the last of the DMT joint a year before. The lupine, at the entrance, were bursting with buds, and the shrubs within were already in flower. I arranged the statues in a sandy niche and then sat facing the Lady and offered her the tumbling coins.

The twigs in the sand grew as a medley of alternating firm and yielding lines that climaxed as the last hexagram of the book, "Before Completion". It indicates a time of transition similar to that between winter and spring, when disorder prevails at first, and then finally order. It promises success but warns against complacency, and says that external forces can only be handled properly when apprehended from the correct standpoint. Three changing lines added to the natural dynamism of the configuration. The first, for the sex chakra, says:

He brakes his wheels.
Perseverance brings good fortune.

My wheels were already broken, so I was more than happy to comply. My main reason for going to Gooseberry Springs was to be near water, but the stream at the end of the jeep trail was an easy walk from the Saddle, so I could also camp here without difficulty. I decided to do so even before reading the second change. This was in the place of the heart chakra and speaks both of trauma and treasure. It says:

> Perseverance brings good fortune.
> Remorse disappears.
> Shock, thus to discipline the Devil's Country.
> For three years, great realms are awarded.

My remorse had already vanished, a fact known to the throat chakra, where the final changing line added to and reiterated what had already been said:

> Perseverance brings good fortune.
> No remorse.
> The light of the superior man is true.
> Good fortune.

I was deeply pleased with the reading and turned to the second hexagram without misgivings, for it was "Contemplation", the sacred mountain, to which the changes led. I stoked another pipe, and the wind god rested for a moment to let me smoke. A red-headed hummingbird, curious at my presence, emerged from the flowers and swam a circle around my head. Its electromagnetic wings were tuned for slow flight, so he drifted while I turned, and we gazed at one another mutually intrigued. Behind him, the energy field of the Chalice became visible. Each thing persisted in its own being, but all were melded in a resonant blaze by the Presence permeating every particle. I was opened to ancient whisperings by reading the *I Ching*, hearing again the timeless secret: it is not we, but the cosmos, which is conscious. The creative power moves, molding the receptive nature of all things, and we, in our time, appear to contemplate the divine meaning underlying the workings of the universe. I listened until I could hear no more, and my reverie burst in a resurgence of wonder: the Dharmakayaic kings retreated into their no-man's-land, the nonesuch became nominal, and the unspoken name melted back to wind.

I had scattered six meditational stones among the statues in the niche. The Presence suggested that I put a lapis lazuli over the tick bite by my eye and direct its energy toward the infected sinuses. The stone was a thin square, so I licked it and stuck it to my eyelid. Then I sat cross-legged and gazed up at the Monuments with my left eye. Purple-headed swifts darted among the cliffs, and the ravens glided above. Suddenly, in a flash of red, a large bird flew over my head from behind and disappeared above the towering Monuments. The lapis fell from my eye. I buried it in the sand for the earth to purify and scrambled to the top of the Pedestal with the binoculars.

I searched the vault of sky for the strange bird and discovered him across the Saddle, riding a desert-side thermal. He was an eagle, unmistakably red, and very large. He knew when I spotted him and moved closer by drifting across the Saddle without seeming to move. I, elbows propped on knees, followed him through the glasses until he was low overhead. He circled above, glided to the next ridge, and settled on top of the tallest snag pine. I studied him and was amazed, for he looked like a flame tipped with a golden aura: bright red on the breast, with dark blue wings, and a head of shining gold. He sat for a long while, allowing my inspection; his feathers ruffled in the wind, and now and then he moved his head. Finally, he lifted off into the air and dropped behind the ridge.

The afternoon wore on in a succession of delightful vignettes. I stayed near the Pedestal and did some barefoot climbing. My feet were tender, so I soon retreated to my shoes and busied myself setting up a little encampment in the maze. I dug a sleeping depression in a side hill under another flowering manzanita. I leveled the area first, making the depression into a triangular hole that left the wind, even at its worst, six inches above me. At three-nineteen, my wristwatch stopped. It was a skin diver's watch virtually impervious to the elements, antimagnetic, and shockproof. I had worn it continuously for eight years without mishap, but the water that had leaked in the day before had done it in. Fortunately, I was too stoned to be perturbed, so I took it as a good omen and went timeless.

When shadows clothed the Lady in her evening's gown, I returned to the stream at the end of the jeep trail to fill my canteens and bottle. Spring in the Saddle was about two weeks behind the Waterfall; the yucca along the trail were just beginning to flower and the air, as I walked into the mountain's shadow, was instantly cooler. I filled the containers and hurried back to the sun. Below me, the ravens were cawing from the direction of the ranch. Their calls grew strident, so

I uncased the binoculars and climbed to the top of a boulder for a better look. At first I saw nothing, then three large birds rose out of the shadows of the valley in an intricate dance. Two ravens were driving off a hawk. The ravens, being smaller, faster, and more maneuverable than the hawk, dove and slashed in passing, then circled above, repeating their attacks. The hawk slipped and skidded, beating the air to escape the snapping beaks, all the time climbing higher. I became engrossed and extrapolated a consciousness that merged with the combat, not as a participant, but as the space focusing the encounter, the field discharging as angered birds.

I was at home in my element and was soon transported in time to my flight training days in the navy, when we used to dogfight among ourselves. I don't remember if it was forbidden, or merely frowned upon, for it could be a dangerous game, but it was excellent practice in the meditation of flying. Two aircraft would meet at a rendezvous and slip into starting positions with one behind the other. We stayed high; our only rule was that the lead plane could not go below three thousand feet. The pilot in front could do anything he wanted to make good his escape; the one behind merely had to follow. The action was fast. A pilot who still had to think about flying could never win, for it was a shell game in which the hand that moved was always quicker than the eye that thought to see. The secret was a technique of awareness similar to the contemplative practice of focusing the mind on a single point of visual reference, then relaxing into the tunnel of space thus created. In dogfighting, the point of reference was the tail of the aircraft ahead. Before the technique was learned, the game was one of frantic maneuvering; thereafter it quieted into the electromagnetic silence preceding sound: the ground which was never seen was never lost sight of, and the target aircraft, for all its gyrations, rarely drifted from the center of the gunsights. I marveled at the birds, whose intricacy of flight astounded me. They knew my game instinctively and had vehicles perfected by millions of years of practice. I followed their dance through the glasses until they, like the sun, disappeared behind the ridge.

As I busied myself with dinner, the night turned cool, then cold. At this time of year, the temperature in any twenty-four hour period could vary as much as seventy degrees, so I had come prepared to adapt. I had not brought a jacket because of the extra bulk, relying instead on three insulated layers: a thermal T-shirt, a heavy cashmere sweater, and a stout leather shirt. Besides these, the tarpaulin and sleeping bag could double as wraps. Tonight, I dressed to the hilt and took the pipe to the Pedestal. The wind was asleep; the night air completely still. The Saddle was filled with a cacophony of insect calls and responses. I blew a smoke ring around the moon, while a nearby cricket massaged my bones with a tingle of ultrasonics. The mountain air was clear, but Palm Springs glowed brownish through smog, while across the desert the San Bernardino Mountains jutted from the pallor like a Doré engraving.

The silence amid sounds is the substance of magic. A paradoxical gateway to this silence is through chanting, so I began a duet with the noises of night. Soon, the repetitive words quieted my consciousness: sounds superimposed on sounds, thoughts upon thoughts, until all steadied to stillness. The moon, bright lady of the night, cast a silver glaze across the sky through which animals of the zodiac strode in succession. Cancer, the Crab, was sidling toward the west; the Lion marched above. The moon herself obscured the Virgin and Scales, while rushing to the embrace of the Scorpion who twisted out above the Monuments. My chanting soon conjured up the Centaur, who carried me off to my sleeping bag and sealed the night with dreamlessness.

FOURTH DAY

Mirrors

I was awakened by the sun cresting the ridge and lay for a while watching it flow from branch to branch of the manzanita. It blazed forth from Taurus, most earthy of cosmic regions, while a world away, the moon moved toward her climax in Scorpio and reflected the taut power of the Bull as the arcane wisdom of the octal arachnid. Full moon energy is delicate. The earth is between her luminaries, and the seductive moon waxes boldly to draw us away from the sun. Focused, stretched, the gravitational field tightens around us; as its spectrum narrows, its energy increases, but the needle it becomes, though an implement of many uses, is fickle.

I felt the coursing energies and anticipated joining them psychedelically. I was not alone in the endeavor, for even officially it was a day for space walkers. The National Aeronautics and Space Administration was setting off another of its remarkable spectacles; this time, hurling Sky Lab 1, a full scientific laboratory, into inner-lunar orbit. The space program's epic dramaturgy was being focused in a search for precise, physical evidence of the universe's many existences, but I, having a more thaumaturgic perspective, presumed that in the Sambhogakayaic mind of earth, NASA was a neo-mythic Titan, master of a new pantheon of lesser gods named in honor of greater ones, who was busy rebuilding truth with his mechanisms. Today, he was casting out a billion-dollar tentacle tipped with an ingenious mechanical eye with which to look at himself and an array of ears to hear what heaven chose to tell. Tomorrow, astronauts would catch up with the laboratory as it skipped along the edge of Dharmakayaic space, man it, and fit themselves into it as biological components in its computer systems.

Since Scorpio delights in laboratories, I assumed that NASA (probably because of the disreputable DNA inherited from his ancestress,

Astrology) had planned his moves with the esoteric connivance of the same stars his creatures conspired to master. The techniques he employed were impressive. Rockets rested on their pads, fueled, their every function monitored and ready. A worldwide communications network was already humming with life, and television pictures were being carried to audiences around the world by binary beams bounced from pre-positioned satellites. The launch, being another first in a series of inaugurals, generated a considerable amount of cultural as well as technological excitement. It constituted a major species event in that large populations of us were simultaneously focusing on a single object, which all could see and hear with unparalleled clarity.

The earth tingled with its cosmological connection, and I, warming in a circle of sun, puffed my pipe and sipped protein in preparation. I selected the things I needed for the day and carried them up to the Chalice. Among these were a DMT joint, which I placed on the shrine with the statues, and seven hits of LSD. The acid had been dissolved in water, dropped on blotting paper, and passed on to me as a strip of little dots. My source, a very discriminating astrologer, had told me they were mellow but weak, probably no more than a hundred micrograms per dot. Trusting her judgment, I took all seven and then settled down to discuss the ambient energy field with the *I Ching*, expecting the first half hour to slip by in pleasant conversation before psychedelic energy replaced the book with its meaning.

I usually consulted the *I Ching* first and only afterward turned on. Not infrequently, the book dissuaded me, and I held off for a more propitious time. Today, however, I had no intention of missing the cosmic show, and being determined to turn on in any case, I had reversed my normal sequence in order to speed up the process. I anticipated slipping into high consciousness on the arm of my old Chinese friend; but as it turned out, he was practicing *tai chi,* and I found myself upended instead. In the fashion of the Tao, he used a throw called "Preponderance of the Small". The hexagram itself is not unfavorable, but it implies restrictions that, in the case of psychedelic tripping, are severe. Even though I was promised good fortune and success, I read the words with dismay:

Small things may be done
Great things should not be done.

The flying bird brings the message:
It is not well to strive upward,
It is well to remain below.

There was a change in the sixth place—a brain-buster for the ajna chakra. The *I Ching* employed the Chinese version of the Icarus myth to shatter my hopes in the complex mirror of its timeless reality:

He passes him by not meeting him.
The flying bird leaves him.
Misfortune.

Then, as if the person unlucky enough to receive the line would surely need help deciphering it, it adds:

This means bad luck and injury.

The second hexagram was the Wanderer, signifying that the quester has lost his home. It, too, advises restraint and it tells how strange lands and separations are the wanderer's lot, that his only protection lies in conduct that is cautious, upright, and steadfast. By the time I had read both hexagrams. I had canceled the DMT for the day, lowered my sights to earthly things, and abandoned space to NASA. Nonetheless, I was determined not to fall victim to a self-fulfilling prophesy, so I busied myself with a series of breathing exercises, then some chanting. Neither worked very well, and the acid came on with an inexorable cadence of woe. My head did not clarify into its electromagnetics but rather expanded darkly as a tuberous excrescence. My mind filled with dank waters; a plug was pulled from my throat; perceptual and kinesthesian spaces began to spin uncomfortably and swirl down as nausea to my stomach. The *I Ching's* advice was to hold to the lowly, so I lay out in the sand, face down, and felt like I was strapped to a propeller.

During the next three hours, I stood up on several occasions, but each time the earth reeled and the sun glared too brightly. A kaleidoscope of discordant colors and fumes claimed the right to inhabit me. Once or twice I remembered the *I Ching* and groaned my approval. Its bird image dominated my discombobulation, circling above like a buzzard, now and then tearing at the throbbing brain tissue that gave it substance. I tried to center the energy but found no skill nor technique, no modality, no method to guide me. Pictovisions of spinning aircraft roared through my head, and I was sucked into an endless dogfight, a miserable affair I knew I had already lost. It ended only when I was blasted from behind into another oblivion.

Eventually, my swirlings slowed and came to a stop. Exhausted, I managed to sit up against a rock, only to have the experience of structure capture my being and clutch me in the cold embrace of stark materiality. As I froze into its features, time became meaningless, for I was a corporeal existence strung together by an insensible web of forces in a space where change was random, spontaneous, happenstance. Patterns appeared. The constituents of matter arrayed themselves like suits in a deck of cards, chose colors, and shuffled irrationally through my head. I dealt a hand, then stood to read it. The first card was the queen of hearts, who, before my astonished eyes, trumped in as the Mountain Lady.

A condemned man, on hearing himself pardoned, could have felt no greater transformation than I. In a moment I was healed. I stood stunned in the ruin of a vast sculpture carved of mountains and was utterly dazzled. My eyes, ears, and skin melted into the synesthetic pre-consciousness of sensation, where a palatable field of aural light replaced my usual sequences of thought and eliminated the phantom of a dependent thinker. The Mountain Lady radiated with a supernal luster; all else glowed in response. The brilliance was intangible, yet perceptible; centered nowhere, yet focusing all things. I shut my eyes and decreased it not at all. It was neither outlined in shadows, nor highlighted by sparkle. Everywhere shone equally with it and served as its reflection. Even my networks of nerve tissue extending from sensation to sentience did no more than create a glass from which this light, seeing itself, returned.

The Mountain Lady lay like lush spring on a couch of sierra. To join her, I escalated through spectrums beyond sight, where we merged, and emerged in a realm whose myriad shimmering shapes were attuned to our breath, attenuated by our thinking. The mountain molded the creatures who molded it, for we were mirrors to each other and superimposed images in the space of reality between.

I came back to myself propped against a rock, ruminating on an old Tibetan tradition that sacred mountains are self-created and only later invite men into their presence. I got up and stretched like a cat, sending electrical energy through still-stunned muscles; then, hoping I had moved into the second hexagram of the day, I set out from the Chalice to wander the mazeways of the Saddle. My instinct was to climb and soar, to view it all from above, but the *I Ching*'s warning stayed my appetite for heights and kept me on the ground, aimlessly walking through labyrinths of flowering shrubs, wind-blown trees, and polished stone. I traveled slowly, paying singular attention to where I put my feet, for the carpet of flowers was alive and singing, and I dared not step on a single voice. Every rock reverberated riddles, every pebble sparkled a secret. Tapestries of mountainscape showed scenes of earth's ancient perfection and shone all around as a glorious Presence.

I moved to view the Mountain Lady from every angle, every vantage, to frame her with yucca and oak, to explore her depths in different lights and shadows. She became image to my mirror, glittering with sonnets of sweeping stone and sermons of crafted space, where I, glazing to glass to glimpse a moment of nonbeing seeing itself as sentience, found her there watching. Time turned into space: light, impinging on a gridwork of light, changed speed for a moment to reflect on the nature of matter and elongated my eyes into the reality of dimensionality. Images of a forgotten epoch appeared. I saw the desert as a turquoise sea reflecting a lapis sky, the mountains as living islands, and the Mountain Lady as bemused by infinity, lost in the eternal delight of giving birth.

The afternoon went by in an amazing way. I watched it progress as a comet of sunlight sweeping across the sky. Time passed without seeming to and the sun shone like a swath of molten gold, simultaneously everywhere along its path. I was seated in the sand below the Pedestal when it disappeared behind the Lady's right arm, emblazoning her with haloes. After a pause, evening came to the mountain, and my stomach reminded me of eating. I had used less than half my water for the day, so I poured the remainder on the flowers around the Chalice and hiked to the stream for refills and a light dinner. I also boiled water to wash my socks, noting in passing that my reserve can of fuel had leaked under the reduced pressure of the mountain, and that three-quarters of it had evaporated.

Back at camp, I hung my socks in the bushes and climbed the Pedestal for an evening pipe. It was not yet dark, the sky an empty silver blue. Across from me, a small rodent darted along a ledge in the face of the Monuments and dove down a hole. I called, but he was gone almost before I saw him, and a flourish of disappearing tail was my only response. During the day, I had seen several of his kind; nervous little creatures scurrying among the three-dimensional mosaics of their cliffside catacombs. With tails held sharply aloft, they raced from crevice to crevice, vanishing and reappearing, vigilant for hawk shadows, alert to the glidings of snakes. I did not know if they were wood rats, or ground squirrels, or chipmunks, but during a moment of tongue-twisted internal dialogue, they emerged as monk-monks, and so they became in my personal lexicon. I called over, whenever I saw one, cajoling him, playing on his curiosity, spanning the distances between us with modulated sound. Occasionally, a head popped up and looked back.

The light darkened to silver gray, the brighter stars glowed through the sheen of the risen but not yet visible moon, and I, enamored, lost myself in the shyness of night. I knew the sky was mistress to many a science of understanding it, and mother to all the arts of love, but my own bias was pragmatic. I knew the stars as a navigator, and trusted their fixity as beacons along my pathways, but I also knew of their many mysterious motions and reflected on their strange ability to satisfy everyone who inquired of them: theoretical physicists had their mathematical abstracts; astronomers, their structured universe; astrologers, their directed forces; and priests, their heavens, all compounded of the same sky-stuff fashioned by human ingenuity.

Heaven sparkled. Her evening star self, bright Venus of many moods, followed as queen after her departed lover, whose royal raiment still tinged the western sky with purple. Above the ranch a single star glowed faintly, an old friend called Alphard the Lonely, the Sentinel Star, and Eagle's Eye, a fit companion to stand guard over the broken fragments of a dream. In my breast, an old emotion stirred, like that felt by a seafarer setting out to sea. It welled up as a vision of my mentors, those who had taught me my ways. I chanted their names to the night, calling out to the six directions, the three times, and the listening Presence.

I grew cold on the Pedestal and climbed down to the warm sleeping bag. By positioning my head to the north, the turning sky wheeled about my feet, and an unobstructed view of the Mountain Lady was to my right. I cogitated on the strange fact that I had seen but one bird all day: a large one, unaccountably in the bushes, jumping from branch to branch. I had seen none in the air: no eagles or hawks, no ravens, swifts, or hummingbirds. I wondered about the astronauts, but was two weeks from the knowledge that NASA had aborted. Not knowing this, I probed space with an empty mind, honing for an uplifting contact, but the morning's *I Ching* prevailed and left me wrapped in my bag on the ground. Suddenly, the moon, which had crept to the top of the Monuments, burst from their crown like a diadem of silver. For an hour, I watched it glide through the sky, then could stay confined no longer and slipped out into the night chill. I danced to the pack for my long johns and sweater, then remounted the Pedestal for a warming pipe of hashish.

Lunar fingers played the earth harp, sending ancient rhythms pulsing through my body. Scorpio rose from the pyramid of rock at the top of the ridge, high above the Monuments. The constellation twisted like a cosmic serpent striking at the perfect disc of moon centered before its mouth. The night was still, the desert clear, and silent cities glittered about the base of the mountains. Suddenly, a bright light lit the sky far to the north, well beyond the San Bernardinos. A second light flared, and a third; the far peaks stood silhouetted in stark white brilliance. The lights hung in the air and drifted slowly down until they were obscured by the ragged horizon. They were quickly followed by others. The display was a touch of official surrealism. I recognized the lights as star shells and parachute flares blazing above the vast military reservation at Twentynine Palms, where I assumed the marines had taken on Scorpio and were playing war games with themselves.

As more flares exploded into prominence, I abandoned myself to visual sensation. My head became a projection room, in which old movies of my days in the navy assembled themselves as content for the silent and distant spectacle. I merged with the pictures. The Pedestal on which I sat became the cockpit of a Neptune bomber wheeling over a black ocean. The sea below was dotted with flares we had dropped to mark our search pattern, and the equally black sky above was speckled with stars. Between the two, we thundered through our maneuvers, playing cat and mouse with a submarine lurking in the depths below. It was a useless game, ineffective and ridiculously expensive, but worth it for me, in that it trained me in one of the latent peculiarities of being human: the conscious use of my magnetic response to the environment for analyzing the prevailing ambience of phenomena. In our war games, a variety of techniques were used to locate the submarine, but the final identification was made with a sensitive magnetometer called MAD gear, an acronym for Magnetic Anomaly Detector. To the electronic senses of this equipment, the submarine was a chunk of iron that altered the earth's magnetic field, causing a discernible anomaly. Having already experimented with LSD, I was aware of myself as an electromagnetic entity. I reasoned that if an artifact of metal, glass, and plastic could detect alterations in the earth's magnetic field, so, too, could my electro-magnetically alive body, for I was subjected to the same changes in the field and had to be experiencing them at some level. Consequently, as the aircraft roared through its intricate patterns, I guided the action with my eyes and hands, but reached out with something else to locate the submarine physiologically. I had little success, certainly nothing to report to the navy, but I got a lot of practice probing the depths of the sea with an incipient awareness, wondering all the while if I were as mad as the MAD gear.

After an hour of pyrotechnics, the marines ended their exercise, and the last flare sputtered out. My awareness was atingle, so I reached out, groping for the geomantic currents that roved the mountain, for the mountain, far more than a submarine, was an electromagnetic and gravitational entity. The night made magic of moon shadows, and an occasional breeze whispered through the Monuments. The reflective slabs of white rock on the Lady's belly radiated a soft phosphorescence. This grew brighter, then tingling threads of energy appeared and danced on her surfaces. They darted about, then linked together and seemed to take nourishment from her towering breasts. The gigantic figure glowed; nodes appeared in a patterned field, and a pulsating aura reached out. Pictures came into focus: faces and silent melodies. Then energy ignited in her womb and deep within her rocky flesh coverings. I watched an obelisk of black diamond come into being. It shone from inside without disturbing the play of energy on her skin, but its clear obsidian luster dimmed all else and left me dissolved in the mysteries of darkness.

Nearby, an owl hooted, telling me it was past midnight and birds could fly again. Distracted, I hooted back. He called a second time, now closer, and when I pulled my eyes from the Mountain Lady, I discovered him sitting a few yards away, on the top of the snag pine of the Chalice. I had not heard the beat of his wings or the touch of his talons on lighting, but, for a timeless moment, we shared a shining space. When he left, I again heard nothing, nor did he seem to go when he disappeared, but lingered as the wisdom of the mountain.

The Mountain Lady

In sleep, I stalked the chambers of the earth, probing with my dream-mind for what my eyes could not see. Gray caverns appeared as tunnels into the blackness of the underworld, luring me to pits hewn of eerie shadow where stalactites of turbid dream-stuff dripped. I paused to watch them grow, but lost my seeing as their shapes took substance from the shadows and engulfed me. A black angel flew through the immensity of domed darkness. The beat of her wings woke me, and I came into day to the sound of a hummingbird hovering over my head. The down draft fanned away the trailing edge of my dream, but I grew conscious slowly, and by the time I opened my eyes, the bird had left. It was too early to move, so I lay for a while, dozed again, then woke a second time to purple-headed swifts swooping from the Monuments and darting about the clearing. One came to a virtual stop near my head, backpedaling the air with liquid wings, and tasted my aura. The hummingbird returned and investigated my hanging socks. I got up without disturbing them and climbed to the top of a sun-tipped boulder, the better to watch their antics.

I was refreshed with the morning, happy and excited, but saddled with a sore, muscle-tired body. My eyes were swollen, my lips puffy and cracked, and I was covered with bites and scratches, all of which itched. Strangely enough, I was not sunburned. I had come to the mountain winter white, but four days of continuous sun had only shaded my skin to medium brown. Earlier in my life, I had sunburned easily. I attributed this later piece of good fortune to the cumulative effect of psychedelic substances, in particular, LSD. These provide access to the electromagnetic body where the organism can confront the energy of the sun in its own domain and there flow with the solar dance, leaving the flesh energized rather than scorched. I looked through closed eyes at the sun's fusing hydrogen and reached out to him as my ontological ancestor, the precursor of my ability to see. His soft radiance penetrated my flesh, and fingers of soothing fire toyed with tight muscles. I relaxed into the warmth, which conjured up bright red dreams of days gone by. I had joined the navy in the early 1950s, just as the Korean War was drawing to a close. Within a year or so, the Russians had set off their first hydrogen bomb, and the bipolar world was stalemated into history. Emotionally, the overriding issue of the day was defense against nuclear catastrophe. The new and most frightening factor in the problem was radiation: a spectrum of poisons that in one form or another could linger for years. A program was undertaken, later curtailed to find an anti-radiation drug that would make organisms impervious to the threat. Unknown at the time, the substances sought were already available in the psychedelics. Indeed, the most powerful of these is the birth twin of the energy whose antidote it is, for both LSD and controlled nuclear power first appeared in the midst of World War II. Unfortunately, by the time the potential of psychedelics was beginning to be realized, the substances had been officially proscribed. One reason for this is obvious. The protection that psychedelics give also gives freedom, because a consequence of their successful use is the realization that survival in our chaotic world lies with one's ability to conform to the earth's changing energy fields and not to the political or economic dictates of technologically terminal power structures. I took the binoculars to the Pedestal and sat to study the Mountain Lady. My plan for the day was to explore her belly. I was giddy with the morning; certain that last night's visions meant I would find some entrance to her deep interior. Her presence was tangible; the emanations of her womb were like those from a great energy chamber in which sentience was being brought to birth. I felt I had merely to follow the promptings of the day in order to enter into her secrets. I studied her contours through the glasses, trying to pick a path through her disarray. The terrain was steep and rocky, covered with tangles of low bush. Shattered piles of stone, encircled by vegetation, extended like chains across her belly. Toward the top, an avalanche had occurred, causing the upper stomach to slide and become an apron to protect her modesty from the prying eyes of the Kali Yuga.

Her natural entrance was sealed, but prospects elsewhere were interesting. Her ankles came together at a fork in the canyon from which I got my water. A short distance up the right fork was a formation of fallen rock that looked like a Greek portico. Its interior was heavily shadowed, and my magnified vision could penetrate no further than the façade, leaving my imagination unbounded space to roam; higher still, on the left side, lay the large, white slabs as though afloat on the tangle. I wondered if they hid doors or were merely mirrors for startling the unwary. The belly itself was a great, cliff-fronted dome, whose distant aspect was of many dark crevices, caves, and rocky overhangs.

I decided to go to the lower canyon, treat myself to a bath, and proceed to the Lady's belly via the Greek portico and white slabs. While filling the small pack, I discovered that the hash pipe was clogged, so I sat down to clean it. I hadn't intended to smoke, but the operation left me with a small ball of tarry goo, which I lit rather than throw away. The smoke was equal to its source and soon had me coughing like a buffalo, while simultaneously catapulting me back into my acid-stoned head. Energy swirls revitalized my tired body, and the world about me returned to its ancient perfection. I stood to stretch, then walked off packless, aimlessly, once more a child wandering the marvelous maze.

The glyphs caught my fancy. They shone from each side, making huge boulders seem like remnants of shattered temples. I could not read the words, and only their exquisite beauty bridged the chasm of epochs. The haunting patterns were both stable and shifting. They wove with time a timeless art, and their indecipherable message, with the patience of the pyramids, spoke to what saw my seeing. The mountain tuned me to its chorus, and I gazed past the boulders at the sky. The Presence hummed the harmonics of earth and steadied to silence; then into this space grew the fairest vision I had ever seen of a woman's face.

She smiled. She spoke. The flowers radiated a response like music culled from light, and the Presence wafted like perfume from the life-layered ground. Time paused. Delight flowed on delight, and only a hummingbird passing before my face returned me to normal reality. I came back to awareness vaguely confused, for I had somehow been assuming that the Presence was masculine, and her being feminine disturbed me. The thought was sufficient to change the gender of the energy, and the face of the radiant woman was replaced by that of a commanding male. He was indeterminably old, well-lined, stark, but equally radiant. Startled by the sudden reversal of the field, I burst into laughter. "Moses, I supposes!" I said, for the stones spoke, and the trees were aflame.

The vision receded, and I set out again, heading for the Chalice and *I Ching*, but I was stopped en route by yet another segment of the same ethereal sequence. A third figure appeared in the sky: an intent and determined younger man. He watched me as though I did not see him, then turned to the side and said, "We have succeeded." The space of the vision expanded, and the two others reappeared. The three held a conversation among themselves, but the words were indistinct, and I did not try to eavesdrop. Toward the end, they looked back, more with curiosity than concern, then faded into the Presence.

Enraptured, I sat in the Chalice facing the Mountain Lady and asked her to tell me about herself. Show me your secret, I thought, tell me how to find your heart. Then, fixed on her form, I cast the coins. The first hexagram was "Biting Through". It speaks of obstacles that have to be forcibly removed, but promises success. The changing lines are enigmatic. The first says:

> His feet are fastened in the stocks,
> So that his toes disappear.
> No blame.

I hoped it referred to the delay of several hours that had already occurred because of my wanderings in the maze, and not to the hazardous terrain ahead, but it also described the Lady, for her feet were no longer visible. The second change cheered me on like a pep talk before combat:

> Bites on dried gristly meat.
> Receives metal arrows.
> It furthers one to be mindful of difficulties
> And to be persevering.
> Good fortune.

I assumed the gristle could be the last of a roll of salami I had packed for lunch, but the metal arrows seemed a bit too archaic for relevance.

The second hexagram was "Splitting Apart". It represents a time when beneficent forces are in abeyance, and dark forces are ascendant.

The advice offered is explicit, but it was unacceptable to me since I was anxious to be off. It says simply:

> It does not further one
> To go anywhere.

I was left in the frustrating state that occurs when the *I Ching* stands counter to the desires of the ego, and the ego, in a quandary, casts about for alternatives. I saw no good ones. I was too energized to spend another day gazing from the Saddle, and too drawn to the Lady to go elsewhere. I set off in spite of the book, deciding as I went that if I found an entranceway, I would mark its location and return later, under better auspices, to enter.

I followed the trail to the stream, bathed, and left dinner supplies, expecting to return the same way by sundown. I slowly made my way up the canyon. The stream went underground almost immediately, for the canyon floor was jammed with layers of fallen rock, and both side hills were choked with brush and cactus. The lower end of the Lady's apron was formed of huge piles of rubble, loose underfoot, but a solid covering. I kept to the right fork and pushed on to the Greek portico. It proved disappointing. There was nothing inside; the formation was but a fortuitous arrangement of more or less rectangular slabs fallen together.

The way became steeper, so I crossed to the Lady's leg and continued along her calf. I climbed until I reached a point opposite the white slabs. They were hidden on the far side of the belly, but I had their location in mind, so I re-crossed to the apron and plunged into the tangle. The vegetation was thick, resolutely alive, and wielded thorns like Cyrano to punctuate its determination to be undisturbed. My path was largely determined by natural breaks in the tangle. I went from pile to pile of broken stone, sweating in the hot sun. I donned the leather shirt when I had to push through particularly high brush, or to slither beneath it, and I reflected stoically on the *I Ching* having me fastened in stocks. When I next glimpsed the white slabs, they were a good distance below me, and a hard way back down. I had already reached the base of the upper cliffs and decided to hold my advantage rather than descend. I moved laterally, exploring crevices and holes as I went, but found nothing of more than passing interest. Finally, I scrambled up the far side to the top of the Lady's belly.

I had climbed out of spring, so it seemed as though I had gone back in time to stand again in April's cool breeze. A copse of dwarfed, windblown trees was showing buds, but no leaves, and the ground cover, though pushing through last year's stubble, had yet to flower. I sat for lunch beneath the Lady's looming breasts. They offered an easier climb than the way I had come, so I let my curiosity overcome my desire to explore her belly further and continued upward, my only worry being my water supply which was almost exhausted after the morning's hot climb.

I went first to the top of the right breast and then crossed the cleavage to the left. Both breasts were well rounded, grassy, and easy to walk; each was surmounted by a stone nipple in the form of a large, ragged pile of red rock. I looked for air vents, cracks, or pores that might seep with secrets from below, but found only fallen stones immovably settled into place. Although no trace of human engineering remained, her contours were as fine as the Venus de Milo. But unlike the Venus, she had no head. A depression was left where her visage should have been, and I remembered the painful vision of her head being blown apart and scattered across the mountains. What remained as her profile seen from the Saddle was but the chance rearrangement of Spitler Peak displaced to the side.

I left the breasts and pushed on toward the peak, but I was magically diverted along the way. My path led me by some boulders, and against one, unmistakably a metal arrow was propped . . . I stopped as though pierced by it, gawking, before I realized it was a six-foot-long iron fence post, pointed at the upper end and tailed with feather-like fins. There were no fences anywhere about, so its presence was a mystery that delighted me as much as its oracular significance. I sighted along its shank, certain that good fortune lay in the direction it pointed. It aimed behind Spitler Peak, toward the edge of the depression where the Lady's head had once been, directly at an old snag pine. I changed course to follow the arrow, wondering what the tree might reveal. A small forest lay in the depression. The snag was a short way in, ringed by tangles of manzanita and scrub oak. I peered through the matrix of branches and saw a small oblong of sparkling white crystal lying at the base of the tree. I doffed the pack and crawled in for a closer look. The crystal was a small patch of snow, due north of the tree and sculpted by its shadow into a hardened mound of porous ice. It was the only taste of winter left about, just enough to provide me with a long drink and a refill for my canteen.

Refreshed, I threaded my way up the backside of Spitler Peak. At the top, I had my first view of the great mountains beyond, for the Lady hid them from the Saddle. They rose in ridge after ridge to lofty San Jacinto, and there, stepped off into sky. The mountain air snapped about me. I huddled behind a rock to light the pipe and then stood to smoke it on the gusty summit. Wind-churned smog was rolling blue brown across the desert, so the mountains emerged from a pallor of haze into brilliant sunshine. I looked across the Saddle to where the Monuments, far below, were small, and the Pedestal barely distinguishable. Suddenly, from the vantage of the Mountain Lady's eye, the scene fell into a new perspective.

The Monuments were one of three sets of cliffs on the far side of the Saddle. Across from them, high above the ranch, was a second set on the same level, and between the two, recessed and considerably higher, was the pyramid-shaped summit of the ridge above. From this, sweeping down in graceful arcs, were two sub-ridges that terminated in the lower cliffs. The whole arrangement formed another gigantic sculpture, comparable in scale to the Mountain Lady, but smaller. It was an animal lying before her. I saw it as a Lion, though it might well have been a sphinx, for the head was gone and lay scattered about the Saddle as boulders. Nonetheless, his ruin was regal, its aura still animated. He was poised in eternal vigilance, tranquil and alert. The whole figure shone, but my eye was drawn to the Monuments, now merely the claws of his right forepaw. My lofty Pedestal was but a mouse mesmerized before them.

Two ridges beyond the Lion's flank, as though thrust up to look past him at the Lady's labor, was the great column of dark green rock standing above Landslide Canyon. It was another major component of the Lady's visual space, and it glowed as a positive pole in the electromagnetics of the mountain. It might have been a serpent once, twisting down the ridge, then standing erect to return the Lady's gaze, but it was now largely demolished. The top portion of the column was broken, and the remainder pitched forward. The exposed end was covered with white stone, which stood out in sharp contrast to the green rock and glinted in the afternoon light. I saw it as a platform of the sun, a sacrificial altar where ancient rites were consummated and Dharmakayaic space touched earth. My head swirled with Egyptian obelisks and the countenances of Pharaoh, while the wind wove strange words through my hearing, telling tales in unknown tongues.

I stayed stoned on the summit for some time; then I found a tick crawling on my stomach and knew it was time to leave. I had enough water to be leisurely, so I decided to go the roundabout way through the forest of the Lady's hair to intercept the trail above Gooseberry Springs. From the peak, I could see each turn clearly, but in the actual going I was soon swallowed up in forest and unable to follow the landmarks I had picked to guide me. Several hundred feet from the summit, I stopped and reassessed my position. Evening was approaching, and I was tired, so I decided to go back and take the easy way down the Lady's left side. I remounted the summit and began again. During the descent, my day warmed into evening, and the lower slopes became more gentle, opening into little, flowery meadows ringed with boulders and cactus. Not far above the trail, I came on an emergency helicopter pad with a concrete tie-down plug in the center, which reminded me how tenuous my solitude was.

I did not stop at the Monuments, but continued on to my dinner supplies. I ate at dusk with the tiny stove casting its blue light over my mood. I was weary from the day's ramblings and a little disappointed that I had found no entrance to the Lady's mysterious interior. Nonetheless, the structure of the ancient temple complex had opened for me, and I pondered on the strange intelligence that depicted itself as the mountainous forms of its creatures.

The Lion

I woke beneath the Lion's paw, conscious of its colossal presence but not at all sure what to make of it. High above was the pinnacle of broken cliffs that I now knew as the neck of the Mountain Lady's regal companion. I decided to spend the day exploring the area and set off to reconnoiter the Pedestal before breakfast. I had never gone to the side opposite the Chalice, for the ground fell steeply to a lower level and the way was choked with brush. Now, I pushed through for a look from that side and was confounded by what I saw. The Pedestal not only resembled a very unusual creature but seemed an artifact, for its style and composition whispered of human design. It was mounted on top of a dome of rock with the appearance of an animal maintaining his perch despite the looming menace of the Lion's claws. The formation was split from end to end, and the right side of the body had fallen away. Unlike the dome, the Pedestal was not a single mass of rock but many boulders cemented together with sandstone mortar. Draped over the whole like a skin was an independent layer of flowing rock, and below, between the Pedestal and the dome, was a layer of milk quartz. Veins of rust drew arcane patterns on the stone, and my eyes were seeing glyphs on everything.

The Pedestal puzzled me. I could not decide whether it was a mosquito or a mouse, for what remained of its shape was too bizarre to be categorized. I wondered if the creature might have been a teratoid: a human-headed bird perhaps, or something entirely fantastic, like a baby dragon. Whatever the metaphor of its outer form, its innards bespoke an electromagnetic design. The boulders were dark red sandstone; the dome, a lighter shade shifting to yellow. I presumed that both colors indicated a high iron content, which could focus the earth's field. But there was also the careful placement of each boulder, the supporting layer of piezoelectric quartz, and the inexplicable veins of rust that pulsed with geomantic purpose. The field was not merely focused but crafted to a high precision, and for a moment I saw myself as a variable component in a wonderful magnetic machine.

I returned for the pipe and hashish, expecting to smoke on the Pedestal, but instead I wandered off through the sloping terraces on the desert side of the Saddle. Years before, the whole area had burned, and many charred snags still stood, while others showed naked, black tops above new foliage. Some had fallen and lay weathering in the sand. My way of walking had become a dance, which often led me along one of the fallen trunks where it bridged a sea of flowers, or offered a puzzle of branches to climb among. Where the flowers were thickest, I had gotten into the habit of stepping in my previous footprints, so my way through the maze was marked by meandering pathways going from snags to clearings to boulders. The less I thought about walking, the more surely I moved, but when I lost sight of what I was doing, I often stepped on somebody or stumbled. Trying not to try, I moved in and out of my electromagnetics; the blinking Nirmanakaya becoming reabsorbed in the Sambhogakayaic field and reissuing from it, back and forth, again and again, in the alternating current of time.

The Presence superseded the cycle of changes. I chanted to the sounds surrounding me and sat beneath a pine to be carried off on a wisp of smoke. Abdominal breathing put me in harmony with the space, but some red ants, claiming the territory as their own, discovered me as fodder and began to graze. I escaped to the top of a nearby boulder, where I sat down quickly, for the hashish had made me dizzy. Or perhaps it was the magnificence of the place that astounded me into sitting, for the top of the boulder projected above the foliage that had blocked my view from below, and the ancient city was now spread out about me. I saw the Lady from beneath her left foot, the Lion in profile, and, two canyons away, the Serpent Tower rising from its garland of forest. Below, the abyss of mountainside fell to the desert and rose again as distant peaks. My ajna chakra pulsed, culling a lost paradise from the transparent whorls of time. Dim chronologies, encoded in DNA, wafted like vapor across the limitless universe and floated as dust on the morning breeze. Here lay the First World of the Hopi and Hindus, before fire tempered its perfection; and here, the Eden of Genesis, before the wily serpent's knowledge of knowledge undid humanity with humanity's own hands. Histories swirled by. Civilization after civilization unfolded like blossoms; destruction followed destruction like fallen leaves.

The vision faded. I had seen the excellence of Eden, whose only flaw was that it contained the seed for degenerate worlds, and I returned to myself atop a broken relic of the same dream. The morning washed through me and soon took me back to the Chalice, where the *I Ching* waited on the shrine.

The first hexagram was "Gradual Progress", whose image is a tree on the mountain, connoting the process by which new growth in a hostile environment becomes firmly rooted. I applied it both to the development of ancient civilizations and to my understanding of them. The changing line warns of danger and counsels caution. I was planning to climb the Monuments and explore the Lion, but the book's advice muted my adventurousness and reminded me that capricious energy fields still eddied through the ruins.

The second hexagram was "The Family". It says that the family is humanity magnified and society in embryo. It also had a special meaning for me because several years earlier when I had asked the *I Ching* about the physiological reality of the chakra system, I had received this hexagram in answer. I subsequently came to see the family as any group of chakra-resonant people wherein a symbiotic, Sambhogakayaic consciousness could, at one level, display itself as a creative mingling of individuals, and, at another, as a transpersonal entity conscious at every point within itself. Now, seated near the foot of the Lady and Lion, I saw beyond our species and perceived a family of resonant energy fields embodying themselves as a whole spectrum of intelligent forces, from the seeming solidity of mountains to the evanescent sentience of organic life.

The resonance without structured that within and called me to the task of scaling the Monuments. The cliffs across from the Pedestal were vertical, but beyond the Chalice they fell back into a steep but climbable slope, which looked like a strawberry pot dotted here and there with tiny terraces, each holding a stunted pine. I climbed among them and finally made my way along a crevice to the top. Veins of rust drew fantastic patterns in the stone, and there were many indications that water had once poured through the area: long channels were worn in the rock, and deep, circular depressions showed where it had fallen on its way to the Saddle. Not even a spring remained on the ridge, but

I conjured up hanging gardens, with multicolored mosses clinging to moist rock faces, and ghostly people bathing in pools below.

The top of the Monuments was made of rounded protuberances of stone, catacombed with rockfall caves, clefts, and covered crevices. I roved about the area, occasionally moving to the edge to lie on my belly and stare down at the Pedestal and Chalice. From above, the Pedestal was as enigmatic as ever, and the Chalice as lovely. Looming above me was the lofty pediment forming the Lion's neck. I progressed toward it along the paw and foreleg, ascending through sloping, boulder-strewn terraces of flower speckled sand glinting with bits of mica. A ruby-throated hummingbird followed, nonchalantly sipping from selected blossoms. At the base of the pediment, he went off around the desert side, and I, after surveying the situation, followed. The pediment was too steep in front to climb, but the far side gave access to the top along the backbone of the ridge. I went to the summit and found it much like a nest, for it was a rocky depression encircled by ramparts of stone and oak. The view was unimpeded in every direction, including up and down, and the air to every horizon was clear.

The catness of the place was pervasive, and I toyed with the riddle of the sphinx, wondering what, in ages past, had risen above this pediment of stone. Mythologies offered a range of symbiotic possibilities. The Egyptians gave the sphinx the head of a ram, falcon, or man; while the Greeks made her a lion-lady fashioned, as befits a goddess, with wings. Her riddle was the mystery history of man, and failure to solve it was fatal, for hers was the duty to guard sacred places.

The wind called through the Lion's throat, reminding me that this mountainous creature was perhaps no more than it seemed, an immense cat, poised and powerful, the guardian of secrets and participant in their expression. Here, as in Egypt and ancient Mesoamerica, the cat was deified and its form deemed suitable for the embodiment of god consciousness—an idea strange to those of us who project a universe without God, or, at best, of God without gods. Our ancestors, however, understood the value of perceiving the sacred in whatever form it chose to display. As refugees on a derelict planet, they saw that every species had its unique talent for survival and that each provided a vehicle for transcendence. Companionship among compatible species was of particular significance, both symbiotically and heuristically. A human and a cat in tune created a creature greater than either, for capabilities melded in the electromagnetics of the combined field. Such a couple were mutual mentors in the development of their essence, co-conspirators in the machinations of the Tao.

My head became that of the Lion and filled with a succession of images in which various animals demonstrated their electromagnetic capabilities. A startled cat became wired, its fur flashing out like quills, while another, staring me in the eyes, raised its hackles hair by hair. A blind bat, navigating by sonar, darted through my thinking and picked off a fly of distraction, while an imaginary rattlesnake coiled to my embrace, radiating a defensive field as tangible as a diamond under water. Then my ruby-throated hummingbird, wings a blur, glided backward through my nest, reminding me that all these capabilities were, as the old Taoists professed, learnable by observant people, and that those who taught the skills were worthy to be honored as vehicles of deity.

I stretched and cleared my lungs with a series of shouts. The wind swallowed the noise and gave it back as a cooling draught. In the distance, the Serpent Tower reared like a beckoning finger. I surveyed the intervening country and mapped a route across. The Saddle trail wound around the base of the Monuments and climbed the Lion's desert side. It crossed his rump and zigzagged up the next ridge to disappear into forest. The remainder of the distance to the Tower was across steep, thickly wooded mountainside. I could not gauge the difficulty of the terrain but decided to find out by inviting myself to lunch with the Serpent on the morrow.

I left the summit and went down the far side of the Lion, past the snag on which the red eagle had perched. The ridge descended in a sweeping arc dotted with large pine trees. The cliffs forming the cat's left claws were less extensive than the Monuments. Parts had broken off and fallen away. The mountainside plunged to the ranch where the distant metal roofs looked like little squares of silver. Across the Saddle, silhouetted against the sky, the Pedestal crouched as a tiny creature before the monumental claws of the Lion's other paw.

I returned across the Lion's chest and spent an easy hour climbing among the cliffs of his neck. They rose like turrets and harbored many interesting crannies, but I found neither deep caves nor air vents. Below his sealed throat were a group of irregular terraces pushed out as the upper part of his chest. Although the area was quite extensive, I had not seen it before because from below, the level areas were indistinguishable from the surrounding slopes. The terraces created an unkempt Japanese garden whose camouflaged purpose revealed itself in an irregular mandala that geomantically energized the space. I let it move me about its peripheries and then settled at the center for a pipe.

Power poured from the Lion and beamed as a pillar of strength to the Lady in labor. A heart chakra resonance, serene, unsleeping, sounded. I chanted a response and then sat as afternoon orchestrated into sunset, and cool breezes called me back to camp. On the trail, I met an organic mandala in the form of a newborn rattlesnake coiled in a swirl of black diamonds on white. His blunt button tailpiece was vibrating noiselessly in concert with his silently flicking tongue and played me the mountain's evening mantra in mime.

SEVENTH DAY

The Serpent Tower

The night was dark, cold, and very windy. Shortly after going to sleep, I woke with my head frozen and tied it in my thermal T-shirt. Later, my makeshift turban blew away, and I had to brave the blistering wind to retrieve it. I wriggled into day with the first light, but as I was dressing, the sleeping bag, foam pad, and ground cloth blew away, so I chased them and retired to a windbreak of bushes.

I ate breakfast with the sleeping bag tied over my shoulders and then threw the *I Ching*. My plan for the day was to explore the Serpent Tower, an enterprise favored by the hexagrams "Fire" and "Fellowship with Men". The first is one of eight in the book in which the same trigram appears twice, standing on top of itself. In this case, fire is doubled, as both flame and the electromagnetic pattern it reproduces. To see these as complementary aspects of a single phenomenon is to see nature in its radiance, a state the *I Ching* calls clarity. The changing line was in the place of the ruler; though favorable, its words bode strange energy, for it promises:

> Tears in floods, sighing and lamenting.
> Good fortune.

"Fellowship with Men" is concerned with the development of a symbiotic consciousness and gives the secret of its success: clarity within and strength without; one yielding nature among many firm persons. The yielding nature is the Tao, which all share, but to utilize it properly one must be unattached to phenomena. Firm persons are those who can yield to the yielding nature, even while doing what they do. For my purpose of understanding the ancient temple, I took persons in the broadest sense and applied the concept to other creatures as well, linked in fellowship by these mountains where a serpent, lion, and lady arose with equal dignity.

I left the Saddle and went up the Lion's desert side. The sun cleared the ridge as I crossed his rump. I traveled quickly, for the trail was long rather than steep. Now and then, I sang a couplet or two, or chanted, fashioning my stream of consciousness into a morning raga. Far off in Garner Valley, steam rose from Lake Hemit, and smoke rose from the cabins clustered on its shore. On top of the second ridge, the trail entered the forest and went off to the south. I left it and climbed a large outcropping for a view of my destination through the trees.

The Serpent Tower stood in the center of a huge amphitheater of forest formed by the convolution of a major ridge. The Tower was the truncated end of a bare rock sub-ridge that projected into the amphitheater like the middle prong of a trident. The terrain was steep, and the forest formed a canopy from below my feet to above my head. Underfoot was loam and humus held in place by tree roots. It slid easily, often covering my low boots as I dug in for support. There were many large outcroppings, and near one I discovered fresh paw prints of a mountain lion, but no other trace of his presence.

Occasional breaks in the forest offered intermittent views across the amphitheater, so the Tower came into prominence as if in a series of photographs. From the side, it looked more like a citadel than a snake, for the sub-ridge became a castle causeway strung across a moat of air. The Tower was broken off below the causeway and cleft in half as though struck from above by a mighty ax. The smaller, front section was pitched forward, leaving a chasm between it and the rest.

As I neared the sub-ridge, I angled upward and emerged above the causeway. The formation was dark green stone, probably iron-rich gabbro. The ridgeback was about ten yards wide but narrowed toward the end and was piled with broken rock. Giant slabs teetered as I crossed them, and crevices opened below. I made my way carefully, often on all fours, checking both sides of the causeway. As I inched out, the forest fell away and left me with an eagle's solitary perspective. The top of the Serpent was fifteen feet below the end of the causeway, and it bulged out to either side in the form of a crescent-shaped platform. Its surface was a three-dimensional mazework, broken irregularly along a vein of schist, with pylons of gabbro pushed up through a rubble of granite. The broken-away section jutted up beyond an irregular chasm.

I climbed down to the Tower and made my way to the chasm. Inaccessible recesses lay hidden below, but it seemed I might see them if I jumped out to the broken, downward sloping tip of the platform. I hesitated for a moment, gauged the difficulty of the leap, and managed to overcome the urge. Instead, I made a circuit of the Tower's rim and settled in the lee of the causeway to smoke a pipe. The sky was clear, and the cool air crystalline. Across plunging canyons, the Lady and Lion lay couched on mountains, seeming to focus the energy of the whole range in the crucible of their encounter.

The rock beneath me tingled, then started to flow. I drew energy from it and felt like an incipient volcano, for the rhythms of earth were rent by the memory of the mountain's epic destruction. My heart was compressed by pain. I reeled, then fell to my hands and knees and toppled forward until my forehead pressed against stone. Tiny points of light burned into my flesh and pierced me with sorrow. I sobbed for that which was irrevocably lost, for beauty blasted to rubble, for life extinguished. I tried to Aum, but could only Ooo. The Presence, nonetheless, responded, and waves of compassion rolled through me.

The pain passed like tattered clouds. I could not move my head for it was magnetized by contact with the stone. Time dissolved, and space became a point of speculation. I strove to see the lovely temple-city as it had stood before the devastation, but striving blurred the image. I was shunted off elsewhere, swirling as a constellation of burnt-out stars in a galaxy of night. My knees, pressed into the uneven stone, hurt, and my forehead was on fire. I sat back gingerly and rubbed my brow. It was pockmarked with sharp indentations. I looked more carefully where it had rested and discovered tiny crystals of mica and quartz embedded in the schist.

Unaware that the energy had flipped me into a backward head, I tried to drink from the canteen, but couldn't open it because I kept turning the cap in the wrong direction. The more I studied it, the more confused I became, and the harder I twisted. Eventually, it accidentally figured itself out, and I got a drink, but the same thing recurred when I tried to put the cap back on: it kept falling off instead. I was in a dream space where subjectivity and objectivity exchanged roles, and every act produced an opposite effect. My ego and its environment were confused at a precarious portal to the Sambhogakaya where reality guarded itself with mirrors. I knew it was not a place I could safely walk away from, so I snuggled against the rock wall and sat confounded by reversals. Left was right, and top, bottom; form was emptiness, and emptiness, form; and every boundary was a two-sided illusion in the drama of mind.

By early afternoon, the sun had mended me, and I was ready to continue. Thunder rumbled in the distance as I returned along the causeway, and cumulus clouds were building on the ridge. I still had the sides and base of the Tower to explore, so I made my way down the slope of the sub-ridge, searching for caves and places to climb the sheer rock wall. I found only rubble and masses of shattered stone, but the descent involved a lot of scrambling and jumping. By the time I reached the bottom, I was hobbling with a twisted and swollen knee, so I decided against climbing the other side in favor of the shortest route to camp, which lay down Landslide Canyon to its waterfall and then cross-country to the Saddle.

From below, the Tower looked like an Easter Island monolith. Reluctantly, I turned my back on it and continued on. The canyon went down like a ship's ladder, and sprinkles of rain from the distant clouds had made it slippery. I paused frequently, once to exchange greetings with a medium-sized rattlesnake draped over some roots. The waterfall was considerably smaller than I expected. It fell over a massive promontory of granite mountainside, but what from a distance had appeared to be water was a three-foot swath of blackened moss, with only a trickle down the center. The water oozed from the cracked rock of the canyon side. I managed to refill my canteen by channeling a stream along a stem of grass, a process that took a few minutes but was no delay at all, for the rock face was covered with glyphs and, high above, the Serpent rose into a cumulus-studded sky.

The top of the waterfall was about level with the Saddle, so I headed off across the intervening canyons. I had to go up three times, and down twice, before reaching my destination. I relied on the Presence to navigate. The northern slopes were thorny puzzles of cactus and agave, and the southern ones were tangled with chaparral. Often I could only see a few difficult feet in any direction, but something animated my intuition, once it even said "Go up!" very clearly, and the way ahead invariably opened.

I rested in the Saddle and put salve on my knee. I poured the remainder of the day's water on the clumps of lupine at the entrance to the Chalice. They were flourishing. Flower stalks pushed up in abundance, and the first streamers of tiny blue blossoms whispered the future of spring.

Arrogant Dragon

I woke in the early light, but lay until the sun warmed my nose, and then lingered for a while longer enjoying the morning. I had decided on a day of rest, but the *I Ching*, when I threw it, was so favorable that I changed my plans. The first hexagram was "The Creative", which, through a complete reversal of the Dharmakayaic resonance, transformed itself into "The Joyous". I decided to more intimately involve myself in the process by eating the rest of the psilocybin mushrooms, even though the first changing line warned of danger, and the second, in the top place, said:

> Arrogant dragon will have cause to repent.

The dragon expresses the attributes of the creative power of heaven. It represents the fundamental dynamic: the arousing force that initiates, sustains, and brings all things to completion. "The Creative" possesses both sublimity and success, and, though never tangible, is ever present. Arrogance is not its attribute, but one that appears in a subsequently arising ego that thereby opens itself to foolhardiness. I knew the place of the arrogant dragon and had learned to want nothing to do with it, so I did not fear the delicate change in the ajna chakra whereby the Creative completes itself and disappears into joyousness.

I was seated on the red mat in a sandy depression beyond the Chalice. The orange sleeping bag was thrown over a boulder, airing. The mushrooms were in the pack on the other side of the Chalice, so I set out to get them. As soon as I climbed from the depression, I heard the drone of a small aircraft coming up from Gamer Valley. I wondered if I should go back and strike my colors or first dig out the mushrooms. Inertia won, and I continued toward the pack, but two steps later I remembered the arrogant dragon: his electricity galvanized me backward, and I fairly tumbled into the depression. With mat and bag beneath the camouflaged tarpaulin, and all of us under a bush, I watched the plane come over the ranch. I looked intently, trying to identify it, and unexpectedly became an eye within the cockpit. I saw through the morning stillness as though I was the pilot, and all the mountain, in its multiple moving perspectives, rippled below. The aircraft drifted across the Lion's back and dropped with the mountain's contour toward the desert. I stayed with it as far as the junction of Gooseberry and Landslide canyons, then slipped back to myself, now standing on top of a low boulder, watching the distant machine disappear.

I mounted the Pedestal to eat the mushrooms, slowly savoring their flavor. Gradually, my body drifted out of its normal chemical focus. Edges blurred. Things began to move and melt together, even as their individual realness deepened. Each item of awareness was equally absorbing; each commanded my attention, came into focus, pointed at something else, dissolved, and disappeared. The cornucopia was inexhaustible, but I emptied it by dismissing my desire to taste its every offering. Thereupon, objects disappeared as such, leaving their supervening field as a network of dancing forces.

My body felt light, uninhibited. I went down to the maze and began to stroll. The rocks were no less sentient than the trees or flowers. All gloried in the radiance of a shared consciousness seemingly composed of every awareness everywhere about, but, in the more sublime reality, composing them of its own essence. I whispered the simple mantra Aum Tao to my feet, until the repetition of words merged with the dynamism of my being. Tao, the patterned perfection of the stochastic universe, and Aum, the creative utterance eternally bringing it to birth, together formed the single Presence underlying every illusion of separateness.

Encapsulated by the phenomena around me, I experienced the day in terms of its entities. The wind was a dragon coursing over the mountain. In some places, he almost bowled me down, in others, he was as still as stalactites. He revealed himself to be a master sculptor of cliffs and gardener of wilderness. He showed me how he twisted trees and taught toughness to gnarls; how he ground rocks for flower food and mixed it with mulch; how he brought water from the ocean for his thirsty creatures; and how, now and again, he pruned them with drought or shaped them with his fiery tongue. I pulled him into my lungs and held him inside like a bottled jinni, making him dance my feet. He stumbled me down the hill until I laughed and let him out, then he wafted along beside me as a carnival of fragrances and startled each flower into talking.

The multicolored meadow burst into a chorus of buzzing chatter, jabber, squawks, and squeaks. Words and bits of sentences rose from the din, so the overall effect was like a barnyard at feeding time, with me the farmer singing along. I hopped and sang, alight with merriment and exhilaration. Then I remembered the arrogant dragon and stretched out on the earth, face down, letting the coarse, sandy soil ground my jubilant energy.

In human physiology, joy is the natural predecessor of enlightenment, for whatever makes us joyful also enlarges the pupils of our eyes, but my hexagram for the day had given me this sequence reversed, so I pressed my face into the sand and invited darkness to follow joy. I was in a terrace below the left foot of the Mountain Lady, and she now appeared in my interior space as a tangible emptiness: a womb spermed with memories of new life. She spoke in the images of the *I Ching*, showing me what I had learned of her since the LSD trip four days earlier. Each day's first hexagram had described the nature of my intention. Since I had used my energy to penetrate to the meaning of the mountain, the second hexagram had presented a conclusion about it. On the day of the LSD trip, the second hexagram had been "The Wanderer", which adumbrated a human role in the drama of the ancient temple. The role was not that of priest or master, but of journeyman and stranger, of one who needed to be continually alert, whose safety lay in proper movement. On the following day, I had climbed the Mountain Lady, to discover that her head had exploded to the oblivion of "Splitting Apart". The day I spent on the Lion was defined by "The Family", which had presented these sculpted mountains as a family of anthropomorphic and zoomorphic beings, once capable of entering into conscious relationships with their dependent creatures. On the Serpent's day, I had explored the nature of this symbiosis in "Fellowship with Men". Now, with the magic of magic mushrooms, I saw the purpose of all this loveliness, for "The Creative" brought forth "The Joyous", the youngest daughter of heaven and earth, and gave her form as the anima of the mountain.

My brain became a critical mass of knowledge, self-sustained by chain reactions of thought and imagery. I experienced the mountain as an electromagnetic and gravitational consciousness molding my perception of it. Yielding nature was dominant: the Sambhogakaya controlled its Nirmanakayaic transfigurations and loosed them to play. Energy transmuted to environment, and back again, over and over, creating mandalas, numbers, beings, and vistas of time. Overwhelmed, I watched, trapped in the knowledge of knowing, but knowing this as prelude to abandoning it. Earth forces tuned my psyche, absorbed it in the crucible of their being, and radiated me outward through the spiritual space of the heavens. I heard esoteric rituals sung and tasted magical dreams. Arcane chambers, misted with incense, opened mysteriously, and mosaics of meditational music merged with the harmony of light. Sacred space, coexisting with the ordinary, appeared shining from beyond a shore where ancient rites of initiation and passage launched earth consciousness into the ocean of time-space.

The visionary surge abated. I separated back into my body and lay echoing a single tone, a resonance of the mountain's mystery. Beyond the excellence of this resonance there was nothing here to be found, nothing to dig for, nothing that could be taken away, for the power of the mountain was as intangible as it was invincible. I sat up and bowed to the Lady. I could not see her, for I was too close to the red sandstone cliffs that supported her foot. These towered above me, elaborately weathered: carved, pinnacled, eroded into gothic splendor, and shimmering from top to bottom with mystic glyphs. I saw them as great tablets intricately inscribed, as cascading scrolls on which the ancient secrets of the world were engraved, and as open books whose pages were tissues of sand blown off by the wind, exposing those beneath. The Presence, whispering in windsong of mantric sound, called them the Footstool of Temporal Wisdom and fluttered their missing pages somewhere deep within my brain.

I walked the lower terraces. Once again, the desert seemed to be an inland sea, and the mountains an Isle of the Blest. I realized I was part of a planetary zoo whose beings were mountains and whose intelligence was the earth itself, taking the forms of a headless lady, a deplumed serpent, a sphinx-like lion, dragons, and I knew not what else. Astounded by the menagerie, I thought of ancient zoos and wondered for what forgotten purposes our ancestors employed their generic cousins. Teratoids pranced through my mind, hinting at hybrid powers that delighted my imagination and appalled my reason, for they filled me with Sambhogakayaic intimations of a controlled, logarithmic expansion into spectrums of symbiotic consciousness.

In the maze beneath the Lion's shoulder, a fallen snag lay across my path. It was partially reduced to dust, and the rest was so filled with dry rot that little more than habit held it together. As I surveyed the derelict, I sensed a rational residue and asked if I might walk his back. He said yes, so I did, and he crumbled as I went. When I reached the bottom, he said, "One walk is all I'm worth, but hope you enjoyed it." I told him I did, then stood gazing at his uprooted end which, in falling, had pulled large chunks of rock from the earth. These were broken, entwined with roots, and covered everywhere with glyphs. The tree had squeezed much of the stone to powder, and more of it was ready to flake away, so I broke off a piece with my fingers. Beneath what I took, the glyphs remained.

Contradiction assailed me. I could not deny that the glyphs seemed as real as the rock that gave them substance, but neither was I ready to attribute human artifact to the interior of a stone. A rational impulse told me that the phenomenon was an obvious mental projection, so I attempted to trace my internal circuitry. Still, I could find no point of separation between what I saw now and what I usually saw. If the glyphs were mental projections, the impulse that molded my seeing them must have arisen from my primitive, preverbal brain stem and contorted the image before I, the subsequently arising observer, could see the situation in toto. Consequently, I could not separate the images without dissolving myself. If, on the other hand, the glyphs were real, if they were somehow attributes of the stone itself, then I was seeing what sight usually hid from itself in the very act of discrimination.

I could not tell which assumption was nearer the truth. Faced with the conundrum, my eyes involuted and saw themselves looking outward from the rock. My body became sandstone masonry from the distant past, and I solidified into a new time dimension, where motility was deep within, and the muses, eonic. Eternity shrank to a probability function, then dissolved into a multilayered latticework of energy to which the material of my stone conformed, so that, from center outward, no matter how broken or abraded, each piece radiated the truth it was designed to embody. As millennia of wind and water wore the stone, new faces continually emerged, and new perspectives eroded into focus. Day by day, the Tao altered its expression in the eternal song of creation.

Caught up in wonder, I met the mountain as a colossal thought. Deciphering the glyphs that reflected this sentience no longer mattered, for everything was pure intelligence, neither separate from myself nor yet quite the same, intangible and yet the clearly shining Presence. All things from my own being outward were suffused with a diamond light, invisible, but intense and determinate.

My mind became a forum in which the age-old controversy between science and mysticism flared up. I slipped to the frontier of my understanding, where physics faded imperceptibly into metaphysics, and champions arose to dispute the boundary. Both scientists and saints agree that this world is some sort of marvelous illusion made up of forces, not things; of probabilities, not certainties; of relationships rather than individuals; but they differ on the nature of consciousness. Mystics say that the universe is a single, unknowable intelligence which, when apprehended in itself, makes its reflection as knowledge superfluous. Science demurs and defines intelligence as itself, the fourth or fifth function of a non-intelligent universe, for scientists deduce our mental complexity from a primal explosion which, blowing outward as a cosmic cloud of debris, coagulated to galaxies composed of such things as our solar system, upon whose third planet intelligence arose as us: a unique, accidental, and perfectly egotistical event.

My cogitation dialectically synthesized into an immense reservoir of joy, from which I awoke sometime later, just as the sun was slipping behind the Lady, erasing my shadow with her own. The wind came back, cool and whispering of new delights. I went to the pack for warmer clothes, and the day ended as it had begun, with the drone of engines in the sky. It was a helicopter, and I had just enough time to re-conceal my gear before it appeared. It passed about a thousand feet above the Monuments and went on its way, but it convinced me to move my encampment down into the more protected maze. When the machine had passed, I shouldered the pack and headed off. I found an exquisite, pine-shaded garden between two huge boulders. It was low, protected from the wind, and hidden from the air; a suitable refuge, I thought, for an arrogant dragon.

After dinner, I wrapped up in the tarpaulin and leaned against a sloping rock to smoke and watch the stars. The moon was hours from rising, the night dark and vivid. Leo strode toward the Mountain Lady, and the Archer, Sagittarius, in distant pursuit, rose from the ridge. I pondered his lineage, for he is one of two teratoids in the zodiac and stands guardian at the earth's galactic portal. The constellation is the mortal remains of the immortal centaur Chiron. The centaur has the body of a horse, and the trunk, arms, and head of a man. His bow is drawn; his arrow points to the center of the galaxy, for the plane of the zodiac and that of the galaxy meet in his domain, and the Milky Way pours through his arms. The Greeks of the Heroic Age said that centaurs were real creatures and that a band of them lived on the wild slopes of Mount Pelion in Thessaly, where they were originally honored for their wisdom and skill at arms. In the end, though, they fared badly, for the Greeks accused them of wantonness and exterminated them. Chiron, the most famous of the centaurs, was honored for his teaching of martial and medical arts. Hercules accidentally wounded him with a poisoned arrow, and Chiron, suffering a pain that would neither kill him nor go away, renounced his immortality and was cast into the sky by Zeus.

Swept up on a mythology of stars, I saluted the centaur and dove into Dharmakayaic space, where I once more confronted science on the near edge of the immensity it held at bay. The solar system with its sun and planets, its satellites, comets, and debris, is big. The galaxy with its hundred billion suns is immense. The universe beyond is beyond conception, and yet all are related by the speed of light, a scientific yardstick that correlates time and space. In one year, light travels six trillion miles, an unimaginable distance. Light from the sun takes eight minutes to reach us and, in a few short hours, is beyond the planetary edge of the solar system, but it takes a hundred thousand years to cross our galaxy. The galaxy, in turn, is but one of innumerable others, all moving away from each other. Our nearest galactic neighbor is more than two million light-years off, visible on clear nights as a fuzzy patch in the constellation of Andromeda. The light we see from there, scientists say, began its journey when Homo sapiens was still a hominoid, and it will continue until long after we are gone. For the mystic, however, light is the nature of reality. It neither comes nor goes and is equally present everywhere, for a particle of light, waving through space, is without existence except as a universal field.

The sky became a mandala. I spiraled in harmony with the spheres and eluded gravity as star lights pulled me into the depths of night. Heaven and the ontological space of the heavens were no different; the one was within, and I within the other coursed the magnitudes of deceptive distance.

The waning moon, flattened with its monthly age, came over the ridge and drew me back to more usual haunts. In its light, the Milky Way faded and disappeared, leaving me in a shrunken universe, bemused by the thought that, whatever it was, the cosmos was mostly nonexistent, for if all of its real stuff were put together within the space science ascribes to it, it would be, relatively speaking, no bigger than the boulder against which I sat was in relation to the whole world.

The Maze

I woke in the maze, amazed, dreaming the maze, wandering the maze, confusing the convolutions of my brain with those of the mountain, and spiraling along both in wonder. I opened my eyes. Leaf shadows on the rock above were calligraphy telling stories of the sun, and a morning moth danced among them as an exclamation point. I got up and stretched, joining my shadow to the others and moving consciousness into my extremities like a cat. I walked off naked into the near mazeway and scrambled about among the boulders. I had done it all before; by now my trails went everywhere, and I recalled my ancestry as a path-following animal. My days had already fallen into a pattern: up at dawn; exercise, breakfast, and toilet; meditation and *I Ching*; off on the day's adventure; water trek and dinner; meditation; bed. The sequence, tuned to the sun, acted itself out, leaving my ego with nothing to do but not step on flowers.

It was a beautiful day for an acid trip. I threw the *I Ching* in a terrace perched like a ship's prow over a rocky abyss. The first hexagram was "Duration", signifying a union that cannot be dissolved by time. The commentary speaks of sacred and ordinary space and says that perseverance in a right course is the key to their synthesis. This, the book continues, is the secret of the eternity of the universe, and it adds that meditation on what gives duration to a thing reveals the nature of heaven and earth.

The changing line, to the part of me who liked straight answers, was annoying: it announces good fortune for a woman, misfortune for a man; but to the part of me who found the mysterious tantalizing, the ambiguity was something to engulf like an amoeba and watch while it figured itself out. The second hexagram was "Preponderance of the Great", indicating too much of a good thing. The image depicting this state of affairs is the ridgepole of a house that sags to the breaking point because its supporting ends are too weak. It foretells a time of dangerous climax, a time for me to be gingerly with DMT.

Four days had passed since my last encounter with LSD, and I felt ready to soar again. The proper spacing between trips is a variable, a matter of tolerance and intolerance. Physical tolerance to LSD, the period that human chemistry partially blocks the action of the drug, lasts about three days, after which the body is again ready for the optimum effect. The mind, however, is rarely so supple. Every trip requires a period of psychological restructuring during which the various insights and reactivated potentialities of the nervous system are synthesized by the developing persona. Generally, three days is not enough time for this process to complete itself, so the high in trips taken too closely together can diminish or turn sour because of our intolerance to psychic change.

I had a small bag of LSD tablets, some colored Sunshine orange, others, Krishna blue. Each table contained 350 micrograms of sacrament. I determined the day's dosage by picking blindly from the bag, one tab at a time, until I had two colors. The first and second choices were orange, the third, blue, so I began the trip with a thousand micrograms of LSD reactivating a tailing of mushrooms.

I chewed the tablets, but kept the mash in my mouth. The acid was absorbed through my tongue and palate and came on first as electric tingles in my teeth. I set off to wander the maze again, and now the ancient city shone forth as a radiant heaven-world. Broken stelae and shattered columns rose around me, the great Lion and Lady revealed their noble forms, and the Presence once more displayed itself as its sacred precincts, whose energy wove a garland of memories through my cellular being.

I thought of other mazeways and wondered why they had been so useful to ancient cultures. The Mediterranean world had many of them, the most famous of which was the Labyrinth of Minos on Crete, housing the dread Minotaur. It had seven crucial junctions; a wrong turn at any of them compounded the problem of escape. The Minotaur, a teratoid of a bull's head and giant's body, fed on the humans who could not decipher the maze before he found them.

I pondered the meaning of the myth, and my mind responded with visual art. I saw the Labyrinth of Minos superimposed on the one I actually walked. Acid etched the scene on the whorls of my brain, and I saw the maze as a training device in meditational technique. Its objective, like that of meditation, was to force transcendence. The solution of the maze was not merely to escape, but to get outside it in a psychic sense, to see it from above as a puppeteer sees his stage and puppet. Thus it was a portal to the earthmind, a schoolhouse of electromagnetic consciousness. But in decadent times, most people had lost the ability to live liberated, and the Minotaur provided the necessary incentive to drive them out of themselves. During the Kali Yuga, terror has often provided the only emotional force sufficient to remerge the Nirmanakaya with the all-seeing Sambhogakaya.

Sound brought me back from the silence of speculation. I brushed against a manzanita whose brittle gray fingers snapped like notes from a xylophone, reanimating my world with music. My feet squeaked soprano in the warming sand, and a cricket added counterpoint. The wind played flute with the trees, organ with the rocks, and swished through the flowers like a ballerina's skirt. The chorus grew and responded to my listening. Birds sang, flies hummed, and a pinecone fell fortissimo to my side after playing Bach on the branches as it dropped. But then, the vibratory spectrum shifted, and individual sounds lost their identities.

I had wandered into a circle of huge boulders and was stopped by their steadying field. The Footstool of Temporal Wisdom arched above like a rainbow, dazzling me with learned displays of deep red and profusions of form. I was assailed by the mystery of seeing and the enigma of light, the particle and wave implicit in each other, the formulations of science in the visions of mystics. The morning's I Ching had spoken of the sacred space of the eternal universe, but my mind retreated before the vast unknowns that clothe the origin and ending of forever. We begin as a quasar and perish as a black hole, during which time the triad of light, darkness, and I who distinguish them weave patterns on the loomings of time.

The sun sparkled from the sand in myriad colors, its prismatic waves shattering into a multiplicity of beams. I strove to understand their essence, but, like the sand, could do little more than reflect on their nature. Light was the glue of time-space, universal and synchronistic. It transported energy instantaneously, and only the interference of thinking slowed it to visible speeds. Dr. Einstein said that if a vehicle could travel at the speed of light it would get to where it was going with no lapse of time. In his hypothetical universe, a round trip to bright Sirius would take seventeen earth years to accomplish. As far as the travelers were concerned, however, they would be back as soon as they left because, from the standpoint of pure light, the universe has no dimensions, and our seeming to see them is but that quirk of galactic time which scientists call relativity, and mystics, duality.

A sunbeam slipped through the sanctum of my space, molding it with delicate arrays of brilliance. In its luster, eternity had no meaning. I watched the birth and death of a galaxy in the space of a breath and saw the universe pulse, much like ourselves. A pinpoint particle of light pierced my eye; a photon, randomly running forever, exploded to new life with a neuron, and waved away. Light does not age; it is eternal: a bearer, not a function of time; an extender, not a component of space. It exists beyond seeing and sees beyond existence. It neither is nor is not, for at the speed of light there is no light, and unchanging essence returns to the mind of God.

At the speed of light, there is no light or limit to the timeless universe: the secret of the stars is our synchronicity in knowing them now as they will be long ago. At the speed of light, there is no light, for knowledge and knowing merge: the Nirmanakayaic corpuscle dissolves as the Sambhogakayaic wave sinks in the megadimensionless, Dharmakayaic field alight with the essence of eternity.

The surge imploded. I woke to myself lying on the sand, staring out at the sky canvas of our blue-scattering sun. I drifted on a cushion of luminous imagery as my mind, rearisen naked, hurried to weave gossamer threads about itself. At the speed of light, I thought, there is no light, for if there was, empty space would not exist, and nothing else would appear. The sun slipped past the zenith. Shadows grew short, then lengthened again, and another hour passed before I thought to move. Finally, I made my way to the pack for a DMT joint. I stuck it behind my ear and started for the Lion's heart, taking the most direct route up the steep, forested slope of his forepaw. Halfway up, in a clearing among tall pines, I was stopped by a darting swift, who announced himself as an usher/actor in the Theater of the Woods and invited me to a matinee. He flashed by my head and began circling around the glade at top speed. He glided and swooped, danced and pranced on air, missing branches by a feather. A second swift appeared and entered the pattern. The clearing was about a hundred feet long, but pinched in the middle like a figure eight. The swifts flew the eight, one on either side, crossing neatly at the center on each pass. Suddenly, a hummingbird darted out of the forest and flew just behind, above, and to the right of one swift. To my amazement, he maintained the position flawlessly. No matter how spontaneously the swift maneuvered, the hummingbird remained tucked a few inches from his side. Occasionally, the hummingbird disappeared in the trees and reappeared like a shot, sometimes next to one swift, sometimes the other.

I was caught in an organic cyclotron, dazzled by the spectacle. My own magnetics responded and I was drawn out and joined to the bird's-eye consciousness that spun the mountain. The new perception was an eclectic composition of binocular and contra-lateral vision that created a psychic dimension requiring a man-bird hybrid for its utilization. I saw and was seen; neither was nor was not; within and without moved effortlessly together, spinning the space within my head, within the mountain, within the richness of the Presence.

I bid the birds good-bye and continued up the Lion's paw. The tall forest became scrub at the top. I ascended terrace by terrace and crossed from the shoulder to the breast at the base of the Lion's pinnacled throat. My path brought me down to the heart and into a circle of white sand in the central terrace, where I looked across the Saddle at the sleeping Lady. She lay in the embrace of a threatening, exciting sky. The desert to the north shaded from yellow to dark gray. Thunderheads were building over the San Bernardinos, towering heavenward like celestial extensions of the mountains, replete with twisted canyons and sweeping ridges.

For twenty minutes or more, I sat mesmerized, joint in one hand, match in the other, waiting for the wind to abate. It did, several times, but I continually missed the moment. Each time, I was reminded of what I was doing by the returning wind; awakened, as it were, by the recreation of the phenomenon whose negation I awaited. Finally, I called on the wind gods to desist and focused my full attention on what I was trying to do. I poised anew and waited. The backdrop blackened. Soon the Mountain Lady was crowned with a nimbus of sky, and the iconography of cloud culled from my memory a place where I had once lived in Hawaii. It was a little hut on the south shore of Maui where the sacred mountain Haleakala meets the sea. The place is named Ol-e-nue-ha-ha, which means "Winds that Laugh at Man" for there, too, the aery gods chortled, swooping from above, bounding, spinning on their heels, and then vanishing abruptly, for a moment . . .

. . . sswtch! I lit the match in an instant's calm, but the wind, half a move ahead of me, blew out the flame before it singed the paper. Chastened, I emptied my head, and with a second match in hand, waited until it struck itself and lit the DMT.

I cupped the joint in my hands against the wind and filled myself with the familiar, acrid smoke. My lungs dissolved. I probed the dissolution with a startled kinesthetic sense, seeking the flavor of the sacrament and hoping for a hint of its still hidden intent. I inhaled again, and my mind poured out through opening fissures in my skull. The light, already brilliant, became exponentially brighter as though tiers of magnesium lamps had been silently ignited, revealing the Mountain Lady in her superlative beauty, palpably alive, though sleeping through the nightmare of her nighttime.

I smoked again and entered the sacred space in which the ancient city still lived. I felt the Lion's breath on my back. The Mountain Lady began to move. She grew larger, more animated, her sleep stirred by the intensity of my fixation on her. I bowed my head and slipped into silence. My hand proffered the joint again, and my lips accepted for the fourth time.

The tempo increased dramatically. The rhythmic breathing of the Lady altered, and the mountain began to pulse. Accompanying this, as though to the beat of a drum, was an incredible metamorphosis of organic into electromagnetic form. The Mountain Lady's warm and vibrant reality was withdrawn into its more fundamental energy matrix. Vision abstracted itself from matter, and the radiance of life dissolved into myriad shifting patterns.

As the movement accelerated, I was sucked into the process. The Lady became a jigsaw puzzle of seething energies. Shorn of her gentle nature, she revealed a demon, a volcanic colossus with a thousand iron leashes and ten thousand glittering eyes. And still she grew, and changed, and turned ever more horrible.

My predicament was inescapable. The world itself decreed my doom. The future assailed me with its finality, for it contained only one sure thing: my death. I sank to a frightened center and there took a stand, hoping to use the catharsis of fear as a spur to freedom, as a needle to burst the bubble of illusion that surrounded me. But the horrible apparition grew ever larger, overtowering, overpowering; her breath, a furnace; her fragrance, a powerhouse shorting out.

Suddenly, from behind, the Lion roared, sending me tumbling forward in terror. I shrank to the size of a flea, while the mountainous paws on either side flexed restlessly, cleaving the earth. I quaked to the planet's tremblings. The trees and bushes of the terrace became grotesque, then horrible, as though devil's hair was freezing to fire and reaching for me as fuel. The light itself became spectral, malevolently intelligent, and vindictively all-consuming.

I was too terrified to close my eyes and reacted by taking several quick, deep breaths.

The vision stabilized at unimaginably hideous and held for a long minute. Then, without striking, the horror slowly began to recede like a retreating cobra.

The joint had gone out. It seemed a maggot in my fingers, a thing to cast away, but some part of me knew better and held onto it until I was together enough to stash it safely out of the wind. I felt like a chemistry set and smelled like a bad experiment, but I could still appreciate the magical perceptiveness of the *I Ching*, for I had certainly sagged under a load too heavy to bear. My timing was off, my body unhinged, my lungs parched, and my muscles mush.

When I felt strong enough to stand, I limped around the terrace coaxing life back into my limbs. Then I gathered my gear and moved back to the granite security of the Lion's throat. I sat on a low pinnacle, letting the cool wind revitalize my stunned senses, but I quickly grew restless and began to climb the rocks. I crossed the Lion's chest and gradually made my way down his forepaw. By the time I reached the top of the Monuments, I felt more agile, so I accepted an invitation from the wind to explore the caves and crevices in the claws of the cat.

I moved quietly but, even so, disturbed some monk-monks. They scurried away and then came back to peer and play, darting in and out of their three-dimensional maze. I laughed at them, and they vanished; I called, and they returned. Sometimes they hid nearby, just out of sight; then, tweaking their tails above a rock, they would be off again. One watched from beyond a crevasse. I asked him how it felt to live in the Lion's claws and what his species remembered of former times. He admitted to great wariness of lions, much delight in life, and, to my last question, replied that I had most certainly come to the right source, for his people were archivists, scholars of this monumental library, and keepers of nuts. He said if I had a question, he would be more than happy to investigate it. I wondered aloud about the consciousness that joined us and, for answer, tweaked my tail at the sun.

After my respondent left, I jumped the crevasse, crawled along a ledge, slid down a steep rock face, and settled under a lone dwarf piñon pine high up on the desert side of the Monuments. The wind whistled above, but where I sat was calm, shady, and cool, so I crumbled some hashish into the pipe and leisurely enjoyed a few puffs of smoke. The storm had gathered more darkly over the desert and was piling up in gray billows above San Gorgonio Pass. I watched while its cascading forms wove tapestries with my nervous system, but twenty or thirty minutes later I snapped back abruptly when motion below caught my eye.

A hiker had come into the Saddle along the trail behind the Lion. A large black dog trotted at his heels. I had the binoculars with me, so I brought the pair into closer focus, wondering if I knew them. The hiker was wearing a broad-brimmed hat and walking obliquely away from me. I was unable to see his face, but at the junction of the trail to the ranch and Gooseberry Springs, he stopped and surveyed the area. He tilted his head back as he scanned the crags, giving me a good look at his profile. I didn't recognize him, and wished him away, but he turned instead and came toward the Monuments.

I took a quick mental inventory of where everything was: the pack and sleeping gear were far down the terraces, well hidden, but the shrine pieces, *I Ching*, and meditational stones were spread out in the natural rock garden of the Chalice. I had a strong presentiment that they were quite able to take care of themselves, so I settled back to watch, wondering if the maze would confound the visitors. The hiker was following my paths through the tangle; the dog had gone off on his own. Halfway to the Pedestal, the man stopped and called the animal. His shouts were barely audible to me, but clear to the dog. He returned to the man, and together they went off across the Saddle. I breathed easier when they disappeared over the Mountain Lady's ankle, but waited a while longer before climbing from my perch.

I went down to the Chalice and sat, hoping to calm myself with the soothing vibrations of a tranquil yin field. I was tired and hungry, but also hyperactive. My mind had been stunned into anxious submission by the perceptual onslaught of the LSDMT synergy. Parts of it were now starting to sputter back into action. I pasted the small square of lapis lazuli to my forehead to steady my brain and placed a ruby in my mouth to extract poisons, then I did a series of cleansing breaths to purify blood and bile. I soon felt better but my restlessness continued, so I left the Chalice and walked down through the terraces.

The maze mollified my mind, and friendly flowers called out as I passed. My care in not stepping on them, nothing more than a subliminal mediation of noticing their space, had matured my side of the relationship, so they were able to speak intelligibly to my spectrum of understanding. They were garrulous, unquenchable, and regaled me with perfumed perceptions. I followed the nuances of their song, which took me to the ship-prow terrace, where I joined their chorus by chanting.

I sat in golden sands and called to the Goddess Tara with cadences older than the Sanskrit that embodied them. I counted the repetitions on a string of bon and sandalwood beads, but the finger motion was part of the rhythm, and the beads flowed on without number. The breeze snatched the sounds from my lips and cast them into the valley full of bubbling storms. My mind emptied, and the last embers of DMT turned to gray matter in the vaults of memory.

Evening came on as I finished. I was calm but emotionally drained by the events of the day and physically exhausted. I stood up slowly, twisting my legs and kicking my feet to restore circulation. I turned while doing so, and stopped in mid-kick. The hiker and his dog were twenty feet away, watching. It was an unpleasant shock, but I nodded a greeting, and they came over. The man had a small pack and sleeping bag hitched over his shoulder, but what caught my eye was his hatband. It was a snakeskin, a headless ouroboros encircling his skull.

He noticed my attention and ran his fingers around the hatband. "It's rattlesnake," he said. "I killed the fucker myself."

It was good for openers, but I had no reply. I reached down to scratch the dog's head. The animal growled and backed off, his tail between his legs, his yellow eyes fixed on me. "Don't fool with him!" said the hiker. "He's crazy." He told the dog to sit, but it refused. "My cousin owns him," he said. "He kicks the shit out of him, so he don't trust nobody, but he keeps snakes away."

There was a pause. I meant to say something, but before I could get it out, he started again. While talking, he unslung his pack and pulled out a chunk of schist. He pointed to an array of tiny, broken crystals protruding from it and asked if I knew what they were. I said probably garnet and added that they were worthless, but was dismayed to see another of the mountain's sparkles being carried away.

He returned the stone to his pack and pushed his hat back to hang by its strap. His hair was just starting to get long. He said I was the first person he had met all day, that he had seen my trails earlier, and had known I was around. When he couldn't find me, he had wandered over the ridge, napped, and come back. He said he was glad to find someone to talk to and began to bombard me with details of his recent past. His monologue was a chaos of personal problems and unrelated snippets of memory punctuated with taut pauses, during which he partially withdrew his attention, not so much expecting an answer as looking for something inside his head. The gist of his rambling was that he had come to the mountains for a few days to unwind.

He had recently been discharged from the army and had been unable to find a job. He was broke, unhappy, and pissed off. He asked how long I had been here, what I did, where I came from. I pointed to my scruffy beard and said I had been here about a week. He knew something of the Brotherhood and began to question me about the ranch and what had gone on there. I told him I knew Frank Scovel and that I had been coming here for years, then I dropped the subject and sidestepped the rest of his questions.

It was dusk and getting cold. The stormy sky was gray on gray, with no stars showing. I wanted to break loose, but the hiker kept on talking. He had just gotten back from a year in Vietnam. I told him I had been there with the navy and immediately regretted it, for he now began to unload his war stories. His memories were garbled: battles indistinguishable from nightmares. Part of him was still trapped in a steaming bunker somewhere beyond Pleiku. He talked as if we had been there together, assuming I knew the details of the heavy action in the highlands where he had learned the horror of war, of fighting an invisible, implacable enemy in an alien land, a million miles from his own reality. Plagued by uncertainty, anxiety, and a lack of belief in what he was doing, he had come to distrust both friend and foe. He hated what he spoke of, but was unable to stop as his compulsion cursed its way through the most awful and deeply etched memories of his life. The dog whined at the growing shadows, but would not take his eyes from me. Without thinking, I put my hand out, but the animal snarled, snapped the air, and slunk back.

I was jolted back to myself, pulled from the magnet of the man's distress by its reflection in his animal. I was drained of energy and was being pumped for more, so during the break provided by the growling dog, I told the hiker that I was tired, that I was going to have a cup of soup and go to bed. He said he would build a fire and invited me to join him, but I declined and slipped off into the night.

My gear was nearby, and I had sufficient water for both dinner and breakfast, so there was no need to go to the stream. I put the stove in a crevice to keep it from blowing out and warmed my hands as the water heated. I drank the soup quickly and slipped exhausted into the sleeping bag. The hiker had settled in the lee of a boulder no more than fifteen yards away. His fire blazed yellow against the turbulent night sky, and jittery shadows sparred with the clouds. The dog yowled, and I, trapped in my own memories of Vietnam, fell asleep.

TENTH DAY

Gooseberry Springs

I slept late and woke tired. I was sore and had no impulse to move, so I lay quietly for a long while. I listened for the hiker but heard no sounds, and I wondered what to do next, but couldn't decide. Finally, I talked myself into the trek to Gooseberry Springs, hoping I had enough stamina to make it. I got up, dressed, and checked the hiker's campsite. He had already gone, leaving a mess behind. His fire was snuffed out with sand, and ashes and charred chunks of wood had been kicked about. The boulder against which the fire had been built was blackened to above my head, and the area all around had been trampled down, as though the hiker had paced like a sentry through the night. I buried the ashes and dismantled the circle of stones surrounding the fire pit by shot putting them away, letting my body act out its lingering pique at being surprised and intruded upon.

I hoped the hiker had not gone on to Gooseberry Springs, but the *I Ching* could have been saying he had, because my day's oracle was "Fellowship with Men", no change. Since the hexagram is favorable and harmonious, however, I assumed that rather than referring to the hiker, it was describing my relationship to Gooseberry Springs, a place I had always known as a center of fellowship.

I pushed the hiker from my mind and set about reducing the weight of my pack by pruning it of things I would not need at the camp. I removed pots and pans, excess food, and water bottles; wrapped them all in the tarpaulin and stashed them in a rockfall cave. I wondered about the shrine pieces in the Chalice, but an intuition told me to leave them where they were, snuggled in the care of the mountain.

My pack was still heavy, and the trail up the far side of the Saddle seemed longer and harder than it actually was. My only comfort was a cooling tail wind. I rested on top of the ridge, at a place where I could look down through the Mountain Lady's ankles to the ranch beyond.

The hiker had also stopped here. I sensed his presence lingering about his footprints and again felt intruded upon. Impatiently, I dismissed the wraith and scanned the ranch through the binoculars. It was quiet in the morning calm, but my eyes were not. They glazed with pictures, as though the glasses through which they looked were screens on which translucent figures aped human manners. A misshapen archetype, one delighting in violence, formed before me and danced out the dementia of contemporary history. The right glass showed soldiers in Vietnam; the left, policemen at the ranch. The images superimposed, as though two hands had come together holding a pistol.

I dropped the glasses and shook my head to clear away the ugly images, but the devil consciousness was persistent. As I watched in fascination, it displayed itself as a semi-eternal quirk in our species consciousness, for the consortium of police that had raided the ranch was driven by the same forces as the Soviet secret police, the Nazi gestapo, and the Roman guard of the Emperor Nero.

The vision subsided, leaving me in a rubble of fallen idols. I had spent fifteen years in the navy opposing tyranny, but had never known what it was until I found it at home. All nations have laws. Each law restricts freedom. Some of these are necessary, but many are not; for some are stupid, others vindictive, and far too many are nothing but rip-offs for the clients of politicians. A nation that condones such laws is more than functionally blind, it is addled, for if the laws are crazy, so, too, are the people who obey them. Today, adrift in the desolation of the Kali Yuga, we multiply such laws, as well as the predatory bureaucracies needed to enforce them. Consequently, the nation becomes ever more ungovernable, and the prophesy implicit in bad law fulfills itself in the re-emergence of the police state. Death is the force by which it rules, and only the dead place their faith in it.

I felt a heaviness, as though a devil in departing had stepped on my head. I set off feeling less energetic than when I arrived, but the way was level, and I was not far from the trail that would take me down to Gooseberry Springs. I arrived at the junction hoping the hiker had continued toward San Jacinto and was relieved to find that he had. I headed down to camp along a fresh, untrodden trail that wound like a great yellow serpent through hedgerows and meadows. Much of the way was steep and difficult with the pack, but the side hills were all covered with flowers whose fragrances flavored my breathing and made the walk seem a pilgrimage to paradise. I was the first traveler of the season and felt pleasantly exhilarated as I climbed the final steep grade into Gooseberry Canyon, but fifty yards below the camp my returning spirits began to ebb again.

Pots and pans and bottles and cans were scattered down the hill. The camp was a shambles. All the sealed drums containing supplies had been knocked over and opened; their contents had been pulled out and strewn about: sleeping bags, pillows, blankets, winter clothes—all molding away. The canvas coverings of both the storage and kitchen enclosures had been pulled down and tattered by the wind and winter. The top of the big cupboard was closed but inside was a mildewed mess. However, the lid of the large tin of food that had stood next to it was still in place. Inside, the tin was dry and the food usable, but except for a small can of meat, everything was starch and sugar: crackers, macaroni, dried potatoes, spaghetti, chocolate.

Despite the wanton destruction of the camp, I felt good being back in the canyon. The forest was soothing and remarkably calm after the wind of the Saddle. Its light was deeper and redder; its solitude more stately. The sunbeams slanted through high, feathery branches, mottling everything beneath, calling forth smells of musty, new life. Gooseberry Spring overflowed onto the pathway and splashed down the side hill through a garden of its own creation.

I spent the early afternoon cleaning the kitchen. Mice had been nesting in the cupboard among a litter of overturned tins and chewed cardboard. In the debris, I found three water-soaked books: an *I Ching*, a *Tao te Ching*, and the early LSD tripping manual, *The Psychedelic Experience*. Beside them lay the weathered remnants of a cardboard mobile whose individual parts were Buddhist mandalas, icons, and mantras from Tibet. The mobile was beyond repair, so I placed its pieces between the pages of my notebook, among the leaves and flowers of my other treasures. I furled the building's ripped canvas like a sail and tied it along the top of the pipe skeleton. I found a rusty rake to clean the area of its winter accumulation of forest floor; then I collected and rehung the pots and pans from the side hill. Finally, I gathered a stash of firewood from the forest and built a fire, but did not light it.

Satisfied with my day's labor, I filled the hash pipe and left camp for the large boulder overhanging Devil's Slide. Beyond the canyon, the afternoon wind danced along the northern slopes of the mountain and howled down the barren ridge above. I crept into a crevice to light the pipe and sat tucked below the boulder for a few furtive puffs. Then, stoned, I climbed to the top and was almost blown off. After a few minutes of sparring with the wind, I retreated and returned to the canyon.

Part of the canyonside was a set of broken cliffs. The sun was shining on them, and there was a place to sit a few feet from the bottom, so I climbed up to it. I had the *Tao te Ching* with me. Occasionally, I opened it at random to read a passage aloud and let the picture it drew carry me off to a self-destructing, conceptual heaven. The alternation of book and reverie, like the warp and woof of fine cloth, wove a timeless pattern from the star-stuff of human neurons.

The cliff against my shoulder lit up, its cracked face arranging itself into a mosaic of meanings. As my eyes drifted over its lovely surface, they were arrested by an organic pattern protruding from the rest, for eight inches of a large rattlesnake extended from a fissure by my foot. He seemed spaced out from his winter's sleep, so I did not disturb him by moving. I wondered if he understood Chinese spoken in English. Hoping he did, I read him some more.

He was still stretched out when I slipped away for dinner. The forest was in shadow and turning cool, so I lit the fire. It was the first I had had since coming to the mountain, and it smelled delicious. I set three pots of water to boil: one for dinner, a second to wash clothes, and a third to wash me. Unfortunately, the top of the fireplace was a thick piece of iron with an uneven surface. It was a fine grill, but a hard way to heat kettles. The night grew darker and colder while I waited, and when I finally got my hot water, it was a late dinner and a cool bath.

Afterward, I stoked the pipe and settled back for an evening of fire watching: a meditational art form whose medium is dancing light. I became entranced by the fire's singleness of purpose, until the Sambhogakaya slipped its Nirmanakayaic fetters and displayed its omnipresence. The fire was no different than I who watched it, for the dichotomy between the subjective and objective disappeared in the invisibly creative Dharmakaya. The cosmos spoke in tongues of flame, and smoke rose as memory.

My gaze swept the surrounding forest where firelight played the shadowmaker's game of multidimensional Rorschach, turning light-molded darkness into psychological manifestations of brain circuitry. I saw eyes in the forest and heard the hoot, howl, and hiss of predators, the rustle of dry branches, and silences contorted by wind. Night pressed in, and hungry spirits called from the trees. I awoke to a paranoid reality and cast it off, murmuring a chant to pacify the shadows. The consciousness of those who had wrecked the camp clung to the remaining clutter, lingering as a social foulness. I bade it begone, then thought again of "Fellowship with Men", the hexagram whose chakra image is a yielding ego with many firm capabilities, the proper deportment of man among men. The night relaxed around me, and, changing masks, reappeared as a pleasant companion, well fed, settling into embers.

The Kings of Old

Morning dreams wove a delicate aurora through the chemistry of sleep. I roved their ionic barrier, now and again surfacing like fish whose chatoyant scales color the translucent water. In the last pageant of the night, two happy children took me by the hands and introduced me to their friend: a very large snake, beautifully spotted, multihued, lithe, and magical. He undulated before us through the nagamudras of mythology, then rose and swam about our heads as if the air were a crystalline fluid too subtle for our senses to perceive. The morning was still, but the motions of the reptile merged with bird calls and insect buzzings, then disappeared into a gnat caught in my ear. High above, the drone of a jet sounded an alarm and nearby, the burbling of Gooseberry Spring called like another child, beckoning me to play.

It was a lovely day, cool in the early sun and calm through the forest. The kitchen smelled of pine and cedar, of moist earth and ashes. Before going to bed, I had put my food in the cupboard, but a mouse had found it during the night and had eaten through two layers of plastic to sample the civilized delights of granola. I prepared a bowl of the cereal for myself and sat in a spot of sunlight in the shambles of camp. I decided to spend the morning cleaning up the rest of the mess, and the afternoon climbing down Devil's Slide.

I took the *I Ching* and my pipe to the edge of the canyon where the forest gave way to scrub and cactus. Here a little circle of flowering yucca, manzanita, and creosote bush surrounded a space paved with sparkling gravel. Two flat rocks stood like a bench and footstool at the far side of the circle, where the view through the narrow entranceway was of descending treetops and distant desert.

The place was cool in the forested shade of the morning, the rock still cold to my seat. As I smoked, a bright red and yellow bird pranced on a branch and sang me a song. While back in camp, a metal drum, expanding with the day, snapped a metallic salute to the warming sun. I reflected that the bird and barrel, like myself and the ears that heard them, were bellows pumped by sunlight and air.

The smoke dried my mouth but whetted my spirit, and I slipped easily into the practiced rhythms of pranayama. My energy became channeled in my upward rising breath that met itself descending my spine as its preexistent pattern. My stomach chakra glowed like the petal of a fire flower, and my diaphragm, its controlling muscle, did a sine wave dance with time, enlivening me, breathing me, caressing my innards. For a while I was my diaphragm, then I became an elfin creature bounding on it as though on a trampoline. Time and again, I arched up, twisting through the space of my chest. Finally, I was pulled into the orbit of my throat chakra and perched there like a pelican by a blowhole, watching the air whistle to my lungs and exchange secrets with the momentarily encompassing flesh.

Suddenly, my throat chakra erupted and burst red about me. I toppled from my precarious perch and fell in tumbled disarray to my stomach chakra. There my trampoline caught me and flipped me back up again. Delighted, I sprang through chakra space, an electromagnetic acrobat contorting among shifting fields of energy. I leaped from the throat chakra to the stomach chakra and was flung back again, beyond the throat, to empty ajna, and the vast realms before space-time existence.

I repeated the sequence again and again. Each time I reappeared in the throat chakra, I dove willy-nilly into the abyss below: a moment, no more, a taste of annihilation, then caught in time's elastic meshwork and thrown free, bounding to unbounded ajna's portal to elsewhere. Beams of sunlight scattered through the forest, adding photonic excitement, and still the vibrant, acrobatic sequence continued, sometimes with slow, graceful motions, sometimes like lightning: throat to stomach to ajna and off . . . throat to stomach to ajna and off . . .

My calisthenics were finally interrupted by a flight of bees that arrived with the sun and set about transmuting the day's radiant energy into honey. The morning warmed considerably, assailing me with a medley of smells. I took off my leather shirt and then my sweater. These activities bestirred me to do more, so I gathered a handful of twigs from beneath the bushes and broke them into long and short pieces with which to construct the picture the *I Ching* would draw.

I set the book before me in the sand. Today I had a specific question to ask, but I was not at all sure how to phrase it. I was back at Gooseberry Springs where this whole adventure had begun, but mysteries had opened to even greater mysteries, and the mountain's secrets were cloaked more obscurely than ever. I had met the mind of the mountain in a thousand disguises, each masking the same Presence; I had seen its majesty, and its ruin; I had felt its benevolent power as well as its terror. Yet, I still knew nothing of its purpose, nor what sublime message all this beauty had been created to convey. Baffled and expectant, I probed the *I Ching* for an answer.

The coins fell, the twigs arranged themselves, and a familiar image formed on the earth. It was that of the sacred mountain, "Contemplation", whose commentary speaks of the temple of the ancestors, mysteriously locked, and says that when things are great, one can contemplate them. Three lines changed: the third, fifth, and sixth. The explanations accorded them are remarkably similar, but, as the energy ascends, it shows a transformation from a subjective to an objective mode. The third line reads:

> Contemplation of my life
> Decides the choice
> Between advance and retreat.

The fifth says:

> Contemplation of my life.
> The superior man is without blame.

And the sixth concludes:

> Contemplation of his life.
> The superior man is without blame.

The second hexagram was "Modesty", whose image is of a mountain sunk back into the earth, indicating the Nirmanakaya reabsorbed in the Sambhogakaya. The book calls this condition the end attained by the superior person. It occurred to me that the image also applies to one's point of perspective, for it is the appearance of a planetary surface seen from space, where mountains, like the gigantic peaks of Mars, disappear in a distant disc of reflected light.

I relit the pipe. The mountain loomed within me, a wonderful entity, a self-conscious, contemplative mind displaying itself as a stage for life. Pondering the *I Ching*, I slipped again into chakra space. Understanding both book and mountain implies being them, experiencing spontaneously the truths they so laboriously expound in words and seasons. To the ancient Chinese, such comprehension was not impossible. They saw themselves and their sacred mountains as superimposed axes of the same universe, whose sensible forms were encoded in sixty four hexagrams.

I became the image I contemplated and pulsed as an overtone of earth, a modulation of the mountain vibrating in symbiotic synchronicity with the cosmos. I reread the text of "Contemplation", was shaped to an identity of understanding, and felt myself a discrete frequency resonating to the pre-established harmony of the universe. The words blew through me like the wind their image raised, and my mind clung to the concept evoked:

> The wind blows over the earth:
> The image of Contemplation.
> Thus the kings of old visited the regions of the world,
> Contemplated the people,
> And gave them instruction.

The Presence in whose presence I sat, sat kingly, while the ancient text revealed his commanding nature. Suddenly, in a moment of intuitive astonishment, I met the venerable mentors of the authors of the *I Ching*, who, for an instant, let slip their accustomed veil. These ancient and eternal kings stand as guardians of earth and give expression to the omniscient intelligence of the Dharmakaya. Focusing their awareness in the charged fields of space, they take life as the tangible nothingness through which the world forever moves.

The earth became a vision in my heart. It promenaded as a great but troubled queen, whose passage was filled with a trillion separate activities. Space itself, as the kings of old, contemplated her in harmonious understanding. Simultaneously, solar winds and galactic currents molded the earth field, shaping it to a magnetic matrix by which the kings of old provided instruction. Under their direction, the mountain had been made to tune its creatures to the changing spectrums of the cosmos, thereby completing the bond between heaven and earth.

The book sang, and music was its wisdom. I resumed reading, but a few moments later, a curious juxtaposition of data exploded in my head. Old and forgotten information synthesized with the morning's speculations in a new gestalt, which left me stunned and wondering. The changing lines in the day's hexagram duplicated the acrobatic chakra sequence I had experienced earlier. Beginning with the throat chakra, I had dropped abruptly to the stomach chakra, and then resonated to the ajna. Numerically, I went from fifth to third to sixth chakra, and this combination 5-3-6 catapulted me back to the moment when that number had been branded on my brain. It was not a measure of time at all, I realized now, but a means of abrogating time, of returning it to its zero point of reference within eternity. The number was not meant to inform me when a particular event had occurred, but rather how it was always occurring. It was a specific chakra code, one whose implementation released consciousness from the bondage of time, for the blameless contemplation of one's life is an electromagnetic correlation of personal freedom.

I contemplated the chakra image that had instigated the insight: two firm lines atop four yielding ones, with changes occurring in the stomach, throat, and ajna. Following the 5-3-6 sequence, the dynamic alteration began with the throat chakra, the seat of the highest level of material existence, the directing agent of individual life. Blameless contemplation here implies purity of motive. This purity, however, is conditioned by bodily existence, all of whose patterns are contained in the stomach chakra. I descended again to that realm to see what determined the choice between advance and retreat. The decision here, too, rested on purity, for the ability to pass from organic to electromagnetic forms of existence is dependent on purity of action, a way of egoless conduct that implies that the body's life-acting circuitry has been rectified to accommodate electromagnetic experiencing.

Energy from the stomach chakra resonated to its upper octave, to ajna, the nonexistent and indescribable. The *I Ching* indicates the necessary direction of movement: a reversal of ego's outwardness, a dissolution of figure into background, a letting go of human focus to drift unencumbered through the contemplative universe, where the pre-elemental nature of consciousness allows for its infinite extension through the subsequent categories of time and space.

Sometime later, I regrounded on my mountain. The *I Ching* lay open on my lap, telling me when, how, and where to cross the great gulfs of space that separate the many within the one. The book had again proved animate, a perceptive and reliable guide, and I saw it in new ways. It was a manual of transcendence, a geomantic codebook for tuning human consciousness to the cosmos, an operator's manual for projection through chakra space, and a navigator's handbook to the pathways of heaven. My mind overflowed with ideas I wanted to write in my notebook, so I returned to the kitchen and sat in the sun on an upright log. I tried to contain fragrances with words and coax lightning into pen strokes. The morning passed unnoticed except for occasional glimpses of the Presence playing in the forest, hiding behind trees, and now and then looking over my shoulder. When the sun became too hot, I moved into the shade and sat on the retaining wall beyond the spring, and when the cool of the forest sent a chill down my spine, I returned to the log. Words, like the kickings of a gopher, spewed from behind.

Nothing known. Nothing intuited. Spatial and temporal frames of reference interchangeably zero and infinity. The excellent conundrum of the Dharmakaya slipping through the contradiction of nonexistence characterizing itself, pretending the absurdity of brain-body location, point-time concentration.

Zero compounded to three. The crystalline Dharmakaya shattered into a gestalt summation of all possible combinations, arose as the Sambhogakaya, and differentiated a Nirmanakaya to contemplate the devolution into egohood of the scientifically precise and magical universe, where order is implicit in chaos, and precision impossible.

Nonexistence robbed me, took away my coverings. Intelligence wore the paper mask of a child, molding life to familiar contours, while the eye of the Dharmakaya looked out. Light showed through holes in the mask, through nostrils, eyes, mouth; through the paper's fibers; through the spaces of molecular structure; it pulsed from within the non-existing atom where form is emptiness and emptiness form, where $1=0$ and $0=1$, and light like life lies empty in the cradle of God.

I looked up from my notebook to the forest and back again. Another blank page beckoned, but what could I possibly write if all knowledge were a mask, an empty shell? What was I beyond a few dollars worth of chemicals hung together on a gridwork of energy, itself tending toward abstraction? My mind poked among the ideas of speculative science, where physicists are currently saying that everything in the universe, all the galaxies, stars, and planets, even we ourselves, is compounded of four fundamental forces. On the theoretical frontier, some say these four are really two, reflecting themselves in the mirror of their mutuality. Others go further, postulating a single source substance as the only fact of concrete reality. Albert Einstein spent his last thirty years working on a unified field theory, but even he was unable to formalize it. And yet this was the starting point of the ancient Greeks who, scientifically naive as they may have been, knew that the physics of lesser forms merge in the metaphysic of one substance, which being non-dual is eternally unknowable.

I was in the abyss of the unknown, so I retreated to the hard rock of science and used its logic to structure the previsible. If all things are but four forces, then consciousness itself has only three alternatives. It may reside in the four; it may be a gestalt summation of the four, whose reality is greater than all of its parts; or it may dwell beyond the four, creating them as its playthings.

My mind toyed with the choices. The first was that of the materialist who sees consciousness as not resident in but produced by transient things, such as our bodies. The second was that of the idealist who sees consciousness in a compendium of its derivative ideas, with, unfortunately, a priori and therefore unknown origins. The third alternative, the tertium quid of unknowable certainty, was the unified field of Einstein's dream and Christ's Father.

My own experience confirmed this certainty, but it left me alone in the irreducible void, so I reversed my intellectual field and tried to induce my way out of the unknown. If electromagnetic theory can explain all chemistry more simply and yet more comprehensively than chemical theory, therefore being chemical theory while obviously not being it, why cannot the unknowable source substance enlighten our essence by being it while not seeming to be it at all? For a moment, science and mysticism met. Mach's principle and Buddha's doctrine coexisted on the dialectical brink of understanding, and the perfection of the universe generated itself everywhere, irrespective of my presumptions.

Noon slipped by before I ran out of words. I laid the notebook aside and basked in the mountain's glow. Soon my body evoked its prerogatives, demanding exercise. I got up and stretched, splashed water from the spring on my face, and drank. I remembered Devil's Slide and the walk I had promised myself after cleaning the camp. For a moment, I contemplated the mess, then decided the cleanup could wait one more day, packed my gear, and started off through the forest.

I stopped for a lunch of raisins and nuts on the cliffs where the funneling trees gave way to steep rock canyon. I took my time climbing down the rock face, stopping in places where I remembered huddling on Iboga, hoping to reactivate the paranormal space I had experienced, in which ancient people encased in light traversed a thoughtful universe. I was partially successful, but too restless after the morning's immobility to delay long enough for the process to complete itself.

The May canyon was lush, more like the vision than the reality of an August ago. Flowering succulents climbed the cracks of the walls, and a small stream, threading in and out of the rubble, laid a carpet of flower-embroidered grass where it went. The space was smaller than I remembered—a consequence, I supposed, of my ability to move more rapidly with a normally coordinated body. Devil's Slide was only about a hundred yards long. The choked up area below it was not really circular. Further along, I descended into a different ecological domain, where the first desert yucca and bay laurel trees appeared. I picked a bay leaf and ripped it in half to inhale. The leaf was shiny and firm, moist inside, and pungent. It cut through my sinuses like a knife. Enjoying the sensation, I inhaled deeply a number of times, then overdid it and experienced one of pleasure's sharp reversals. Like eating ice cream too fast, an icicle of pain pierced my forebrain, bringing tears to my eyes. When it passed, I congratulated the tree for its fragrance and collected leaves for dinner spice.

I detoured to the old gold mine but spent little time at it and continued on to the limits of my previous excursion under Iboga. Here the canyon was narrow and clogged by rockfalls and thickets, into which the stream disappeared, to re-emerge below as a waterfall. To the side was a little cave where I had sat before. I sat again, letting time play games with my memory, wondering who else had also sat here, and following the speculation as it took me inexorably back to my Iboga people. Somewhere, I knew, they dwelt, still tied to this slumbering mountain by filaments of dream stuff and a promise of return.

The bottom of the waterfall was inside a cave, whose entrance, when seen from above on Iboga, had seemed a perpendicular door, promising evidence of human handiwork. However, my plumb line and measuring tape were still secure in the pack at Gooseberry, for the information they could provide no longer seemed important. I climbed down. The cave was but a cave, a humid desert grotto with trickles of water flowing down through thick beds of dark green moss which covered the walls and hung luxuriously from the ceiling. A reflecting pool at my foot doubled the scene, and the runoff disappeared under rubble.

At this point, the canyon was V shaped. It twisted ahead, so the prospect all around was of walls, and the only direction I could see was up into an oval of blue. I kept going, eager to see around the next bend, and found the same prospect repeated, for the canyon S turned like a snake. After another half hour, I decided I had seen enough and turned back.

Above the waterfall, I again picked up the trail of my Iboga trip and climbed the far canyon-side to walk the ledges of the shattered wall above Devil's Slide. Across from me, the great boulder squatted precariously, reminding me again of the feelings I had had about human participation in the destruction of the mountain. Pained memories passed through my mind, but what I saw was conditioned by my more recently acquired knowledge. Human beings were no more required as the willful demolishers of the ancient order than they were as its architects and builders. We came as caretakers, not kings, and left as homeless émigrés.

I was back at camp by twilight. Soft gloaming crept through the forest, and the tongues of my fire talked to the night, mesmerizing me and sweeping my circuits like magnetic erasers, editing the day into molecular configurations and relaxing me into a state of controlled somnolence. The categorization points in my visual pathways relinquished their time consuming activities, and my visual cortex opened more directly to sensible reality. How different everything was from my seeing of it. How much more wonderful!

The fire, growing tired of conversation, fell to coals. I remembered the mouse in the cupboard, so I put my food in the metal drum, leaving only heavy plastic bottles of oil and honey and a bag of vitamins on the shelf. Before sleeping, I decided my itinerary. Tomorrow, I would rest and clean the camp; then, on the day following, if the *I Ching* concurred, I would keep another tryst with the Lady Iboga.

TWELFTH DAY

Birds and Bees

The day began with me being foiled by the mouse who, it seemed, was a bogus health nut. He had chewed through the bag of vitamins, eaten his fill of their sugar coatings, and had left me with a pile of naked tablets, somewhat desanitized. An oriole came for breakfast, staying low in the forest, while high above, a large green bird with a bright yellow head watched from a bough. Woodpeckers were active, talking in code from cedar to oak, while the more domestically inclined wrens pranced in the humus of the kitchen, hunting bugs.

The morning was an invitation to pleasure, so I dug through the pack for my stash of Oaxaca and then sat on the retaining wall, cleaning it. The dry, slightly resinous texture delighted my fingers. I must have radiated contentment, for the hummingbird from the day before came over to watch the operation, suspending himself in the space between my eyes and hands. His face was bright red, rippling with different shades, and his back flashed electric-hued rainbows as he flew. He hung on the periphery of my sight, quite intent on what I was doing, so I explained the process as I went along. When I had finished, I held up a California joint for his inspection. He responded by helicopting to the trees, then diving to the kitchen pipes, and putting on a remarkable display of birdobatics. Back and forth he went, darting from cupboard to can, zooming around a wire, over a branch, spiraling up along the chimney, then down to the woodpile, and out of sight behind the fireplace.

When, after a few minutes, he rested on a twig, I applauded him heartily. Then, sticking the joint behind my ear, I gathered up the *I Ching* and headed for the circle of bushes at the edge of the canyon. My friend followed discreetly behind, inventing diversions. He played a game, and finding it fun, played again. He hovered above my collar until I turned, then he followed behind my head completely out of sight. I snapped around in the opposite direction, but he was too quick for me and remained invisibly behind. Then, sliding around to the front, he did a pirouette and darted away, only to wind around a tree and slip behind me once more.

He came with me into the circle of bushes. I lit the joint and blew him some smoke. He went up to taste the attenuated plume at ten feet and then dropped down to tell me about it. The gist of his remarks was that he preferred his ecstatic perfumes directly from the blossom. Then, miming his meaning, he dipped his long beak into a tiny manzanita flower. His wings, a blur, held him stationary before it, and I marveled at the energy he used in sipping for so meager a reward. He picked up on the thought and told me he drank only essence, whose conversion to energy was different than digesting leaves or leaf eaters. His flight was like shivering from delight; he hummed a song, and his wings followed the melody through the forest.

Having sipped his fill, he went off and left me on the rocks, staring at my feet where a wounded bee was stumbling about. The bee tried repeatedly to fly, but was unable to do so, and in his efforts careened about, bumping into pebbles and small rocks. "Well, little fellow," I said. "You seem to be in poor shape. "I'm not a fellow," she said. "And my present state is no cause for concern."

"Excuse me, Ms. Bzzz," I said, somewhat taken aback. "But your wings are tattered, your left middle leg is dragging, and you seem to be very much a derelict."

The bee stopped and combed herself. Her armor-clad body with its furry feelers emanated a peaceful field, and her abdomen moved like a beckoning finger. "Come closer," she said. "Look into my eyes and see why I have no worries. The hive is a goddess, and I but a gleaner of pollen. She is our consciousness, and I only her fingertip."

I bent over and focused on the two black ovals that dominated her head. They were composed of thousands of single lenses that combined to form screens where pictures were displayed much as on television. The images were alluring. For a magical moment, I gazed into the hive where the Presence was established as royalty amid a swarm of activities. The vision was of a truly elegant creature, a hydra whose thousand invisible tentacles were tipped with delicate, organic sensors and essence-collecting instruments that together wove a vibratory pattern of queenly sentience over acres of mountainside. The hydra glowed under the intensity of my gaze. It delved into my brain patterns, then metamorphosed its central feature into a human head. Transfixed, I thought of Medusa, but then the lady smiled and I was not turned to stone.

"Good morning," I said.

"Indeed it is," she purred, in a voice soft as honey, beguiling as a flute.

"I think you must be a Gorgon," I said. "A very beautiful one."

"Thank you," she replied. "But I know little of snakes, for I am a creature of the sun, whose nature is light."

Her words belied the vision. The face on which I gazed was deep blue-green projected on a field of purple shadows, so I told her she seemed more of earth, of the dark element, and chthonic mysteries.

"The sun is my lover," she said. "I exist only to offer him my darkness. Hived, I hide within, to lead him stealthily to my chamber along many a devious pathway." She hesitated, then beckoned me closer.

I bent until my head was well below my knees, but the hydra-face vanished, and I saw only the bee with her bulging eyes sparkling like domes of black crystal. Her other eyes, on stems, poked through the heavy plating of her external skeleton, and it occurred to me that this was an amazing creature to be a flying animal. She was not built like a bird or bat, but like a tank; hardly what one would expect of an air machine where lightness is a virtue.

I was just going to ask her about it when a gleam in her eye caught mine and presented me with the answer I sought. A sunbeam, slanting through the forest, was trapped and focused by every facet of her eyes. Each lens fed a beam of light into dual-purpose neural cells that were sensitized to retinal seeing, but were also solar batteries that powered the flying tank. I was astonished. "Why you run yourself directly off the sun!" I exclaimed.

She began moving back and forth across a small rectangular area that, during the course of her meanderings, lit up like a tarot card. She talked with her motions. "Creatures come here to be combed," she said. "The sun makes one many, and the mountain makes many one. We live in a mirror. I look in and see you; you look in and see me."

I told her I had a pocket version of her mirror and, when she inquired what I meant, produced the *I Ching* and asked if she cared to look into it with me. She was intrigued and urged me on. I explained how the book worked and showed her the coins. To her, they were metal millstones, so I threw them carefully to the side of her tarot card and built the hexagram of twigs above it. The first hexagram was the "Well", signifying the unchanging center of human social organization. It was particularly appropriate to Gooseberry Springs but, when I read the commentary to the bee, she took it to refer to the hive:

The well nourishes and is not exhausted.

The well means union.

The well shows the field of character.
The well abides in its place, yet has influence on other things.
The well brings about discrimination as to what is right.

There were two changing lines. The first was ill-omened, and I could not help but feel it applied to my companion. It says:

At the well hole one shoots fishes.
The jug is broken and leaks.

She picked up my thought immediately and admitted that the line probably referred to her present condition, but pointed out that it was I who had thrown the coins, and that I should not be so quick to assign their consequences elsewhere. I agreed and suggested that we share the second line, too. It says the well is dependable, that one can draw from it without hindrance, and promises supreme good fortune. The bee, very pleased, walked a hieroglyph for the hive.

The second hexagram was "Development" whose theme is the attainment of one's proper place through the ordering of phenomena. I started reading it aloud, but before I got to the judgment on the configuration, the first changing line of the "Well" exploded into manifestation. The bee was listening from the top left corner of her tarot card, when she was suddenly attacked by a ferocious, red-and-black soldier ant. The ant hit her broadside, and the motion caught my eye, distracting me from the book. The initial charge was so savage and well aimed that the bee tumbled a good three inches, rolling over and over again.

"Watch out'" I yelled, but before she had a chance to regain her footing, the ant was on her, slashing at her sides and wings. The bee kicked back, stumbled to her feet, and rumbled away. She was enormous compared to the ant, but clumsy, and her sting was useless against so small and quick an opponent. "Do you want some help?" I asked.

She thanked me and said she'd handle it herself, but the ant promptly butted her, tumbling her six times. She got up and thundered about, buzzing furiously and fanning her wings like burp guns, but her ammunition was spent, and the ant hit her again. By now, the contest had become so one-sided that I saw the bee as a bulging barn on stilts and the ant as a goat butting against its bottom in full confidence of winning the grain inside. The bee, however, was granted a reprieve by the very ferocity of the ant. As she waddled along the edge of a saucer-shaped depression, the ant struck again, rolling her all the way to the bottom. But this time supergoat had knocked the barn into the next county and could not find it again. While the ant raced around the rim of the saucer, I put my foot down, and the exhausted bee climbed to the top of my shoe. I crossed my legs, lifting her to safety, and the ant, off on another scent, disappeared down a hole.

I let the bee sleep for a while, and when it was time to go back to camp, I settled her securely on a manzanita branch. The forest was perforated with sunlight, but still cool. I surveyed the wreckage of the campsite and decided to begin by repairing the storage tent. I examined the gear and put what was usable back in the barrels, which I sealed and covered with the ripped canvas.

The job took several hours, but I was in no hurry. I was, however, interrupted once by still another bee: a huge, black carpenter bee shooting at me straight from the *I Ching*. While I was digging a hole to bury the rotted gear, I began to wonder who had torn through the camp in such mindless rage. As I engaged in a series of mental skirmishes with my fantasy villains, my energy increased, and I dug with remarkable fervor. Focused on imaginary devils, I blinded myself to the real world. I had just thrown a shovel of dirt into an adversary's face when I heard something that made me look up. The carpenter bee was zooming toward my forehead at top speed, already too close to avoid, and looking like a musket ball about to demolish me. At the last possible moment, she veered away, going straight up as though she had ricocheted from my skull. It happened in a flash. I reacted after the fact and snapped my head back to see her disappearing in the trees. Over before it began, the encounter was nonetheless therapeutic, for the bee had cracked my neck like a good chiropractor and filled me with enough adrenalin to dig ten holes.

It was well into afternoon before I had restored the camp to some semblance of order. I had uncovered many reminders of the Brothers, and of Frank Scovel before them. I found a peyote drum and rattle, both still usable though well weathered. A funny old hat in the storage bin filled my memory with a face, as did a science fiction anthology with a friend's name on the flyleaf. Above camp, stuck in the ground among the roots of a large pine, I discovered another old friend called the All-Purpose Walking Stick, patiently awaiting its next companion. The stick was bare wood, polished by the hands that had held it. Its name was carved along its length, and its old leather thongs and faded feathers still hung from it.

When the chores were completed, I took the stick, rattle, and drum, along with my pipe and reading material, to a sunny spot in the forest. After smoking and playing with the instruments, I turned to the book, *The Psychedelic Experience*. Based on The Tibetan Book of the Dead, it was one of the first Western attempts to correlate psychedelic and mystical insights, and it provided timely instructions for dealing with altered states of awareness. Both psychedelic and mystical intuition show that the ordinary and the enlightened mind are themselves not different, except that a veil of existential ignorance hides the one from the other. Physiologically, this veil is a net of psychic states radiated by brain circuit dysfunctions, indicative of incomplete maturation. As ego and id, consciousness confounds awareness, trapping it in lower forms of expression. The book offers terse instructions for escaping these traps, because to be entangled in them is, in a manner of speaking, to be dead. In reality, *The Tibetan Book of the Dead* is a call to the living to assert their immortality, a process natural to our species, and one greatly enhanced by psychedelic substances.

I thumbed through the book, reading here and there as a word or phrase caught my attention and drew itself out as an excursion through the mechanics of mind. Later, the sun made me sleepy, so I lay on my stomach and dozed. I was awakened by a most peculiar sensation. A hummingbird, I assumed was the same one as before, was hovering over my back, fanning down a cooling zephyr as feathery and fine as a lady's blowing in my ear. I lazily turned my head to thank him, but the motion sent him off, unseen, into the trees.

Evening was coming on, and I was hungrier than I had been since coming to the mountain. Although my belt had tightened a notch, my meager rations had seemed sufficient, but now I went through the camp supplies with the relish of one famished. For dinner, I decided on spaghetti with a spicy tomato sauce, and while the water was heating, I made a candy bar of chocolate, honey, nuts, and raisins. Unfortunately, I made more candy than I wanted, and the spaghetti water never got beyond a low simmer. The result was too much dessert before dinner, followed by a starchy mess of tomato pasta. Before turning in, I remembered the mouse and left him a little pile of granola on the cupboard shelf. I went to bed with a lump in my belly, hoping for an early start in the morning.

The Lady Iboga

I awoke in the predawn darkness and watched the last quarter moon filtering itself through the treetops, breaking its beam into the electromagnetic matrices of watching night. A shaft of silver found its way through the foliage and moved amid shadows across my face. I wondered if the universe were no more than this: an alteration of light and dark eternally exchanging places, chasing one another through time, through the series of sleeps and wakings we call life.

I dozed off and dreamt I was in a very large bed. It was hand hewn and covered with colorful fabrics. I was not alone, for a baby was with me, snuggled against my side, and seeming to belong to me. I woke again, puzzled by the child but knowing its mother had been the mountain. I pondered my responsibility toward it. What could I tell it of the strange place into which it had been born? How does one properly educate a child in a topsy-turvy world run by inferior men, blindly acting out the imperatives of the lower chakras? I was caught in a dialectical dilemma that pitted ethics as a set of behavior-orienting instructions for successful social life against the special ethical orientation that allows an individual access to his electromagnetic mode of consciousness. This mode is the perfect expression of ethical behavior, but it appears so sporadically during the Kali Yuga that a magical child, while needing to learn it, must not expect to encounter it often.

I lost myself in questions until the moon lady prodded me with her toe, scuffing the earth near my head with one of her numberless beams, itself but a pale memory of the sun's brilliance. The beam became a tunnel of dream-stuff, so I ascended it and might have been gone, except, like Lot's wife, I turned back to look. The earth lay like a sleeping lady on a bed of stars. She seemed on the verge of wakefulness, about to open her eyes, to yawn, stretch, and reach for her child.

It was still dark when I slipped from the sleeping bag. A chill was in the air. My breath crystallized to heavy vapor, and my clothes were stiff with cold. I had an uncomfortable belly and a sinus headache, so I took some homeopathic pills, two aspirin, and a thousand milligrams of vitamin C, determined to right everything immediately. The mouse had taken the granola and paid for it in fertilizer. I gave his offerings to the forest, then made a protein drink and took it and the *I Ching* back to the sleeping bag.

The forest was beginning to redden as I settled cross-legged on the bag, with a moth-eaten gray blanket over my shoulders. I wondered about the ambivalent Goddess Iboga and thought about the coming day; then I reached out to the not yet visible present with my tumbling coins. The reading was terse: one hexagram, composed of a single trigram, doubled. The trigram connoted thunder and portended explosive energy. The hexagram was "The Arousing (Shock, Thunder)". I was wary of it because I had turned on after receiving it before, and remembered dazzling, if disconcerting, performances. The judgment on the hexagram explains the problem:

> Shock brings success.
> Shock comes—oh, oh!
> Laughing words—ha, ha!
>
> The shock terrifies for a hundred miles,
> And he does not let fall the sacrificial spoon and chalice.

Power is implicit in the configuration, but the Nirmanakayaic controls over it are minimal, for it is released directly from the Sambhogakaya. Somatically, every fiber of tissue can be highly energized, but the result is psychically unpredictable and can be far more intense than anticipated; similar, perhaps, to sticking a finger in a light bulb socket in order to comb your hair.

I put the book aside and surveyed myself. I was not yet feeling as well as I would have liked. My headache was neutralized and my sinuses had started to drain, but the spaghetti was still a ball of cement in my stomach. I weighed the alternatives and appealed to the Lady Iboga for a hint of her intentions. She remained mute, so I fell back on my own resources. I finally decided that the ayes had it, for the expectation of tapping into all that Sambhogakaic energy tipped the scales in favor of tripping. I presumed I could ride out any psychedelic storms, but the *I Ching* had given me no changing lines, so I knew the pulsing energy would be consistent throughout the day.

The Iboga was stashed in the Saddle because I had earlier decided to use it there. Of all the places on the mountain, the terraces seemed the best for re-establishing my tenuous communication with the visionary people. It was a good walk from Gooseberry Springs, and I would be unsteady on the way home, but I figured I would be together enough to get back by evening.

I sat for a time before leaving, cleaning my pipe like a gunslinger cleaning his pistol. I smoked the black, resinous residue, filled the small pack with essentials, tucked the red mat under my arm, and left camp before the sun had crested the ridge. I was exhilarated as I started down the trail; my soreness evaporated and a wave of new energy carried me along. Ascending the steep draw was effortless, like floating. I slipped unexpectedly into my heart chakra, which shone with the loveliness of its own presence. I followed where it led, journeying its labyrinths along the trail I walked. Ecstatic tears ran down my face. I tried to chant, but the words caught in my throat and changed to a deep, Aum'd laugh. Everything I looked at had the power to spark joy, and every now and then I caught glimpses of the ancient city.

In the vicinity of the Lady's ankle, I rested on the red mat, wiped my forehead with a red handkerchief, and noticed that my ankles were hidden beneath red socks. Red is the color of energy, of passion and power, and my morning had been dominated by it. Dawn had been crimson, then scarlet, and the red-headed hummingbird had paid a visit as I smoked. On the trail, a red stone had flashed in the early sun, prompting me to pocket it as a shrine piece for the trip. I decided that red was the day's color, promising excitement, but then I recalled the old seafarers' refrain:

Red sky in the morning,
Sailor, take warning.
Red sky at night,
Sailor's delight.

I shivered to think what lightning would look like through a ruby faceted by Iboga and wondered if Amitabha, the Red Buddha of Immeasurable Radiance, was smiling on the mountain.

I went on to the Saddle to where my gear was stowed. I took the tarpaulin and Iboga to the terrace shaped like a ship's prow thrust above the abyss. I spread the tarpaulin over the mat and put the *Tao Te Ching* in the sand, with the red stone on its cover. The vista was of mountain and desert. I used it to settle myself, breathed deeply for a few minutes, then swallowed one of my two capsules of Iboga.

There was smog over Palm Springs, a brownish fuzz across the desert, and a high band of dust overhanging everything. There was no wind, and the haze-filtered sun warmed me sufficiently to sit naked. For the first hour, I was vaguely impatient. I climbed around the immediate area, exercising and chanting while I probed for early symptoms of the Iboga in my body. The drug came on very slowly. It began with a sense of increasing heaviness, a certain physical malaise, and a gradually increasing pressure in my head. This was not unusual, and no worse than I had expected, so shortly into the second hour, I downed the other capsule.

My sensory impressions began to alter. My brain became a quaking bog that melted into fluid and oozed down my face. My visual field dissolved and came back differently: more organically animated, more totally involving, more chaotic than I liked. I tried to stay centered within the developing kaleidoscope. Chanting did not work; sounds got caught in my drying throat and rasped uncomfortably. I turned to the *Tao Te Ching*, hoping to stabilize my spinning with its words, but I found I could not read them because they circled erratically around the page, the tail of one sentence attaching itself to the beginning of some previous one in a meaningless jumble.

My body became heavier, more nauseous, and turned inexorably rancid. I wanted to roll over and curl up on the mat but fought the feeling with the remembered values of an erect spine. Something moved on my forearm. I brought my wrist close to my face and focused on a tick wandering about. I remembered my resolve to leave places where I found the predatory little devils, but knew I could no longer do so and took it as a bad omen. I half stood and staggered to the front of the terrace, where I loosed the tick to the gathering breeze. Everything spun as though the whole mountain was being stirred by a monstrous spoon.

I fell to the mat, but managed to sit up. My world was an old Victrola, where I, impaled on the needle, ground against the record, while the trees played the opening movement of the day's windphony. Through a moment of controlled dissonance, I tried to stabilize, but into my turmoil another, alien influence penetrated; a distant, muffled roar as of thunder, pulsing to the throb of my brain. It grew louder, more mechanical, and was closing me in. I managed to stand, wobble for a moment, and peer over the lip of the terrace. My disintegrating vision fastened on the source of the sound: a helicopter was charging up the mountain, straight at me, and coming fast.

I splashed to all fours on the sand, spinning wildly, not quite sure what was happening but very sure I did not like it. I scrambled toward the bushes. My feet caught in the tarpaulin, and I pulled myself under the branches with it tangled behind, only to look back and see the red mat in the center of the terrace twirling like a bull's-eye at a shooting gallery.

The roar of the machine was horrendous, but I tumbled out, grabbed the mat, and crashed back into the bushes. In the midst of the action, I flipped into a dysfunctional and miserably altered perceptual state. My body seemed to be moving in exaggerated slow motion, while within I was hyperactive; neither mode was coordinated, and when I finally plummeted to the ground, I was panting wildly and gaping back up through the shattered glass of my visual field.

The noise exploded. The helicopter came over the lip of the terrace like a rocket, clearing me by no more than fifty feet. It was a huge marine gunship with its throttles wide open, taking its crew on a mountain lark. The Saddle rumbled as it thundered through, its tutelary wind devil chasing behind. My shocked psyche reacted with visions of Vietnam, then of the ranch, and of police raids from the air.

The metallic banshee disappeared, taking its wind devil and shriek with it, but the silence it left behind was warped and re-echoed endlessly. I crawled out with the mat and crumpled up on it, completely unsettled. My head was spinning to a vortex of black static in which intricate swirls of color ignited to spectacular incandescence. Fireworks fell in patterns of Persian perfection, then sputtered to bloody red walls dripping gore. Infernos blazed in my skull, but I could no longer bear to open my eyes to escape them, for the light was too intense, and when I pressed my face into the mat, clouds of gray and green smoke tumbled through my confusion.

As though to multiply my discomforts, the day worsened. The breeze, warm at first, turned cool. It strengthened to wind and soon was driving scud clouds through the Saddle. I could not tell how fast they were moving, or even in which direction they were going. I looked and saw, but could not assemble the pieces of my visual field. I knew only that clouds dashed through my perceptual space. Then these changed to swords and slashed at me with cold blades of contempt.

The chilling wind cut through my torso, forcing me to pull on a T-shirt and Levi's. It took an aeon of effort to get into them, exhausting me. Minutes later, as the increasing dourness of the day forced another response, I pulled on more clothes. Each piece was an enigma. Cloth tubes and button puzzles perplexed me with their intricacies, and waves of anger surged from my stomach to the impotent stubs of my arms.

As the weather deteriorated, my internal environment matched it, step by step. I went from nauseated, to miserable, to hurting badly. By the time I finally pulled myself into my leather shirt, none of my movements were coordinated, and all were incredibly difficult. I doubled up on the mat; my head racked with pain, my throat desert dry. I tried to stretch, but my stomach cramped, pulling me into a tight fetal position. I opened my eyes, saw double, then triple, then watched multidimensional reality melt like dirty snow and pour through me as icy gray water.

The Lady Iboga had come on like Lucrezia Borgia, and I was filled with gruesomeness. Images appeared, only to age immediately and wither, turning to mold, then slime, in my brain. Pain contorted my face and burned my eyelids. My throat hurt as though something were caught in it. I coughed and swallowed, trying to spit it up, but it only grew more bothersome. I found the canteen, outlived the eternity of trying to open it, then drank some water. It soothed the membranes of my throat, but accentuated the discomfort. It became imperative that I get whatever it was out. I got to my knees and, with my face pressed in the mat, tried harder, pulling with all the muscles of my neck. Suddenly, I succeeded, but it was not what I needed at all, for the presumed obstruction was apparently the valve in my gullet. I could not cough it up, but I did something to it that caused a searing pain, after which I could feel the valve lying limp in my esophagus and throbbing like an abscessed tooth.

My whole body was an instrument of torture. My awareness jumped from one hurt to another: each parlayed its intensity of pain into the excruciating focus of everything else. I crawled ten feet from the mat and tried to throw up, but the different parts of my body worked against each other. My stomach contracted to expel, and my throat simultaneously did the same to retain. I pushed my fingers into the back of my mouth and managed to force a regurgitation. Nothing much came up, and the effort left me exhausted. A few minutes later, I retched again, spontaneously, but little more than bile appeared. The Iboga had long since been absorbed into my system.

I had hoped the retching would help, but it didn't. If anything, I became sicker, and I was also aware of being very cold. I crawled back to the mat, wrapped myself in the tarpaulin, and once more contracted into the fetal position. My internal light show was an interminable, Dantesque nightmare, a pummeling by fiery fists and hurricanes of smoke.

I heard another airplane and knew that I couldn't move. I cowered under the tarpaulin, hiding from the noise that screamed through me. It neither grew louder, nor went away and sounded like many motors. I peered out into the dismal day. My pupils were dilated and everything was too bright, but the sky was empty. Only the trees glared down, waving their limbs wildly as the wind howled through them, mimicking a squadron of bombers.

An agonized epoch passed. The wind sliced through the tarpaulin, and icy needles of pain pierced my layers of leather and cloth, splaying my organs as though the skeletal fingers of death had opened my innards to their master's breath. Hoarfrost formed on my bones, and sheets of ice cascaded down my breast. Consciousness seemed a thousand miles away. From its insouciant distance, it conceived the idea of leaving this windy promontory, of going elsewhere to find shelter; then it sent the message by squeaky, static-filled wireless to the contorted creature trapped within my body.

It was almost noon when the idea of moving took hold of me and gave me a focal point beyond my pain. I was unable to sit, waves of nausea still washed through me and pulled me down with their undertow. But every time I surfaced, one thought recurred, one thing was imperative: I had to leave this place.

I dragged myself to a boulder and managed to prop up against it. The sun was obscured by the building storm. I started, very awkwardly, to repack the things from my pack, but soon forgot what I was doing. I discovered myself taking them out again, and then could not decide which way they were supposed to go. I lost the *Tao te Ching*, which was sitting right next to me, found it, and misplaced it again. Eventually, on the edge of panic, I gave up packing and tried to put on my shoes. I was more successful, even managing to tie a tangle in one set of laces and to push the other set down in the side of the shoe.

I put the mat under my arm, the tarpaulin over my shoulders, and stood up with the aid of the boulder. My head spun, nausea erupted from my stomach, my knees buckled, and I fell back down. A long while later, I remembered that I was trying to do something. I started to get up again, then realized I did not know where I was heading. Confused, I could not move for several more minutes, because I had no place to go. Finally, I remembered the depression behind the Chalice, my final camp at the Monuments. It was well protected and would be warm. The distance was little more than a hundred yards, uphill, and I knew the way well through the maze.

I stood up again and took my first step toward the Monuments. My shoes were like buckets of lead. It took a determined effort to move them, while everything else danced with abandon. I staggered a few steps, gyrating wildly, then tripped over the tarpaulin and fell in a heap. I doubled up in pain, but even this was swallowed up in a more frightening phenomenon: the staccato pounding of my heart. It raced like a buzz bomb, screaming in on target, ready to explode.

I lay for another ten minutes. Gradually, my heart slowed down; when it no longer rasped in my chest, I stood up again. I doubled up with stomach cramps and could only see the ground directly below me. I watched my legs walk me around in a little circle, trip over each other, and fall me down in the same spot. I had only succeeded in trampling several clumps of flowers, so I added remorse to my other woes. I thought of the fields of flowers yet to cross and saw myself as an engine of destruction careening to its own salvation. Time passed. I got to my hands and knees, crawled five feet and collapsed, gasping for breath, again fearful that my wildly pumping heart might suddenly quit.

I tried once more, on all threes. The tarpaulin and mat were under my left arm, and my right was stiffly out in front like a crutch. It added stability, but did not work very well because I tended to pivot on my fist and go off down hill. Vertigo assailed me. I fell, got up, forced myself to walk, one foot after the other, a step at a time. I fell again, but this time when I looked up, I knew I was lost. My visual field was like a tumbling gyroscope. I knew where I had been, and where I was going to be when I got there, but where I was, except excruciatingly here and now, eluded me. My world had no referent. Things existed independently, isolated in space with neither purpose nor direction. I recognized everything, and knew nothing except that I was heading up the side hill. But even this was questionable, for I could not tell which way was up. All the contents of my visual field were freely exchanging places, rolling about, appearing upside down, disappearing.

I could see the way I had already come by the swath I had left, so I tried to continue in the same direction, but I was completely at the mercy of my legs. As soon as one of my feet left the ground, it was entirely on its own, and I followed where each, in turn, took me. I went fifty feet and collapsed again. I managed to tuck the mat underneath me as I went down, and tried to wrap the tarpaulin around me, but I was unsuccessful, and the wind flapped it about my carcass like a shroud. I was compressed to an agonized ball of protoplasm so completely marbled with pain that I could not tell if I was freezing or burning. Before I found out, the ball exploded, hurling psychic fragments across the abyss. When these came back together, I found myself hovering above my own head, entombed in an eerie and unbridgeable silence. Below, my body was torn by the raging storm of planetary reality, while I, a wraith watching its writhing, dreaded my return.

The anguished body rose up, and I staggered on. Breathing was torture. The air rasped like a sandstorm across my voice box, and my sinuses were so completely blocked that my eyes bulged with pain. I forgot my earlier disaster and again tried to cough up my gullet valve, nearly strangling myself with agony. Moving was the only purpose I had, and I pushed on, gasping air through clenched teeth, knowing this awful sickness would pass, provided I could outlive it.

Eventually I came to the place where I had spent my first night in the Saddle. It was some distance below the Monuments, and not where I had been aiming, but the sleeping depression I had hollowed out beneath a tangle of bushes was still usable and sheltered. I crawled into it and wrapped myself up on the mat. I was inches below the howling wind and, for the first time since the hellish gale began, no icicles pierced my body. Time slowed and pain pulled out like putty. Thoughts flooded my brain with dark waters of depression, and memories from the outer, distant world surged in like swill.

I was waylaid by visions of Sambhogakayaic finality. I saw the world unplugged, its network of political powers and economic cartels disintegrating. Amid showers of sparks, junction box cities and industrial switches shorted out. Tangled nexuses of copper and glass fused in the heat of ungrounded power, as earth herself withdrew her favor, supporting human hubris no longer. Men acted out their parts, pouring oil on the fires, while arms merchants, as priests, worshipped at earthen altars with candles of napalm and smokestacks of incense. Flames swirled up in a mighty holocaust in which the divine androgyne appeared as a fire spirit, wearing a harlequin's mask. The mask came into focus, grinning seriously, its features bifurcating into those of Teddy Roosevelt and Queen Victoria celebrating their Plutonium Jubilee. The lips puckered, and the fire spirit sucked everything else in through the mask's mouth, then sucked in the mask as well, leaving me in utter darkness from which, with a horrendous roar, a lady in armor came forth riding a chariot of stars drawn by the winged horse Pegasus. She thundered by and disappeared into cosmic gravel, whereupon an arms merchant, robed in black, returned, sweeping up.

I became the dirt beneath his broom, and then a wheel, rolling downhill. The tempo increased. The wheel spun as a centrifuge with me strapped to its accelerating periphery. I was compressed by the laws of physics, and space itself became heavy. My features contorted, froze into a grimace. My body stiffened, became rigid and brittle, and then was pulverized. My crumbs compacted to a dense semblance of self that was pulled down and swallowed into the depths of the earth, where Pluto ruled with leaden jurisdiction.

My boundaries dissolved. Chthonic forces claimed me as their own, digesting the solid rock I had become. My brain congealed around the thought of Nietzsche that Satan is gravity, the Law by which all things fall, and I fell in silent, measured swirl to the deep darkness of earth.

I settled into magma, but the sense of falling stayed with me, and pressures built. Heat made light from its own intensity, and dull red lava turned to fiery golden plasma. I began to glow, then glazed over with adamantine defiance. It availed me nothing. Fingers of compressing force enfolded me, and I grew smaller under duress. Pluto as hot Hades slipped between my atoms and announced his presence with a burst of iron sparks. Voiceless, I called out to him, appealing for freedom.

The sparks formed a blazing countenance that spoke, and the reverberations from an immensity of sound echoed through my beseechment:

> Gravity is the hold of creation on itself. Liberation is freedom from gravity. Decrease your mass. Enter the state of dissolution and be gone, for without mass there is no gravity, and unchanging essence resides in the mind of God.

The fiery countenance exploded. Duality dissolved. Energy disappeared as the speed of light squared and zeroed in on the totality of reality. In the quantum leap to zero, space too evaporated; for without mass, there is no space, and gravity waved good-bye to the receding stars left dangling in the universe of derivative form.

I gasped, and woke to myself still huddled on the cold mountain, aware of the icy wind howling above. I did not remember where I was, how long I had been there, or what was happening, except that my body was relentlessly painful and even thinking hurt. My head was under the tarpaulin, but it took me some time to realize it, and I thought at first that evening had come. After a while, I recognized the camouflage pattern on the cloth and poked my head out. Tumbling clouds continued to pour through the Saddle, but there was a break in the overcast, and an errant sunbeam told me it was late. I wondered how I would ever get back to Gooseberry Springs, but knew that I had to or I would freeze in the night. Then, in one of the day's most distressing sequences, I pictured my sleeping bag, the only object of desire left in my world, blowing away down Devil's Slide.

I sat up and let the wind splash my face. It did so with slivers of ice. I waited several minutes, trying to settle my body and formulate a plan.

The early part of the night would be moonless, and I had little chance of finding the camp in the dark. I wondered whether or not to retrieve my pack as it was now in the opposite direction from Gooseberry Springs. I was tempted to leave it, but I knew I would have no peace until I returned for it and finally decided it would be easier to get it now.

I stood up and clung to the bushes until the reeling world slowed down; then I staggered off, hoping to recognize landmarks as I went. I was unable to think in terms of the sequence of places I needed to cross, but they fell into order as I passed. I rested often, and became lost frequently, but I found my way by continuing and coming to someplace else that I recognized. I could see further downhill, and I rolled that way when I fell, so my navigation was surer than before and eventually brought me to the ship's prow terrace. The gear was as I had left it, though now covered with sand.

My hands were like boxcars trying to pick things up with sliding doors. Somehow I managed, then got the pack on my back, and set off. The stash place was nearby. I clumsily folded the tarpaulin around the box and pushed it back in the cave. From there I continued up the hill, but almost immediately became lost and fell. When I came back to myself, I couldn't remember if I was still looking for my gear or if I had already found it. The pack reminded me, so I crawled off uphill.

Relief flooded through me when I stumbled across the trail on top of the Saddle. I was pretty sure I could not lose it, because it cut through thick brush for most of its way, but I soon wandered off and fell again. When I recovered, I was confused and only inadvertently regained the trail. The sun had long since dropped behind the ridge, and the gray gusting storm darkened the transition to evening. I was prodded on by fears of a wintry night, but I could only move at an excruciatingly slow pace. I drove myself on, fading in and out of physical reality, often awaking on the ground, but still on the trail, still going someplace.

The wind along the ridge was like a storm of ice; its screaming so weird that it tattered my psyche. I staggered through it, wounded, panting, heart pounding; my mind awash with frightening images. The sky darkened as I reached the steep downgrade to Gooseberry Canyon. The draw was more sheltered than the ridge, but equally difficult. I stumbled and fell through long periods of not knowing up from down. Somewhere I wandered off into a side draw and only discovered my mistake when I became closeted in forest. I kept circling in a small cul-de-sac, peering through the deepening dusk for a nonexistent trail ahead. I finally found my way back because the draw was a funnel that emptied where I was going.

The lower section of the trail was badly eroded, so I was able to follow along its gully without straying. It was almost black in the forest when I crossed above Devil's Slide. I was relieved but so exhausted that the final climb to camp required four rest periods. At last I crawled over the lower retaining wall and into the sleeping area, feeling ahead blindly with my hands. The sleeping bag was where I had left it, weighted with rocks, and thoroughly inviting. I collapsed on top of it and later crawled inside.

Never before had I felt such relief. My whole body relaxed, taking my mind with it. The change happened so quickly that it felt like I had been struck on the head, the blow driving out everything else, including pain. I was amazed at the transformation. I warmed up, my sinuses cleared, my heart mellowed, and the multitude of discomforts throughout my body evaporated. Not only did I no longer feel sick, I felt positively buoyant, and waves of delight washed through me. My first response was to giggle, but I soon rolled up in a tingling ball of contentment and tuned in to an evening of theater.

I lost sight of my body, but this time as a child let loose in a fabulous fantasyland. My internal landscapes became brilliantly clear, alive with lights and colors projected by the patterned functioning of my nervous system. Visions of aquatic loveliness formed around the reef where my organic and electromagnetic beings met and mingled. The water grew warm, came to a boil, and changed to steam. My eyelids heated as though beams of powerful radiation were pouring through them. I felt no discomfort, for I was the source of the burning energy and enjoyed its intensity. I followed the beam backward into my inner circuits and arrived at my heart, which was happily pumping fuel through the anti-entropic furnace of creation where blood burned to life and remained blood.

The sequence sputtered out, leaving me alone with the night. Half-formed insights lingered on the edge of my understanding, tempting me with conceptual knowledge. I unzipped the sleeping bag, pulled myself part way out into the chilly night, and rummaged through the pack for my flashlight, notebook, and pen. I scribbled a reminder of what was already vanishing from memory and slid back into the bag to be overwhelmed again by colorful vignettes.

The writing set the pattern for the night. Perhaps one out of twenty excursions into Iboga's palaces left me with verbal content, some of which I managed to jot down. Often, however, I was waylaid en route to the notebook. Finding the flashlight, opening the book, using the pen: such things diverted me, and I forgot what I wanted to write. Sometimes I wrote with the pen upside down because the beam of the flashlight playing obliquely across the page cast shadows that I couldn't distinguish from ink. Once, I became so fascinated by the flashlight that I used its beam to erase my memory, then wondered what had left me thunderstruck a moment earlier.

Throughout all these gyrations, my body channeled energy smoothly and felt wonderfully alive, but occasionally the oppressiveness of the day reasserted itself, not as pain, but as painful insights. From one excursion into nowhere I came back as a leaf of gold that quickly tarnished to economic significance. Growing possessive, I tried to hang onto the gold, but it corroded in my hands as though eaten by acid. Soon, only a web of yellow lines remained which, just before it dissolved, spelled the word money.

Blackness ensued, molding itself into a dark chamber, which grew lighter as I materialized into it. The chamber became a college classroom where a professor was lecturing: "Gold is the abstract of value," he said. "Money is the abstract of gold. Credit is the abstract of money. When you are forced to deal with the abstract of an abstract of an abstract, you may safely conclude that a shell game is in progress, that you are the mark, and that the golden pea is in the hand of the money managers." The professor turned around and scribbled something on the blackboard. He turned again, standing in front of what he had written so that I couldn't read it. He continued to lecture: "The value of money lies in the rectitude of the government that issues it. When that government is corrupt, you are, in fact, valuing its ability to lie to you and basing your hopes of future prosperity on the advice of shills whose own profit lies in statutory dishonesty." He paused for a moment and glanced into the classroom. His eyes were magnified by thick glasses, but he did not seem to see me. "Who are you?" I asked, and my impropriety caught his attention. He stared down at me for an uncomfortable moment, but just as his eyes sparked with interest, he faded from my sight. As he disappeared, the blackboard showed through him, and I caught a fleeting glimpse of the first line he had written, which merely said: Professor Shadowmaker, Dept. of Human Frailty.

I rolled uneasily in the sleeping bag and curled into a ball. Energy poured out through my feet and encircled me. I grew warmer and began to perspire slightly. The air in the bag ionized, and sparks played along my surface. They pushed out into the darkness, pierced my nylon container, and glowed as faint, phosphorescent filaments near my head. One danced to my nose and leapt off. I followed along, soon becoming lost in the strange contours of night. The forest took me to itself, and I prowled as a hunter, hoping to find another, but found only myself, lurking in shadows, hiding, trading masks with yesterday and tomorrow and then hanging them back on the branches of time. I longed to burrow into the gray-green earth, to be brother to roots and worms, to cogitate as a carrot denying the benefits of motility. I saw, but was not seen. I heard, but made no sound. Webs, like glistening nets of fire, glowed about and through me, and I became a mycelium sprouting magic mushrooms from my tongue.

The mushrooms dropped their spores and rotted. I fled within, but my landscape changed to a ghetto, and a city revealed itself, only to sag like the fungi on my tongue. I heard the sputtering of termites, and decay crawled from sewers. Cracks showed in the walls of my cement and fluorescent brainhouse, then the ruin dissolved to me, curled in a bag, brooding, lapsing with transience and a taste of wonder, my own forgetfulness strung like lights across the emptiness of mind.

The shadowmaker returned, different now, wholly enchanting. She offered me a cup of Lethe in answer to my questions about her and rove the nighttime with laughter. I saw, and then there was darkness: yin-side of sun, earthlight, and moon mysteries eclipsing to deep red. I opened my eyes. Change patterned the night and the wind wove dark branches into a twilit tapestry of the shadowmaker's art. She crossed the ridge as the moon goddess, and her gaze, like some obscure pull from heaven, drew me out until I lay like a vapor about myself, floating in silent exultation.

The vapor rose, and I rose with it, wooed by the queen of night, lifted by her from my bed of mountain. Her silver aura was turned to lace by ice-crystal clouds, making her seem another Gorgon with hairs of sentient light slithering into space. She was veiled, more than half shadowed, turning to crescent in her stately exit, and displaying night and day as functions of a sphere awash in invisibly streaming light.

I drifted outward. The shadowmaker laughed softly, like a woman in bed, and moved closer. Her arms spread like bat wings over the whole world. Her fur rippled on the edge of ionized space. "Come," she whispered. "Explore the shadow."

A force from the mountain like a plume of heated air pushed from below, increasing my momentum. I flowed into space, traversing the earth's coned shadow that, like an artist's pencil, doodles endlessly on the zodiac. I added my own exertions to the upward flow and swam through the hiatus of sunlight like a pearl diver pulling for the surface.

Far out in the night, I rolled to my back and rested. The dark disk of earth barely covered the sun. The corona glowed warmly, and streamers of fire leapt forth, turning the spectacle into a gigantic eye hung in the emptiness of space. The earth a black pupil encircled by the blazing iris of its life. Sunlight and shadow intermingled like sound and silence in the symphony of being. My eardrums, skull, spine, organs, and extremities pulsed to the complex theme, which encoded my being as part of itself, and dumped me, strung out like a series of binary numbers, on a passing beam of sunlight.

I was imprinted with a planetary mandala, encompassed by it, and conjoined with others in it; and yet, I alone dove into the ocean of radiance and streamed outward as a living memory of earth encased in sunlight. I was aimed by the archer into the dark clouds that clothe the center of the galaxy. The earth shadow shrank to a dark spot and dissolved in the celestial effulgence that encompassed all space. The velocity of my beaming slowed in the escape from relativity, then stopped altogether. I hesitated on the edge of dispersion. A mysterious silence reached to where I lay wrapped in forest, grounding me without recalling my spirit. I listened. Silence became sound, and darkness light. No words preceded meaning, nor any images, yet the vision completed itself.

I awoke in a strange and beautiful place, where stars abounded like pebbles on a stony beach, and waves of inner-galactic intelligence washed over them, enfolding me in voluptuousness. Space was alive in its matrix of stars, even as I was in my sheath of coded light. For a few moments, the Lady Iboga's mirror mirrored the magnetic speculum of space. Then it shattered into prismatic splinters, and the polarity of the field reversed. Energy poured through in a torrent of confusion, plunging me into the unimaginable chaos of primal phenomena.

My body snapped to with a myoclonic jerk, pulling me from the ancient domain of magic that lies but a millionth of a second before now, aswirl as the ocean from which each new moment arises. I gulped the damp night air and lay gasping until I settled back into my body and remembered where I was. I opened my eyes to look at the moon goddess once more. She seemed to be blushing, for her lover, in hot pursuit, was calling her to her day's disappearance.

FOURTEENTH DAY

His Serpency

Dawn came on as a symphony of color followed by its conductor, who smiled briefly, but was preoccupied and parsimonious with his encores. His light was pale, without warmth, and the riotous colors of his coming quickly diminished to cold blue and watery gray. I had no desire to move, so I stayed in the sleeping bag for several hours, watching mosaics, holographs, and epochal histories materialize and pass away. Everything was vividly multidimensional, and every impression pulled me into its own spectrum of experiences. The intensity and delicacy of the forest shades were separate dimensions, as were the qualities of sound and the exquisiteness of detailed forms. I succumbed to them all and ran like a spider among the glistening webs of my universe.

About midmorning, I moved to the kitchen, built a fire, and set three pans of water to heating, for washing, soaking my feet, and making tea. The mouse had left four calling cards. I cleaned the shelf, swept the leaves from the kitchen, and basked before the fire with my feet in a pail. The Iboga rushes were still as intense as during the night, but spaced further apart. During the physically lucid intervals, my body was unsteady, but seemed together, and the sponge bath revitalized it.

I soon felt strong enough to take the *I Ching* to my circle of bushes. Once clear of the forest, I looked up the long slopes toward cloud-shrouded Spitler Peak and felt the Lady looking back. Her breath was cool, so I wrapped the blanket around me and cast the coins. The hexagram grew as an alternation of firm and yielding lines, each in its appropriate place, the balanced but unstable condition of "After Completion". It portrays a post-climactic time when the transition from the old to the new is completed. All things are systematized, and only details need attending to, but it is on these that the success of the enterprise rests. While reading the commentary, I suddenly realized that I now had all the information I needed to understand what the mountain was telling me, but I was also aware that the data had not yet been fully assimilated, and I really did not know how much, or what, I knew.

The two top lines of the hexagram changed. The fifth is a paean to simplicity. It says:

> The neighbor in the east who slaughters an ox
> Does not attain as much real happiness
> As the neighbor in the west
> With his small offering.

The sixth line is a warning:

> He gets his head in the water.
> Danger.

This brought a wry smile to my lips, for I felt I had been drowning for much of the past thirty hours, and I wondered why the book was a day late with its counsel.

The second hexagram was "Grace", beauty of form, whose image is fire breaking out from the secret depths of a mountain and illuminating the heights above. As I read the commentary, another of Iboga's tides began to rise, and it overtook me at the place where the book was saying:

> By contemplating the forms existing in the heavens we come
> to understand time and its changing demands.

How strange it seemed! How upside down that the contemplation of space should reveal time, and that of time educe space. Their mutual dependence is the key to their transcendence, for somehow nothing matters, and things come into existence by themselves.

Iboga's tide rose in cleansing waves from chakra to chakra. Soon, I was drenched in the unadorned Presence, and I experienced the identity existing between the abstract of ideas that constitutes our understanding of the universe and the patterns, which we as individuals and societies act out in our behavior. Great themes of astronomy, astrology, physics, metaphysics, mathematics, and myth passed in profusion and culminated in a vision of pyramids and ancient observatories. I saw men spending their lives in contemplation of the heavens, and saw how they saw so clearly. Their cosmological ideas were the Dharmakayaic programming for their Sambhogakayaic archetypes, and these, in turn, underlay their ability to see and move correctly.

The waters of Iboga reached the ajna chakra and swirled silently about my head. A cool plunge lay ahead, but I remembered the warning in the *I Ching* and held back, clinging to the shore of remembrance. I thought of other disciplines where cosmological data were used to structure consciousness, not only through the tuning of temples and alignments of magical cities, but as when the Magi came together under a star, or a hero was brought to earth on a comet's tail. I also remembered the yoga aphorisms of Patanjali, which describe meditations on the sun, moon, and pole star for bringing forth knowledge of the cosmos and of its many mysterious powers.

My theater of abstractions emptied and was replaced by a succession of human faces, beautifully etched. They were saints, sages, and scientists, whose disciplines had molded their features to super mundane serenity. How different in visage, and yet how similar they seemed. Each had spent a lifetime fashioning consciousness, until, like a cyclotron with a focused beam of energy, his mind channeled intelligence into objects and read the reflection as knowledge. I was overawed, but the Lady Iboga smiled at my seriousness. As a majestic dakini, she scoffed equally at lifetimes, disciplines, and miracles, for she could convey in a moment that toward which the others pointed, and could dissolve all questionings into the Presence they probed.

I grew cold on the stones and returned to camp to stoke the fire. My face and hands warmed quickly, but my feet stayed cold, so I started dancing to thaw them out. Soon I was singing. The tune was a hybrid of "Singing in the Rain" and "Mac the Knife," but the words were my own. They kept popping at me from nowhere and often had me doubled up with laughter. My vocal cords added to the hilarity. They were out of tune and produced a dual sound, one part fainter and slightly behind the other, so that each word had a rasping echo and wobbled strangely.

I was soon warm, but I continued to waltz around the kitchen with abandon. I climbed to the top of the pipes, hung from my knees, and sang a boisterous ditty to the upside-down trees. Eventually, my exertions made me thirsty. I flipped to the ground and cakewalked to the spring, but as I was going to my knees to drink, I froze. Stretched out on the other side was a sizable rattlesnake, apparently come to drink, who was watching my antics with a dispassionate eye.

I was startled, then delighted. He was no more than two feet away and quite unperturbed. I was amazed that my commotion had not kept him off, for rattlesnakes are usually shy, but then I realized a deeper purpose to his visit. I bowed to the Presence, then sat cross-legged across from His Serpency and chanted AUM. The snake did not move at all. His head was three inches off the ground and pointed at my own. I knew he did not see well, and was deaf to most airborne sounds, but he might have had infrared sensors, and he certainly had an uncanny way of translating earth vibrations into striking pictures. He was over three feet long, and thick. His colors were red and golden brown through which faint black markings showed, and on top of his skull, astonishing since I had never seen such things on a snake before, were a pair of stubby horns.

We mellowed into each other's space. I tried to think of ways to bridge our genetic communications gap and continued to chant. I tried one, then another, but soon reverted to a simple AUM. The snake remained motionless. I remembered the first changing line of the morning's hexagram. His Serpency and I were neighbors. The stream divided us, he to the west, I to the east. But I could not remember the rest of the line and did not want to go get the book for fear of ending the encounter. All I could recall was that one of the neighbors had it better than the other; then I realized that I was much too busy thinking to enjoy what was happening.

I relaxed and focused on the head of the snake as a meditational point. His energy became visible to my ajna chakra, appearing as a helix of pulsing light. It drew me into itself, or rather, a presence formed between us which, interpenetrating both, revealed itself as compounded of each, yet different from either. Certainly it was not snake, because it was all me, but with some other fraction added that complemented my being. The circle of my persona became an ellipse whose foci circled each other. The new circle had a consciousness to which I was but a fraction, so I dropped the lower half and became whole—a number within a number scintillating to a hybrid sentience of untested potential.

Within this new, man-snake consciousness, the Presence revealed itself as essence. The world displayed a different aspect, magically altered, sensuous in undreamt ways, peaceful. Suddenly, a voice in very distinct English said: "I am all these forms here present." I snapped from my reverie and looked about, but my only companion was the reptile, who remained immobile.

I became aware of the cold ground, excused myself, and slowly got up. I fetched the blanket and noticed my camera sitting on the cupboard shelf. I asked His Serpency if he would pose for his portrait, which he did, remaining unconcerned even when I poked my glass eye into his aura. I sat back down, more warmly wrapped, and again projected into the space between us. The water burbled below, and objects lost their separateness. My mind toyed briefly with the koan of the heart sutra, then form became emptiness and the Gordian knot of consciousness untangled into a thread of vapor.

The strange snake-man peered once more from the edge of my darkness. He smiled with my lips, and with my darting tongue tasted the sweet musky odor of forest. My hands coiled themselves into mudras, and my fingers wove a pattern of organic communication to the reptile. I chanted AUM three times, and, when I completed the third, he withdrew his head from the water's edge, very slowly turned to his right, and started back along the path. I had not seen him drink and feared that my presence had deterred him. I got up and turned to go, but before I had taken a step, he raised the tip of his tail and shook it once sharply. The rattle electrified the air and sent a galvanic tingle down my spine.

Six feet from the spring, the snake turned from the path and glided into a crevice of the retaining wall. As his head disappeared he rattled a second time, and moments later, just as his tail slid into the wall, he gave a final salute. I waited for a minute, then went to where he had vanished, got to my hands and knees and peered up under the rock. He was nowhere to be seen.

I remembered a book I had once read, in which a Hindu holy man fed saucers of milk to the cobras of his wild place, so I mixed a bowl of powdered instant and placed it before His Serpency's den. The clouds were nipping the treetops and there was distant thunder. The wind was moist, promising rain, so I decided to rig the tube tent. The tent was an eight foot cylinder of thin vinyl, which was set up by threading it along a nylon cord tied above the ground at both ends. The Iboga sidetracked me, however, and I was tangled up for twenty minutes before getting it right. Unfortunately, the tent then slapped like a sail in the breeze, so I dismantled it, leaving one end of the cord tied to the hitching post and the sleeping bag inside the tube, under rocks.

When I finished, I looked again for His Serpency. He had reappeared and now was coiled a few inches back under the wall. Two folds were visible, one directly over the other, with his head centered above, pointing out. I greeted him, and we looked at each other awhile; then I got up and, as an afterthought, placed the *I Ching* next to the milk as a surrogate to continue our dialogue.

The afternoon wore on. Both clouds and temperature dropped, the wind picked up. I huddled before the fire with the blanket around my shoulders and was still cold, so I got the sleeping bag and wrapped myself in that. I warmed up quickly and was soon absorbed by the fire. On a burning log without bark, worm eaten, and charring to bas-relief, the Lady Iboga drew pictures with flaming fingers. The Mountain Lady appeared and smiled at me. Across from her on the darkening log was a great bird standing alertly, watching her, and beside him, a Madonna and Child. The bird burst into flame, rising as a firebird, spirit of light, transformation, and disappearance. I thought of Garuda, the god-bird of ancient India, who was regarded as the Semblance of the Divine Sky and Lord of Life. On the blackening log, flames fashioned his feathers and animated him with the primal force of creation. The worm etchings at his feet caught fire and turned to white-brown snakes writhing in the inferno. As the log transmogrified into fiery coals, the reptiles arose in the form of a nine-headed Naga and merged with Garuda. The two became a flaming feathered serpent, passed into smoke, and disappeared.

I awoke from my dip into timelessness pondering the alterations of form that clothe the functions of time-space. Everything that exists comes and goes through the door of the Dharmakaya, where it is molded to the time and place of its appearance. The phenomenal universe exists as patterned hierarchies, each a reality whose totality is more than the summation of its parts. The difference between summation and totality is also the Dharmakaya that informs every part with the sentience appropriate to its extension in being. The error of the Kali Yuga is to conceive intelligence as intrinsic to the human mechanism rather than to form. And yet, to perceive reality as form is to misperceive it. Our nervous systems are not the authors of our experience, but the structure of it, and only one of an infinitude of ways by which consciousness talks to itself.

A sacred mountain is another way, much like ourselves, but grander. I slipped back into the memory of the Mountain Lady and saw for a moment how the ancient temple city had transcended its inhabitants. It had stood not as a testament to human ingenuity, but to our astounding good fortune, for it was a creation of earth herself. The earth was awake when the mountain was born, and we who were her creatures shared that awakeness. She spoke, and we spoke with her, becoming part of an earth consciousness reverberating through electromagnetic space.

The mountain was the earth's tongue—a singing temple where various creatures met in a clairvoyant matrix and merged, creating a new consciousness of the earth's tendency to think through an accumulation of its component forms. Then, timed by the moon, pulsed by the sun, and called forth by the impatience of the galaxy, the earth spoke into the listening ear of the Dharmakaya. Her words were a dragon formed of lion, serpent, eagle, man, whose accretion of psychic potential revealed the new entity, a probing earth-consciousness freed from the restraints of terrestrial life. The Sambhogakayaic earth mother perfected the mountain as her instrument for speaking to her cosmic brethren, and each of her lesser forms miraculously shared in its life.

I came to myself thinking no jewel in the world is so valuable as the clear perception of dirt, no sound so pure as the silence from which it issues, and no thought, however sublime, that is not a distraction. A white tear rolled down the Lady's arm and engulfed Gooseberry Canyon in cloud. The mist smudged the far trees to a milky invisibility through which the tips of their branches floated like wayward strands of hair. My feet became rooted to the ground by tendrils of electricity. I grew silent and felt the Mountain Lady's heart beating through my soles, tuning me to my fire, its ashes, and the earth below. The earth was waking up! I felt it in the marrow of my bones where my jelly was aligned to the polarity of the planet and my neural sensors responded to tentative, precursory currents of reversing energy. The earth was waking up! For millennia asleep, turned inward, her creative currents phased to regeneration and healing, she now trembled before the advent of her new day. Planetary poles were beginning to shift, north becoming south, and south, north, as the Moebius strip of earth's infinity turned its one side inside out. Poqanghoya and Palongawhoya were yawning, manifesting as unfamiliar, fluctuating forces to trample night and herald in the new age.

I woke up thinking of the Kali Yuga and how difficult was the death of desire, how cold the calamity of thinking. The stormy wind was compressed between the lips of the canyon and whistled through the trees. It had blown the sleeping bag from my shoulders and chilled me to the bone. I retrieved the bag and wrapped myself more tightly, but I continued to shiver. I recalled the Tibetan yogi Milarepa, renowned for his austerities and the miraculous powers these induced. In one meditation, he performed the feat we call hyper-pyrexia, whereby he regulated his body heat and sat comfortably naked through a Himalayan blizzard. I was too spaced out to try it myself, so, when an errant gust again blew the sleeping bag from my shoulders, I cried out: "0, Milarepa! Where are you now that I need you?"

About two minutes later, another gust twisted past my leg, flipped open my notebook and fluttered its pages. The book was stuffed with inclusions, and before I could close it again, a single piece was plucked out and tumbled across the kitchen. I quickly retrieved it and discovered to my surprise that it was the heaviest piece in the book, a section of the cardboard mobile I had found in the cupboard. On it was written the sacred mantra AUM MANI PADME HUM, in red, white, blue, green, yellow, and black Tibetan script.

This response to my call alerted me to the synchronicity of the Presence and hinted at magical things in the air. My antennae slipped out and my body warmed to the experience. I went to the pack for the pipe and hashish, and on the way noticed that the *I Ching* had also blown open, its pages dancing in the wind. I started to take it to the kitchen, but a gentle voice asked that I leave it to flutter before the watching eye of the reptile.

I filled the pipe and crouched under the sleeping bag to light it. A few tokes later, I re-emerged and again confronted the fire. I began chanting softly, using AUM MANI PADME HUM to tune me to the flames, but no sooner had I called out HUM than a movement in the forest caught my eyes. I glanced up to see Milarepa stealing through the glade, and no snippet of logic arose to erase the vision. Caught, he lingered for a few moments on the far side of the kitchen, smiling at my delight in discovering him.

I bowed as the apparition faded, murmured an AUM TAO, and closed my eyes. The Lady Iboga, stoned on hashish, slid a crystalline screen before the velvet of my lidded sight, beyond which, so close I could feel his quiet breathing, stood a black lacquered Buddha, opening and closing a gate. The gate and the wall in which it was set were latticeworks of energy whose iridescence outlined the Buddha from behind.

I passed through the gate and entered an opalescent hall. Energy splashed down my chakras like water in the hanging gardens of Babylon. Reaching bottom, it moistened the root chakra and grew upward as kundalini, the serpent power. The serpent slowly uncoiled and climbed to my solar plexus, then circled my stomach, mouth agape. Its tail arrived as its head returned, and its jaws bit down on its nether end, creating an ouroboros that turned until it became a wheel of glowing electricity hung in the space before me. This became the steering wheel of a car, which my hands held as I drove along a narrow country road. Ahead, on the blacktop, was a snake, so I pulled over, got out, and followed the reptile down a sandy draw, but before anything could transpire between us, a sheriff's car screeched to a halt on the road. The sheriff jumped out, pulled his revolver, and took aim at the snake.

"Don't!" I yelled, and my cry shattered Iboga's picture screen. I awoke confused, having just jumped to my feet. I was hunched over the fire, staring into the forest with none but myself to confront.

Evening came on. I made a cup of broth and sipped it while peeking in on His Serpency. He was as I had seen him last, but despite hours of immobility, he was alert and seemed comfortable. I bade him good night and took the sleeping bag to the tube tent. My exhausted body quickly melted into the ground, and my mind seemed clearer for being free of the impediment.

A new cloud dashed through the forest and matured into flowing billows. I lay on my back, looking up through the trees. The moving mists blotted out the higher branches and gave a new sense of depth and perspective to those below. Suddenly, I noticed something that had not been evident before. Far above, a large broken limb had fallen and snagged among others. It hung over me like the sword of Damocles, swaying from side to side. It was shaped like an inverted V and seemed firmly snagged. There was no cause for alarm, so I closed my eyes, but the image remained in my sight as though my eyelids were transparent. Soon the branches began to phosphoresce and take on new shapes as though rearranged by fingers from a different dimension. A colossus grew and stood monstrously astride the canyon. He was woven from filaments of terrestrial power, and crackling electricity danced from his figure, shedding light on his crystal-studded countenance, from which an intensity of searing intelligence glinted. He was like a Titan grown from the head of Gaea; his objective was dominion. I felt no fear, but curiosity at the temerity of a being who, in grasping his prize, had become rooted to the earth and immobile. He scowled at my indifference, then withered back into the Presence.

Around midnight, I dozed. When I woke, I found myself simultaneously at three different places on the mountain. I did not know where they were, but I was aware of each and every nuance of the three locations and experienced them as focal points in the sacred space of the temple. The reality of the perception was absolute, and as it faded I glimpsed the abstract pattern that underlay the structure and sentience of the ancient complex.

I drifted to sleep, or into a blackness that mimicked sleep, of which I had no remembrance. Later, the wind howled me back to an amorphous consciousness. It began to drizzle, then rain. I slid out of the sleeping bag, slipped it into the tube, and hurried back into it. The rain increased and played variations on a theme of vinyl above my ear. The music drew me through an endless tunnel of sound and then stopped without my noticing. When I opened my eyes, the new day's light was glowing orange through the plastic.

FIFTEENTH DAY

Tourmaline Castles

The morning was cold and the sky overcast when I hurried from my coverings and quickly dressed. I added the gray blanket and wore it like a poncho, with my head stuck through a moth-eaten hole in the middle. The milk in the snake's dish was lower, but whether it had been drunk or had evaporated I could not tell. His Serpency was lodged in the same place, but had shifted the position of his coils and head. He eyed me impassively, his tongue gliding out to taste the space between us. I felt his intelligence and became aware of a question that arose between us concerning the organic forms that electromagnetic entities assume, and how these both entrap and express energy.

I thought of the *I Ching* and conveyed the impulse, telling him the book was the law for such entities. Since he had been exposed to its flappings the day before, I presumed he would appreciate a demonstration. I fetched the book from the cupboard, showed him the coins, and explained how they were the entranceway through the randomness of phenomena to the law of being. Then I threw them, telling him what I was doing while I did it. The words I used were for my own sake, but, although octaves lower, they resonated with the field that enclosed us both and made the communication intelligible.

Neither the motion of the falling coins, nor that of my hands, disturbed the reptile. The first hexagram was "Innocence (The Unexpected)". It was surprisingly appropriate, for it represents unimpeded energy returning upward to the source, the image of the serpent power. In response to our question, it implied that spontaneity in organic forms results from being free of electromagnetic blocks: the ego and its ideas must be empty and everything else full. For me, it foretold a day when naiveté would be a virtue; when innocence relying on electromagnetic integrity would best the wiles of calculated action.

The first changing line counseled perseverance. It says we cannot lose what really belongs to us, and so we should have no anxiety. The second change was a semi-ominous puzzle. It says:

Use no medicine in an illness
Incurred through no fault of your own.
It will pass of itself.

The second hexagram was "Providing Nourishment". It describes this function as the foundation of organic life, but points out that the proper ordering of life—nourishment of one's electromagnetic totality, is the true sustenance of the superior creature.

The snake's tongue arched out, forked, and touched the space between his eyes. It held for a moment, then slid down his snout, became a single spike, and disappeared in the tiny black hole in the center of his mouth. I took it as a salutation, returned it, and went back to the cupboard for breakfast. I prepared extra milk and refilled the snake's bowl; then, taking my pack, started on a trek to the Saddle. I had decided to spend the day exploring the formations of pinnacled rock leading out to the Footstool of Temporal Wisdom.

The morning overcast was burning off, and the sun was enticing fragrances from the forest floor as I left Gooseberry Canyon. I chanted as I rounded the rim above Devil's Slide, but as I started up the steep hill, the chant subsided to a whisper, then to heavy breathing, first through my nose and later through my mouth. The exertion focused energy in my legs, but my mind, unoccupied with the chant, became prey to less subtle thoughts. I dismissed them, one after another, on and on, until they left me free of everything that being an identifiable ego implied. Empty, yet magnetized, I drew a succession of personalities to myself and watched them pass in stylized profusion. There were artists, craftsmen, thinkers, a soldier, a teacher, a traveling man, a hermit. Some stopped briefly, but retreated before the exertions of my body; others luxuriated in it. Then the succession focused on a face from my memory, and I recalled Tim Leary saying that we could be anyone we wanted to be this time around.

I remembered when the jubilant sixties were falling before the drab powerhouse of the seventies, with its crush of inferior men. Timothy, in a Socratic farce, was imprisoned for challenging the validity of the

American dream and questioning the values on which it was foundering. I grew as heated as my body, and a blast of reactivated anger obliterated the pain of my aching muscles. I drove on until, suddenly, there was an explosion beneath my feet. I followed my hair straight up in the air, and landed like a cat on a dog's back, ready to bounce off in any available direction. Fortunately, the cause of the explosion, a six-foot blacksnake on which I had almost stepped, was already forty feet away, moving with astounding agility up the rocky canyon side. He reached an outcropping, draped himself about the top, and gazed back to examine the impudence that had enlivened him.

There was a chortling in a corner of my mind, as my Chinese friend clucked over his unexpected success, but he was charitable and reminded me to review the abrupt sequence of events before they vanished, taking their significance with them. I realized I had been taken by surprise because I had been thinking instead of watching what I was doing. I had set my body on automatic pilot, while I went spinning off in my own imperium. I realized this dichotomous existence was what the *I Ching* means by an improper ordering of life. The electromagnetic world is the realm of freedom to which we instinctively aspire, but the organic world is full of danger, and the two must be integrated before a superior person may be said to exist.

The blacksnake acted as a tonic, and for the rest of the climb I was uncaring and exuberant, albeit observant. At the top of the ridge, I left the trail and went along the rounded plateau of the Lady's lower left leg. The major flora were cactus and scrub, above which towered a series of castellated outcroppings of rock. Many varieties of plants were in flower, including some which had not been evident a few days earlier. The blue lupine had filled out, while Indian paintbrush, penstemon, and red sage clustered about marbled boulders and wind-stunted trees.

There were seven castles of rock extending in a broken line to the top of the Footstool. It was not difficult moving between them, so I went from one to the next exploring their battlements and turrets. They were sculptures of weathered sandstone, boulders swirling in light and dark layers, and megaliths sparkling with mica and pyrite. Some showed water hewn depressions or deeply cut channels, telling of times when streams had flowed and fallen from terrace to terrace.

Flights of multicolored butterflies fluttered wherever I went. In a raised area of one of the castles, a sandy, egg-shaped depression, perhaps thirty feet long, formed a natural courtyard with shimmering, frescoed walls. I jumped into it as though pulled by a vortex, then continued to turn, spun by a subtle but powerful field constructed from the emanations of the rock. A small indentation in one of the rock faces, about waist high, caught my eyes. It glittered with a sprinkling of tiny tourmaline crystals, and reminded me of the profound experience I had had with other crystals on top of the Serpent Tower.

I put my pack aside and knelt before the rock. The indentation was just large enough for my forehead to fit snugly within. The rock was cool; the crystals pressed into my brow like needles, and I felt energy flowing from the stone. Fingers of force penetrated my skull to tinker and toy with my mind. I became aware of intricate, multidimensional patterns of dark blue and deep maroon lines crisscrossed on a field of black; the entire construct moving with mesmeric intensity to the deep sentience of matter below.

Prompted by subtle forces, I shifted my position. My chin dropped to my chest, and the crown of my head replaced my brow against the crystals. There was a moment of adjustment, a reordering of coordinates. Then the laser-like patterns reasserted themselves, but they now embodied consciousness and, like sentient magnets, drew me to them. I relaxed and involuted to a mysterious place wherein a galaxy of living stars radiated warm acceptance. The feeling originated everywhere within me, and I dissolved into its ecstatic field.

Sometime later, I awoke to my Nirmanakayaic self, stretched out on the far side of the sandy depression. I was alive purely as an instrument of delight. Above me, the Presence hovered like a murmuring mother watching over her crib. She lifted me to my feet and helped me take steps, walking me back to the magic rock and once more putting my head to its crystalline lips. Empty space, void and trackless, yet filled with an enormity of sentience and an infinity of the possible, engulfed me. Stars appeared to glide endlessly on course, now and then colliding in masterful, explosive displays, as titanic forces unleashed their fury, and fires glowed with the enlightenment of primal creation. Marvel on marvel unfolded, reached a peak, and ceased, abandoning me at last to tranquil desolation. Through this darkened realm, an ancient burned-out star passed, a hoary remnant of yesterday's creation wandering erratically through space. It seemed a harmless derelict, a cosmic ash, and whirled back to the yawning Dharmakaya leaving barely a wake in the emptiness.

Later, seated in the sand, my head still spinning but wonderfully clear, I bowed to the Presence. It manifested everywhere in the fluid nature of things, and flowed through me, raising a question. I simultaneously experienced the answer, for circuits deep within my electromagnetic being had been touched. I wondered how it had been accomplished, how it was possible for these bare and ancient rocks to retain such residual power. Then certain, paradoxical things became apparent. Whatever had occurred had required no time for its completion, yet timing was essential. A momentary connection had been established in time-space, and I had been at a proper place to ground it. What had occurred had not happened in ordinary space, yet the positioning of my chakras had been crucial. I understood what had been conveyed, what ancient promise had been fulfilled, but I knew nothing whatsoever. As the Presence faded, even this unknowing disappeared, leaving me wrapped in wonder like a man who had just found the world's most precious treasure and, quite as unexpectedly, given it away to a passing stranger.

I continued along the ridge, investigating the rest of the castles, walking the mountain as a geomantic entity, and delighting in its forms and fragrances. The end of the plateau was made up of the red sandstone pinnacles of the Footstool. I had lunch on a balmy promontory, next to a granite boulder etched with very fine, parallel lines, an inch or two apart. They seemed too straight to be natural and reminded me of an expanded diffraction grating, a capacitor, or perhaps an antenna. Across the Saddle lay the Lion, the Pedestal tiny beneath his paw, and further off the broken Serpent Tower. I had no trouble seeing them as they had been, for even in their epoch of decay they radiated their timeless meaning.

After lunch, I explored the cliffs of the Footstool and then smoked a pipe in the upper Saddle. I felt lazy and lay in the sand while the sun arched across heaven, splattering the mountain with dappled colors and puffy cloud shadows. I considered going on to the Pedestal and Chalice, but my tired legs said no, and took me instead along the easiest route to the top of the Footstool. I returned along the line of castles with mounting excitement, for I planned to stop once more at the courtyard of my tourmaline palace, but though I walked back the way I had come, I became completely disoriented. I recognized nothing and though I spent a full hour crossing and re-crossing the area, I had no success.

Frustrated, I sat down to have another pipe, hoping it would clear my head. While preparing it, however, I recalled the line from the *I Ching* that had advised me to use no medicine. I put the pipe away and appealed instead to the Presence to ease my predicament. There was an immediate response. Almost in words, I was told to go back to the spot where I had left the Gooseberry trail that morning, and to return the way I had come. I did so. Fifteen minutes later I was back again, but now I was able to go directly to what I had been searching for. Everything was as I remembered it: the high enclosure of eroded rocks, the sheltered courtyard, the tourmaline-speckled portal. I was amazed and befuddled, for I had certainly been through here several times in my hapless wanderings, but had not seen what I had surely looked at. The Presence smiled at my dilemma, but only hinted at the subtle truth that our solid world is less solid than it seems.

I was footsore and weary, but the long downhill path to Gooseberry Canyon was a visual fantasia of elongated shadows and lush, afternoon colors. Back at camp, I checked on His Serpency; both he and the milk were gone, but whether or not they had gone together was a moot question. I built no fire, being too tired to tend it, and too hungry to wait. Instead, I heated water on the pack stove and prepared a prefabricated feast of freeze-dried shrimp creole. It was the first full meal I had eaten since the Lady Iboga had so thoroughly flushed my system, and it tasted of ambrosia all the way to my toes. Afterward, I went directly to bed and lingered in an alpha state only long enough to watch evening open into night.

Much later, past midnight, I dreamed, or perhaps I woke, for my eyes seemed open, and the thinning crescent moon hung just as it should have, yet was brighter than when it was full. It filled the forest with streaming lights whose presence seemed to stifle sound itself, and even my breathing made no noise. The air was a liquid opalescence, washing through me like an ocean current through an old ribbed skeleton. The Presence invited me out and clothed me in darkness, on which the night lights etched a vision of women speaking:

"I am the sky consort," said the crescent lady moon mother.

"And I the earth mountain," said one from below.

"And I the sea between, which none have ever seen," said a watery voice. "Showing semblances of something dreamed." My heart palpitated, caught, and beat again. It attracted attention, and as I lay in hushed expectation, the sea, ever so softly, spoke again:

> There is one thing every man knows:
> That which he seeks is nothing now.
> So men seek for nothing.
> The wise for now.

Straining to hear more, I sat up in the sleeping bag, but the conversation drifted into a filigree of motionless branches filtering moonlight and disappeared in the matrix where night becomes light, and dreaming, sleep.

SIXTEENTH DAY

A Summons

I woke to blackflies and butterflies buzzing over my head, and several hummingbirds bobbing above my torso. My favorite was among them. Because of his flaming red head, I had named him Amitabha Bird, after the Red Buddha, but this was something of a misnomer. Only his face was red, the rest of him iridescent green. When, after breakfast, I settled in my circle of bushes, he perched on a branch next to my left ear, from where he talked to me, very seriously, in a high-pitched squeak.

I became entranced and could feel him tuning me, drawing me into an electromagnetic consciousness. Like the bird's wings, my mechanisms functioned without my involvement. There was nothing to do, nothing to hold onto, and how foolish, I thought, to grasp at a higher consciousness that itself must yield in order that the purposeful fingers appear. The chemical cannot comprehend the electromagnetic field, nor the current. There is merely an intuition concerning the inevitable progression. The Dharmakaya encompasses the Sambhogakaya, which embodies the Nirmanakaya. Of these, the first and the last are alone; the first, because it is the only essence of everything, while the last, perceiving this, shrinks the perception to itself and imprisons it in ego.

The bird stepped into the air and slid into the space before me. I marveled at his electromagnetic integrity and at the freedom this gave him, for he was continuously recharged by the ambiance of the mountain. I pondered how difficult it was for our species to attain a similar degree of organic liberation, and I recalled the great variety of techniques we teach each other in order to learn the trick instinctive to the bird. We have long used structured meditational systems, yogic disciplines, martial arts, Zen slaps, herbs, weeds, cacti and mushrooms for this purpose; and now, because of our technological competence, we can also employ electronic stimulators, biofeedback devices, and synthetic pharmaceuticals: all to learn, or relearn, our ancient, ever-new consciousness and make it relevant to the modern world. And yet the modern world, like that of Rome two thousand years ago, condemns this knowledge, and I was reminded of my brothers whose pursuit of it led them to prison or to being fugitives at home, exiles abroad.

Amitabha Bird darted into the forest and was back in an instant. He had no allegiance except to the moment, and he trusted himself to act correctly. His consciousness was so intense and precise, it startled me into perceiving our species as functionally blind, lumbering giants, who grotesquely claimed the right to murder every life form on the planet while dismantling all of its habitats for profit. Amitabha Bird agreed, but reminded me that there were reasons why our modern world is so vastly inferior to those great civilizations that preceded it.

How mysterious it all was!—this resonance to partial identity and mutual understanding. Did the bird speak or merely enliven my imagination? Was truth a song, or did he sing words? I could not know, nor did it matter, for the psychic event was real, and the bird, my brother. He darted off again, reminding me of my own day ahead. I decided it would be my last at Gooseberry Springs and wondered how best to spend it. My energy was low, so I decided to stay around camp and tune in to the rhythms of the forest.

The *I Ching* lay on the sand among a scattering of white flowers. I switched to a cross-legged position to consult it, but my knee was bothering me, so I shifted until my foot was on the ground and the sore knee next to my cheek. In doing so, I slipped into a familiar position, that of a small jade statue of Bodhidharma that I had often admired. A strange sensation spread through me. I felt as if I had become the statue; as if each particle of my body had been replaced by milky green, translucent stone, and I took on the serenity conveyed by the artifact.

The hexagrams reflected this state. The first was "Pushing Upward", presenting the image of a young tree growing up through the earth. It is composed of the same trigrams as "Contemplation", but in inverse order, for there a mature tree is depicted standing on earth. The judgment on the hexagram has three spurs to action:

> Pushing Upward has supreme success.
> One must see the great man.
> Fear not.

Departure toward the south
Brings good fortune.

I immediately rethought my plans for the day. I was on the northern slopes of the Mountain Lady; departure to the south would take me to her. She, as a great lady, could stand stead for the great man and fulfill the condition of the oracle. The changing line seemed to assume I was going to visit her, for it advises that:

If one is sincere,
It furthers one to bring even a small offering.
No blame.

I had little to give but hoped if I left a few nuts for the squirrels, it would suffice. The second hexagram confirmed me in my change of plans. It was "Modesty" which admonishes one to carry things through. Its image of a mountain within the earth bespeaks electromagnetic completion.

A morning breeze stirred the bushes and enveloped me in a cloud of perfume. I was opening my canteen to water the source of the fragrance, when I was struck by the Chinese symmetry of my stay at Gooseberry Springs. The second hexagram, "Modesty", was the same I had received the day after my arrival at camp. Now it recurred on the day before I left. The first time it had resulted from changes in "Contemplation"; this time, from "Pushing Upward". It seemed to indicate that although the polarity of the two days was reversed, the results would be similar. Previously I had met the kings of old and had gone down to Devil's Slide; today, I would go up to the Lady and perhaps encounter a great personage.

Despite the favorableness of the oracle, the first half of the climb from Gooseberry Canyon was long and laborious. I stopped often to rest my legs, and once, exhausted, dropped heavily to the ground. When I got up, I noticed I had squashed a small plant beneath me. I became contrite, and my mind filled with speculations about death. I knew an essential function of the Nirmanakaya is to protect itself against death and, by extension, from ego death as well. Wise men of all times and places, however, have countered this limited understanding with the unconditioned declaration that there is no death for consciousness.

Such a concept is a paradox for the encapsulated ego, but if accepted, frees one from fear of the unknown.

I apologized to the little plant and was immediately filled with its freshly-crushed fragrance which structured itself as words. "We are not like people," wafted the fragrance. "We are differently conscious. When one of us dies, there is no diminution, and when all of us die, we hide in seed, and if the seed disappears, we catch a passing wave. I am eternal and can never be lost, because I always happen again." I was about to reply, but my clumsy karma completed itself first, when an ant and two flies simultaneously bit me as I stood.

I started on my way like a burst of pollen, and soon, much to my astonishment, was completely lost. I had somehow wandered off the clear and familiar trail, and when I awoke to the situation, I no longer knew whether it lay to my left or right. It was as if Iboga's magic mirrors had reappeared and transported me to a different world. I found myself in a strange but calming energy vortex, which I explored by emptying my head and steadying into its radiance. Suddenly I was flooded with a clear, visionary intuition of a brother who had died a few years earlier on the other side of the mountain. The intuition transformed itself into a remembrance of the man, then into the perfect present, where the Presence, shining through the trees, reminded me where I was.

I found the path without difficulty and went on to the top, feeling stronger with each step. At the juncture of the trails, I rested and mapped a strategy, then headed off cross-country toward the Lady's belly. The way was tortuous, winding through rocky areas flanked by scrub and cactus, where the stone moved underfoot. I crossed little flower-filled meadows among knee-high hedges, skirted areas of thick packed shin daggers, and crawled beneath tangles. The exercise was revivifying. I luxuriated in the musculature of my body and became absorbed in the yoga of moving. Consciousness flitted from sense to sense and then blended them all in a symphony of color, fragrance, and form given voice by my squeaking boots, birdcalls, and the windsong of rustled leaves.

Everything filled me with an immensity of sensation. I moved into a little clearing studded with fractured chunks of milk white quartz. I was stopped, spun around, and dropped to the ground. For a moment, I lay in a swirl, but this soon subsided, and my mind opened to a vision in which I saw the Mountain Lady's face with perfect clarity, exactly as it had been. Her countenance was more exquisite than life itself, for it contained more than life. Her skin was milk white quartz, her lips—rose. Vegetation framed her with hair and defined her features. A marvelous shrub, of a species unknown to me, formed the irises of her eyes that encircled crystalline pupils. Its many flowered tendrils undulated in the force field of the Lady's gaze, which was visible as beams of energy pulsing to and from the sky. Her left eye drew power from heaven, focusing it in her brain, where the benevolence of the universe transfigured itself into the creativity of the earth. The energy then radiated back through her right eye as a numinous stream of planetary information.

How elegant that face! How sublime the radiance of her smile! How well she followed the sun with her seasons! She flowered and pined, grew, polished herself with waters, with tears. Enraptured, I watched with my heart, until the face receded into its context in the reclining figure. I lifted my face and gazed up at her belly and breasts, where the seen and the envisioned merged. Stumbling to my feet, I let the Lady lead me on.

I crossed an outcropping of shattered white boulders embedded with milk and rose quartz, which I now knew had been the brain stuff of the Lady, the gemstone of her radiant presence. I sat among them, filled with a peculiar ecstasy of longing, a nostalgia for lost loveliness, realizing that these were the remnants of the jewel through which the kings of old had expressed their presence. The Lady smiled at my sad reverie, then with her eyes showed me her cosmic lover, opening me to the sentient space through which she, we, and our solar system move. There was a kiss, a brushing of ionized lips across her cheek, whisperings. For a moment, the universe was grounded, its incessant spirit tamed and made manifest by a mountain whose Lady slumbered beyond the edge of forgetfulness.

A force pushed me up and set me on my way again. I walked like a man drunk. The Lady's belly, with its avalanche scars and apron of brambles, its cactus, thorn, and jagged rock, seemed a garden of rarest delights and filled me with wave after wave of happiness. I made my way to the far side and sat on the white stone slabs that had originally triggered my epileptoid reaction to the mountain's destruction. Today they were benign and revealed the Lady as archetype of Eve, Gaea, and Tara, of the Empress Spider Woman. She was the universal mother in labor, a child of earth, yet manifestress of the universe and birthplace of creatures evolving eternally through the Presence.

By mid-afternoon the visions had passed. I was left spent on the rock, emptied and alone, energyless, and without care. I put up my sails and caught a passing breeze. It carried me across the Lady's belly and back to the trail. I continued on to the castles of rock and duplicated in infrared some pictures I had taken in color the previous day. Afterward, I sat on a battlement to smoke a pipe. I stayed to watch the sun drop behind the Lady, burnish her with gold, and halo her in purple. Satisfied, I wandered aimlessly down the long draw to Gooseberry Springs, to dinner and bed.

SEVENTEENTH DAY

Atop the Hill

Dawn woke me like an old friend, softly, with fingers of gold. It began with the treetops aglow and worked its way down, brightening as it came. Near the ground, the breeze conspired with it and swirled dusty pillars of light among the bushes of the side hill, rousing them to morning. The day was warm, and the forest was soon alive with its usual bustle. I sat in a spot of sunlight to nibble breakfast, assailed by the extravagance of my visions of the mountain. They seemed out of place, irrelevant to the accustomed life around me, and alien to the biospheric activity that marked the surface of the planet. I felt no need for distant places in time or space, and yet, like a volcanic plume on the mountain's side, I was filled with the magma of memory, and dazzling spurts of vision erupted in my sight.

I walked out to the circle and sat, pondering pictures. My rational mind confronted me with a battery of questions, to which I responded with silent bafflement. What mystery made this ancient temple, and what magic made me see it? What was this power that conspired with rock and spoke through mountainous sculptures? After a while, my cogitations resulted in a specific question, and I turned to the *I Ching* for an answer. Today I wanted to know what I knew more than what might happen to me, so I rolled up all of my doubts in a ball and threw it with the coins, asking specifically about the purpose of the mountain. A single hexagram was forthcoming. There were no changes, no alteration of its stately image. The *I Ching* responded once more with the sacred mountain, "Contemplation".

I sat with the unopened book on my lap, recalling the meaning of the hexagram. A person in the contemplative state and a sacred mountain are identical in that both express alignment with the one axis of the universe, along which the kings of old conspire with the earth and her creatures. I opened the book and read the hexagram again.

The mountain expressed itself clearly. It made no mention of perplexity, so I felt it wise to presume none. I dwelt instead on the given image and endeavored to conspire with kings. As my mind became still, I saw the earth as a living crystal suspended in space, tuned to a sentient cosmos. She was a middle child of an infinite family, stretching from quark, molecule, microbe, and man, to solar system, galaxy, and universe without end. All was in the palm of God's hand, and He with the eye of eternity gazed on all, equally, simultaneously, uninterruptedly: His gaze was the kings of old, forever attendant on His creation, ever watchful, ever filled with appropriate response.

I drifted into an eddy where thoughts again assaulted me, making mockery of my knowledge. I remembered the wretched condition of the modern world and wondered at the indifference of the kings. If they were eternal, they were now present, but must surely be looking the other way.

My face flushed with anger. A volatile consciousness, bordering on rage, throttled my equanimity and woke me to the conative process I was undergoing. I backed off and cooled down. The Presence, unperturbed by my disturbance, reminded me that pogroms and poverty occur when people worship such idols as money, power, and orthodoxy, but that no one is forced to worship false gods.

My mind turned on itself, confronting me with the madness and meanness of our species. I relived war. For fifteen years, it had been my calling, and I had always accepted it as a necessary part of an irrational process. Now my cynicism collapsed. We were but lemmings by a sea of blood, creatures driven by a need to self-destruct. Our brains have grown more lethal with every success, but the age-old ethical questions have remained unanswered. Why are the vulnerable exploited, why does power breed stupidity, why do the inferior aspects of the species so often triumph over our ideals, and why do the kings of old play only chess with earth? I thought of the wars I had known, and I wondered who had won and who had lost. What had Korea or Vietnam done for us? The Presence, in a kingly way, refused my pawn and showed me a queen whose dazzling raiment was the tapestry of Oriental culture from Buddha to Gandhi, from Confucius to Mao Tse-tung.

My Chinese friend called me back to a magical present, and I woke to myself in the City of Backward Changes, where causal processes are completed before they begin. A tangible time-aura encompassed events, and I existed in a warp where I saw things happening before they actually occurred. I thought of a tick, visualized it, and sometime later found it crawling on my leg. I also had a presentiment about the ravens who had played on the wind during my first day in the Saddle, and shortly thereafter large shadows slid along the side hill as the big black birds glided into the forest.

The tick reminded me that it was time to leave Gooseberry Springs, and that my days on the mountain were drawing to a close. I returned to camp and straightened it up for the last time; then I assembled the large pack and tied the sleeping gear beneath. Before closing the cupboard, I spread a feast of granola and sesame crackers for the mouse. I expected the walk to the ridge to be difficult with the heavy weight on my back and consoled myself that it was the last hard uphill climb I faced. As it turned out, however, the trek was easier than ever before. I chanted a Hindu mantra as I left Gooseberry Canyon and switched to a Buddhist one as I rounded Devil's Slide. Neither of them suited my mood, so I discontinued chanting. My body, however, was surging with energy that increased each time it was given vent. I sang out a resounding Aum, followed by a resonant Tao, then, much to my delight, I came up with a sprightly rhythm that matched my stride, accompanied by the words:

0! Holy Lord Jesus,
The One
Who most pleases
The people who we are
    Aum Tao . . .
0! Holy Lord Jesus,
The One
Who most pleases
The people who we are
    Aum Tao . . .
0! Holy Lord Jesus . . .

The repetition soon emptied my mind of trivia and put wings on my feet. I glided up the hill with ease, accosted by every passing beauty: veined rocks and moist-red earth, new flowers with butterflies to fondle them, the quartering moon through quivering aspen, and purple finches answering my song.

Twenty feet from the top of the hill, the last section of trail became steeper. I was happily plodding along, head down, pack balanced above me, not even aware that I was nearing the end of the climb, when I stopped for no reason and looked up. The trail, like a stream, meandered through flower-strewn grasses, and the trees to either side opened up as though I looked out from a cornucopia. Luxuriously laden branches silhouetted the deep blue sky and, standing between them, caught somehow in the tunneling matrix of my vision, was the Presence.

I saw this very clearly, yet there was nothing to see. Unadorned, naked, without form or substance, utterly intangible, and completely alive, this stood atop the hill and told me of Its standing. I gaped, then saw through, and beyond, to where a pure white cloud was born, nursed by the wind. The cloud took the shape of a dragon, complete in every detail: wispy mane, fiery breath, gleaming claws. His scales were magic mirrors reflecting the glories of earth, and I looked into them, seeing unearthly beauties. Then the dragon changed into a swan and swam off, leaving a wake of invisible bubbles.

I pushed on. Where the trail dipped down into the Saddle, I met a gopher snake sunning himself. He lingered for a portrait of his heat waves, then glided off. I continued to the Monuments and left my pack in the enclosed area below the Chalice. Then taking the pipe, I climbed to the top of the Pedestal to smoke once more in the lap of my dreamland.

What followed was like a movie. Some frames were thoughts; others, visualizations: a collage of memories, tinted with brush strokes of intuition and washes of fancy. Again, I watched the mountain's epic devastation, this time in silent wonder from afar. I relived the experience of flying the North Atlantic, of seeing the great meteorite and its fiery impact. I watched the earth tremble; then I refocused on the mountain. In exquisite, painless, soundless slow motion, I watched it disintegrate and fall as rubble. The earth reeled, dispelled her surface consciousness, and retreated to her healing core. Millennia passed in an instant, the mountain weathered to its present aspect, and a cooling breeze dried my cheek.

I returned to my pack for the camera and set off randomly around the Monuments and through the maze, etching fragments of what I saw on the silver of film. I soon came to one of the places where, entangled by the Lady Iboga, I had rolled about on a field of flowers. I had expected to confront devastation, so I was pleased to discover that hardly any trace of my passage remained. The sun, wind, and rain had done their work quickly, and all the flowers had recovered. I was sure they would never speak to me again, but again I was wrong.

They laughed aloud and assured me that they had enjoyed my rolling around on them. Many at once, then one by one, they recounted the tale of my hapless adventure. They swept me up in their narratives, and I saw myself on that wintry day, clutching the tarpaulin and mat, stumbling endlessly through the maze. My tormented body staggered through the howling wind like a toy figure in a bonsai pot. It tripped and fell, contorted, and rasped for breath. I felt no pain. It was only another silent movie, another visual memory acting itself out exogenously.

The sequence ended in merriment, for all the flowers started laughing, and I joined in. I chortled off, following my faint traces to where the rest of my gear was stashed. It was adequately, but clumsily wrapped, and its disarray transported me back again to the Iboga trip, this time with a deep sense of wellbeing. I took out some food, and although it was only late afternoon, I went off to the stream with the canteens and cooking gear. On the way, I marveled at a yucca I had often greeted in passing. It had then been bursting with buds but now was a glorious sight in full flower. I regretted not having the camera and decided to get a photograph of it later.

I was back at the Monuments for sunset and was just starting to fill the pipe when I remembered the small packet of marijuana buried in the Chalice. I dug it up and rolled a joint. I smoked on top of the Pedestal, adding a red ember to the convocation of pink, orange, and purple clouds disporting on a field of deepening blue. I remained until I felt the need for my sweater, then turned in instead of putting it on, anxious to get an early start in the morning for what would be the last acid trip of my stay on the mountain.

The Ancient Wanderer

There were meteors in the night, and I, out again from under the canopy of forest, woke and watched, quick to applaud their momentary, farewell debuts. The moon was off with the sun, leaving the field of night to the dimly streaming Milky Way, and the sunstars of our vicinity. Their crystalline shimmerings were muted by the lights of Palm Springs, but the majestic procession could not be stilled, until a red glow in the east became pink clouds bleaching to white, a brilliant orange sunrise, and the buzzings and birdsongs of another day.

I was up with the pink clouds, ate breakfast, and chanted the sun over the ridge. A few frames of infrared film remained in the camera, so I climbed to the top of the Monuments and photographed a bird's-eye view of the Pedestal and Chalice, curious what the heat-sensitive film would see in the still cool rock. My main objective was to complete the roll so I would not have to contend with changing it during the trip. When I finished, I loaded my last roll of color film and filled the small pack with what I would need for the day.

My plan was to turn on with LSD on top of the Serpent Tower and later, to smoke DMT. I lacked only the concurrence of the *I Ching*, so I took the book to the Chalice and sat facing the Mountain Lady. I was lightheaded and threw the coins high in the air, watching them turn over their answer as they fell. The first hexagram was "the Cauldron", or Ting, and is very favorable. The Ting is a ceremonial vessel from which food was served, and nine Ting were the symbol of sovereignty in ancient China. The Ting customarily resided in the family temple, where it was used for offerings to the ancestors; but at important feasts, the living were also served from the Ting. Thus the hexagram represents the continuity of human DNA, and I hoped it might also contain a key to its coding. The commentary on the image says that the superior person consolidates his fate by making his position correct. Since fate, in its physiological aspect is determined by DNA, I took it to mean that if I put my body in a suitable environment, I might actuate some primal genetic potential. Since the judgment on the hexagram promises success and good fortune, I assumed the Serpent Tower to be such a place. The changing line reiterates the good fortune but warned me to be cautious about where I went. It also mentions that there is still food in the Ting, prompting me to see the mountain as the Cauldron, where offerings were made and things blessed.

The second hexagram was the "Wanderer", as it had been during my full-moon trip two weeks earlier. It explains how to behave as a guest and stranger and emphasizes that it is a great thing to grasp the meaning of the time, for one is outside, in a strange land, and necessarily yielding.

I returned the *I Ching* to the large backpack and squirreled the whole thing away under some bushes. Then, crisscrossed by straps from the small backpack, two canteens, and camera, I set off up the trail. The morning was clear and verbosely alive. I sang as I went, now and then bubbling over with laughter. On the grade of the long switchback, a stillness fell about me, and I too, lapsed into silence. My heavy breathing was soundless, my footfalls felt rather than heard. At the crest of the second ridge, I climbed a huge boulder to view the Tower through the forest, but I was unable to see it. I knew its location, so I plunged off along the steep slope of the amphitheater and soon found traces of my last passage. I made no effort to follow them and generally stayed higher on the slope. Eventually I emerged above the great, rubble-strewn causeway leading to the broken Serpent, beyond which lay the Mountain Lady in splendor.

I rested for a while, then removed the acid stash from my pack and selected blindly from the bag until I had two colors. The result was one Krishna blue and two Sunshine; altogether, a thousand millionths of a gram of sacrament. I chewed the tablets, feeding their essence directly into my eyes and brain. The immediate response was a tingling in my teeth, and when I swallowed, a salutation/supplication to the Lady:

> Guide thee well my mind, my Lady
> Guide thee well your mind
> Guide its dreamings and its thought . . .
> Take me from behind

Guide thee well my eye, my Lady
Guide its motes and beams
Fill its seeing with your sight
Make it as it seems

Guide thee well my tongue, my Lady
Temper taste and talk
Bless these lips with song and speech
Soar me like a hawk

Guide thee well my arms, my Lady
Hold these fingered hands
Wield the pencil and the knife
Scribble in my sands

Guide thee well my legs, my Lady
Step upon these feet
Walk me as I walk alone
And find me when we meet.

I moved slowly across the causeway, exploring crevices, peering down precipitous sides, and crawling along ledges. A contingent of purple and green swifts discovered me and darted about enjoying the adventure as much as myself. At the end of the causeway, I confronted the climb to the top of the Tower. The acid was coming on quickly, and my body trembled as I made my way down. I was filled with an urge to continue over the last gap and jump out to the fallen-away portion. Fortunately, another part of me emphatically refused. I went instead to the western side of the platform and stowed the pack, camera, and canteens in shaded niches.

My body, covered with cold sweat, was shivering and shaking from the acid rush. I took off my shirt and sat in the sun, knowing I would be warmer as soon as the perspiration evaporated, then quivered until it did. I felt very weak, and soon even sitting became impossible, so I sprawled out full length on a shelf of white schist, oblivious to its embedded crystals.

The acid ate through my body, dissolving it. Rushes of energy, uncoordinated, came and went. For perhaps an hour the exculpatory process continued. Old behavioral circuits were demolished or refurbished; new ones, tentatively established. Showers of light turned dark, stillness supervened, and I, neither uncomfortable nor compelled, neither asleep nor yet awake, outwaited the necessities of an acid ablution.

Toward the end of this period, my consciousness re-emphasized its Nirmanakayaic aspect, and I was overwhelmed with feelings of desolation. I saw both past and future in terms of suffering, rejection, and pain. At first, these swirled about me ominously, then they became a torrent that washed me away. My body was racked with sobs, and tears ran copiously on the rock. I was battered by the ethical conundrums of my own life, and flayed by the endless cruelty of the world. The whole episode lasted five or ten minutes. Then, as quickly as it had commenced, it was gone, and my mind underwent an almost instantaneous reversal.

The transition was an ecstatic crescendo. That which was shattered became unified; that which was agitated, steadied; that which was full became resplendent. I breathed a deep sigh and relaxed completely. After a while, I rose to my hands and knees and looked about. Above, below, and beyond me, the whole world opened out in shining perfection. All wealth paled before the beauty I saw, and my heart, emptied at last of sorrow, opened like a blossom to the sun.

I got to my feet and walked among the rubble of the platform. My body was stunned with amazement but responded easily to its supporting environment and moved me with care. On the far side, it sat me on an overhanging ledge. A small bush poked out beneath my foot and beyond lay a thousand feet of shining space to the treetops of the plunging canyons. The swifts swept around my head, calling to the wind with piercing shrieks and filling my mind with the vibrance of pure sound.

I felt powerful, swirling energies. My body responded, my forehead glistened as its electromagnetics focused the force, impelling it inward and downward. My root chakra glowed like burning magnesium, but the energy was cool and controlled. Its radiance extended outside my body, and linked with the electromagnetic structure of the Serpent Tower. A pulse of energy ascended, discretely, from chakra to chakra. It leapt as sparks to the heart and fountained to the throat, where a single drop was caught and collapsed to a ball of fused brilliance, which burst into a universe of structured light spinning galaxies in free-flowing space.

The top of my skull dissolved in radiance, filling my brain chamber with a deep, still pool of opalescent liquid. A quantum of energy fell like a drop of dew and silvered the surface, which then shone like a magical mirror. Above and below reflected one another as well as themselves, their intermingling images configuring a multidimensional reality. The surface of the mirror bisected my eyes, and I saw myself as a creature of ten charkas: ten spheres of differently pulsing energy, five in the existent mirror below, five in the sky above, casting down images, gathering reflections.

A pulse began from the top, from out of the sky. Its appearance lighted up all my spaces, but then it entered time and ran me like a gauntlet. It pierced through my liquid surface like sunlight through clear water, bent slightly, then bottomed and bounced up again as kundalini, the serpent power, conveying the reality of the Dharmakaya into time-space as the image of what, but a moment before, it had prefigured by its descent into form. The serpent spiraled upward into the all-dissolving light, and I, coming back to myself, reached for its disappearing tail.

Permanence flew apart like pomegranate seeds that, blood red, rolled the rivulets of my brain and dripped from my hair into crimson oblivion. Dazed and delighted, I fell back onto the rock shelf, for none of my muscles cared to hold a body so otherwise abandoned . . . Self-luminous splendor rested in the void of annihilation. My residue was sucked into a black hole and disappeared, dying to be reborn as its sun, elsewhere. A bubble appeared and expanded, pushing away the primal blackness. The Presence as the omnipresent pivot, pump, and pulverizer, pulsed orgiastically and like a lady lay me open. I saw fifty million years in every direction, and tentacles of brain tissue read epochs of history, like Braille, from the dermatome of the eternally real.

A hundred billion images simultaneously danced on a single retina, trifled with the pictoscope of mind, and vanished. Before I thought, the earth thought for me, and I like an infant watched my dreaming mother bedeck her ages with unending configurations of Nirmanakaya. I took my place in the stream and drifted to the edge of dark and distant things, where a whirlpool pulled me down into another, newly arising rapture.

This, too, fell away, and my mind opened to a vast and empty distance. Time was without movement or beginning and yet formed the things that passed within its ken. I saw a sun appear, and with it came planets tuning its vibrance to a symphony of lives. With measured gait, through me, they moved, while I, as tenuous as the void, filled the immensity of abounding space and found it everywhere a firmament of forces. Hierarchies of intelligence were molded to gladdened life and sang secrets of that Presence wherein the structure of cosmic intelligence mirrored itself as the universe of form.

The visionary sun shone with the brilliance of its cosmic essence. Accompanied by planets, satellites, and force fields, it spiraled through me, displaying its many-leveled sentience. The system formed a unity, all of whose parts knew themselves as members of a solar family. They talked and played among themselves and, in some mysterious manner, cavorted with others who inhabited a congruent matrix in the parent galaxy. For a moment, I eavesdropped but heard no more than murmurs of delight before space itself, like a dark cloud of its denser material, wrapped around me. Caught unaware, I struggled like a child with a blanket, until my head poked out to a real and dazzling sun, whose searing Sahara beneficence enlivened my whole world, and with equal dignity, cast me as shadow.

I was parched and returned unsteadily to my water. I drank, then settled back against a shaded rock, the open canteen forgotten in my hand. Like water, I slipped through the closed places of life and swirled about guarded treasures. A trove of rare and costly things appeared, but my unbiased Nirmanakaya accepted nothing. The treasures formed a mandala from which the Sambhogakaya opened out as pantheons of ancient knowledge. From out of time, vast libraries appeared, aged to dry tinder, then burst into living flame when touched by a remembrance of the Dharmakaya. Everything was synchronistic, all thoughts concise. No causal process appeared before form froze it to recognition; neither manifestation nor meaning; nothing to be noticed by that which would dally in time.

Galaxies spun, spent their energy, and spawned. Time, like a cannibalistic fish swam through space, mouth agape. I floated within it, seeing my own evanescence magnified to a purview of the modern workaday world, caught in its cycles of weekends and vacations, vaguely oppressive, toilsome, punctuated with periods of sleep, boredom, and restless leisure.

Somber time chortled in my ear. Other dimensions had he, and some he showed in holographic detail: the time of a mathematician toying with infinitesimals, and that of an astronomer playing with infinities. Chronologies of history unrolled like embroidered tape, and the epochs of anthropology stacked up like reels. Finally with modest dignity, old Chronos unveiled an ancient splendor: the unending time of childhood, filling itself with fantasies elsewhere true.

Then time turned to stare at me, blinked like his seasons, and pushed me out into an ulterior illusion. I tumbled headfirst to the unreferential now, which, like blue sky hiding stars, hid all other times from view and skewered me on its intersection with space. Here, time and space mirrored one another, and I the eye before beheld their changings and was satisfied.

I awoke to the canteen in my left hand and my fingers screwing its cap back on. I returned it to the crevice and stood again in the sun. I needed exercise, so I did some twists and stretches and began climbing about the rocks. I soon came to a large gabbro protuberance, about ten feet tall, which stood like an old black tooth on the forward lip of the Tower. The shelf at its base slanted into the abyss between the two portions of the platform, blocking the view down. It sloped steeply, so I lay on my belly and inched out, peering over the edge. The position was hazardous but the perspective fascinating. The rock plunged vertically in sliced planes and cleavages, framing both sides of the chasm with jagged sky. Fifteen feet down was a ledge, beneath which the two columns of the Tower were close enough to climb between. Below this were other ledges and rock jams that would have eased the going if I had been climbing, but they blocked my view and hid several interesting recesses, any of which might have been an entrance to the Serpent.

I felt a strong urge to descend into the fissure but knew I would have to return the way I went. I eyed the situation critically. My only problem was the first fifteen feet, but this seemed insurmountable, for my body was in no shape for gymnastics. Instead of pushing on, I rested with my chin on the rock and lost myself in the patterns below. The sun poured over my back and streamed into the abyss, where shadows like sirens molded my gaze and invited me to descend. But I, flattened on the rock, set only my fancy free. Immense were the halls of that distant time, whose doors were unsealed for a moment and swung inward. The earth shifted, exposing her broken heart. I trembled on the far side of anguish, then appeared within the Lady where she slept, nursing a wounded brain, her daytime forgotten, her nighttime a tangled dream of history's tattered web. Pain and suffering gushed from her shattered cup of sorrows, and bottomless was her despair.

My heart was compressed under the onslaught. It glowed, became magnetically critical, and drew the rest of me to itself, where the nightmare resolved into a deeper perfection. I saw the Lady in her eternal aspect, immortal, flawless, forever most lovely. As Mother of Ages, she showed me our ancient brethren and the times before she, devastated, had slipped into herself to sleep and heal, to gestate a new world from the relics and remembrances of the old.

Mighty were our ancestors in the secrets of the earth, for they were the voice by which she spoke to her kindred, even as eagles were her wings; cats, her wariness; and serpents, her extension into darkness. Binding these into one consciousness, she projected an earth impulse into space. In a mountainous womb, the assembled entity was fused with an umbilical cord of earthcore energies and loosed to the perfecting power of the Dharmakaya. There it was purged, ungrounded, and dispatched, to appear elsewhere in the earth's stellar matrix of compatible heaven-worlds. An earth lover, lost in the galaxy, dreaming an unthinkable thought, was reawakened and brought to birth on another, distant world; there to be honored and tended as a guest until returned through the medium of mind to the magical mountain of earth. The chasm cooed with wind, and I awoke to the mountain as though it were within me, suspended like an ovum on the blood-rich placenta of the earth. I was filled with wonder, for its form and my own were the same. The serpent was I, and the lion, and I the expectant one whose belly was teeming with cosmic life. From me, galactic spirits emerged to walk my earth as Nirmanakaya, as children of my family. Magnificent were these teratoids, creatures of elsewhere: tranquil, energetic, golden breasted, aura-encompassed. They told wonders through the medium of mind, till I, confused, knew not whether I listened or spoke.

The wind woke me by its absence, and I became aware of my ears straining after the Lady's last whisperings. She ended with a feathered sigh, like angel wings beating the air above me. I listened awhile, then looked up. Amitabha Bird was hanging two feet off in the abyss.

"Hello!" I said. "What are you doing here? You're a long way from home."

"Watching you," he replied. "And I'm not very far from anywhere."

I looked past him to the treetops of Gooseberry Canyon poking above the ridge from the Mountain Lady's shoulder. "I guess you're right," I admitted. "But how did you find me?" He scooted to six inches from my nose and looked me in the eye. "Truthfully," he confided. "You are rather difficult to lose. Everybody keeps telling on you, besides which you throb."

"I do?" I asked. "I mean I know I do, but I didn't know it was noticeable."

"Of course, it is," said the bird. "Your head is as red as mine and thumping like a pheasant."

I blushed at the reproach, but it added nothing to my color, for my face was already fully flushed from hanging over the edge. I wriggled backward up the slope. When I sat up, everything inside me snapped and crinkled. I looked quickly at Amitabha Bird, but he ignored my noises and disappeared down the fissure.

I spaced out while awaiting his return, but when after a few minutes he did not re-emerge from the chasm, I went back to the canteens and treated myself to more ambrosia. The drink was one of the most amazing I had ever taken, as though a mummy, after ten thousand years in desiccating sands, had been resuscitated with a chilled glass of champagne. My body tingled with exhilaration, and I laughed, then shouted for joy. My voice projected to the encircling crags, who gustily sang it back, for the midday wind was stilled, and the retiring nymph, Echo, on the loose. She teased me, led me on. I called out AUM, and she responded AUM. I sang a loud TAO, and the whole amphitheater hummed with approval. Breathing deeply several times, I snapped my diaphragm and let out short, staccato bursts: BU-DA! BU-DA! Echoes like lightning strikes reverberated from every side. The noise was notes. I called it music and let it orchestrate a symphony of radiant sound thoughts. In the midst of this, the mountain manifested as the Ting of the morning's *I Ching*, and I as a nibbler at the feast. My body overflowed with ecstasies, and I dropped to my belly, to cling to the warm stone and gaze from my precipice at the deep valleys below.

A distant cloud, like a wisp of smoke, reminded me that my pipe and hashish were also contents of "the Cauldron". The pack was at my side, so I fumbled with my funny fingers and soon had cannabis clouds issuing from my mouth. Like cleansing vapors, they polished the mirror behind my eyes. I saw it seeing me seeing myself, then watched it laugh at both, but while thus distracted, an intimation of something profound slipped past my thinking and vanished before I grasped it, leaving naught but the knowledge that the last moment is first to be nonexistent and takes with it what it will. I smoked again and backtracked to the immediate past, but found only my mirror reflecting the future. Like a photon, I bounced off and reentered myself inside out. Mirror images clung to me like static, and words echoed before they were spoken, sounding riddles:

> The only future is the now of the Tao
> The only past has passed
> So running backward out of time
> Is neither slow nor fast.

It sounded like gibberish since I was already caught out of time, and I wondered how I could escape if running forward was now backward. An ego, one of many in my stable of determinatives, rose to the occasion and disputed everything by maintaining that it was not *how* but *when* that was important. The mirror before my eyes reflected my thinking by fogging over, but then an unseen finger wrote words on the steamy glass:

> When should be forgotten
> When is not a fact
> When is when the now again
> Continues to come back.

It was too confusing, so I got up and walked in a little circle, shaking my head. I spied the chasm dividing the platform and remembered I had been unable to climb down into it. Thinking a second try would divert me, I went back and bellied out again. Amitabha Bird had been waiting below and took to the air as soon as my head appeared over the edge. He slipped through my aura and figured out immediately what I was up to. He spoke, and I clearly heard words in English: "No need, brother," he said. "I can tell you all that is down there."

I thanked him, but told him I wanted to see for myself because I was sure I could make it. I became actively involved in planning the initial descent. Amitabha Bird stayed a few minutes to observe my fumbling lack of progress and then flew off without comment. Shortly thereafter, I inched back up and returned to the canteens. I supplemented a drink with raisins and dates. For dessert, I had another pipe, and for pleasant company started a conversation with the Mountain Lady. I looked into her hidden eyes and saw the whole mountain contained in its creatures, yet containing them. I strove to see deeper, to grasp an unthinkableness, and like a child about to be conceived was enveloped by the imaginings of my mother . . . The sacred mountain thought, remembering its origin. Simultaneously movement and echo, grand designs and gracious implementation of powers: thus did the lovely Mountain Lady come to birth, molded from earth by the fingers of God.

I bowed before the weight of the ephemeral vision, and, though gazing at the rock at my feet, I saw the firmament above. Dark stone mimicked the emptiness of space, from which a current of energies poured down as sentience, existence, and life, revealing the Mountain Lady as a self-conscious, self-formed artifact. Through her the earth articulated essence and spoke through time in the oratory of creation.

Supernovae flashed as she slept, woke, and slept again; always to new wonders, new dreams. She now drifts on her primal source to the place in time of her next awakening, and morning dreams, like clearing storms, dispel the illusion of sleep. I stood, and the pillar on which I stood reached to heaven. Light touched the limit of the universe and was back again. A ladder it was, a staff, a pole, a pillar of fire, a tongue of earth, an axis of creation . . . and on this I rose . . . till she, in holy wonder, cast me down, and I awoke upon a pediment of rock, with all my dreams spread out before me, unforgotten once again in the re-emergence of time, and time's mistress, herself a beckoning presence, wrapped round me like a robe of unburning fire and warmed her mountain with a radiance of light.

I remained for a long while gazing at the desert. Then I returned to the edge of the chasm, drawn once more to find a way down. Again I failed, and did little more than lie out on the rock for more excursions into stoned consciousness. They soon woke a thirst, and having finished the large canteen, I started on the small one. I realized I was consuming water more rapidly than I had expected, for it was still early afternoon, and leaf-like, I was expiring to the sun. I slowed the process by sitting in a shady crevice; then I ate more raisins and remembered the DMT.

I groped in the pack for my special joint and discovered the nylon cord for stringing the tube tent. I had forgotten all about it but immediately decided it was what was needed for conquering the chasm. Leaving the joint where it was, I returned to the abyss. Somehow I managed to tie a bowline in one end of the cord and throw a loop around a boulder. I pulled on the cord as hard as I could. It was thin, stretched considerably, and cut into my hands, but it held. Feeling somewhat less than secure, I snaked my way down the sloping rock face, keeping the line taut behind me. I went further over the edge than I had dared before and almost reached a point of no return, but the nylon became so taut I feared it would snap. I used it to pull myself gingerly back: then I gave up on the whole project and looked in vain for Amitabha Bird, who might have told me what lay hidden below.

Disappointed, albeit relieved, I exchanged the nylon cord for the DMT joint and spent the next fifteen minutes wandering the platform in search of the best place to smoke it. I finally settled cross-legged on a level stone above the chasm. Ahead was the fallen-away lip of the Tower, and beyond, across the divide of time and space, lay the Mountain Lady in the lap of majestic San Jacinto.

The sun was high over my left shoulder and brilliant in the clear air, but it became even brighter as the first of the DMT's acrid smoke caressed my lungs. Space turned to diamond in which all appearances were fissures, creating irises and dazzling reflections. Enraptured, I smoked again.

Softly radiating, the Mountain Lady beamed back my love. She moved as though gently breathing, and all the great mountains behind her filled with wonder. She sighed. All else became more still than ever before, and beauty, like moisture, condensed from the air.

Unnoticed, the joint again found my lips, and my undoing progressed like a blossom opening. The flower was the lotus of the Lady who, in a most ancient language, spoke.

Said she words so very lovely
Spoke she things I cannot say
Told she memories of tomorrow
And the grandeur of her day.

Sang she music of her chambers

Hummed she chords that ringed like trees
Played she notes of clearest timbre
Through her owlings and her leaves.
Whispered softly, whispered softly
Whispered tenderly to me
Who like flotsam on the ocean
Told of what no one could see.

Olden dreams forever fallen
Ancient memories laid to rest
For the presence of the Lady
Stilled the tremblings of her guest.

Till her world became a wonderland
Where sun and son did meet
In a burst of golden innocence
Beneath her prismed feet.

Whose firm flesh was nothing solid
Whose domain was all things gone
Whose one step took one to nowhere
Like a half remembered song . . .

My head dipped, shifting my gaze to my bare feet. They were utterly relaxed and shimmering, sentient in their walking ways. My hands touched the upturned soles, and my fingers caressed the shoe-softened surfaces. Then, slowly, my hands turned palm up, exposing their own self-consciousness to my eyes. They were independently alive and exuded the most intense loveliness: each pore pulsed with life, each cell sang an anthem. Under my scrutiny, the flesh metamorphosed until it was covered with a mazework of intricate glyphs, so small my eyes had to multiply their lenses in order to distinguish them. Each glyph was amazingly delicate, but they were so thickly concentrated that it seemed as if all the glyphs of the mountain had been compressed to the size of a glove and slipped over my hand. The electromagnetics of flesh became visible, radiating mandalas. The pattern of glyphs began to structure my mind and hint at their decipherment. My gold and silver rings, like cyclotrons, focused flowing energies, and shafts of light poured from my fingertips.

Unity, like a whisper bursting a bubble, completed the complexity of mind with its fleshy extension. My hand composed my head, and I, intelligibly lost in the Dharmakaya of proto-space-time, swam as an ancient entity through the soft radiances of nowhere. Untutored and unalone, I navigated by hand, for inscribed across my palm was a multidimensional chart of the heavens, and the places to which I was attuned were marked by points of irresistible light.

I outwaited an eternity; then my fingers closed, and the palms turned inward, shyly taking themselves from my view as though I had gazed too long on their nakedness and was in danger of succumbing to their beauty. A wavelet of energy pulsed from my throat chakra, ran down my arms, and crested magically in my hands. They lifted from my lap and began to form patterns in the air. Coaxing and corralling energies, they built them up and bound them with threads of remembrance. As weavers they wove pictures and told stories to the sky, who responded with other fingers that played my chakras like a harp.

The joint was out, less than half smoked, but I had no urge to relight it immediately. I leaned back and lost myself in the immensity before me. A half hour later, with the DMT experience fading, I again studied my hand, hoping to find a clue to the secret of the glyphs. They were no longer visible, though the flesh was still pulsing slightly and was aesthetically alive. But I did not understand it and felt perplexed. The Presence wafted through like a zephyr, reminding me that my hands were completely alive to their own domain and that I did not have to understand them, because they understood themselves. Then, as though to emphasize this, consciousness itself became tangible for a moment, and I saw an infinite series of structured matrices wherein the asleepness of individual identity confronted the mysteriousness of others in dream worlds of separate-seeming entities. I saw that my hand and I were neither separate nor the same, neither attached nor unattached. Consciousness was universal, everywhere centered, every center seeming separate. My body and I, like sides of a pyramid, joined in a higher order dimensional space, whose mystical angularity molded my many faces and composed the substance within.

The afternoon colors were beautiful, so I took the camera and climbed about the platform taking pictures. Afterward, I repacked the pack and found another spot to continue with the DMT. From where I settled, the large protuberance on the platform's lip partially blocked the view ahead and loomed above me in geometries of broken stone. I decided to ascend in stages, so I stuck the DMT joint between my toes and stoked the hash pipe. I took two hits on it, hyperventilated until my system was suffused with oxygen, and lit the DMT. I held a lungful of smoke as long as I could, watching in fascination as my perceptual networks shifted from organic to electromagnetic modes of functioning. Then they melted into the content I contemplated.

The mountainscape transfigured. I saw the great peaks of the San Jacintos as the sacred mountains of China, and flowing from them in stately procession was the long lineage of Chinese emperors, from Fu Hsi to Mao Tse-tung. The peaks became the mountains of heaven, not so much a view as an encasement. With another toke, the reality-vision emptied of meaning, transcended samsara, and left me in a shimmering void.

The megalithic protuberance rearing before me caught my attention. It was animate as a gigantic serpent's head whose fiery, bejeweled eyes stared down at me. Scales of organic stone shifted like iron mail, and a palpable force issued from the creature's mouth, grasping me like a prehensile tongue. It tried to draw me in, but I held my place. Suddenly, with the awakening of a deep genetic memory, its form encompassed mine, and vast powers conspired to undo the universe, encircle it like an ouroboros, and remake it anew.

Theriomorphic forces filled the space of the encounter. A beam of energy surged from the Tower, gushed from my head, and fountained up for a thousand feet. I soared on it while that within which knew my going, drew me out to the eurhythmic ether, where a hybrid sentience awaited an earth pulse to depart.

I called again on the DMT to hasten my departure. The smoke dissolved my lungs, and the remnants of my body crumbled into the void. Seemingly liberated, I steadied for the leap, but death himself, the dark angel, loomed before me. He spoke in majestic tones with utter finality, saying that all besides himself was illusory, that none escaped nor departed his hold, that neither hope nor faith prevailed beyond his portal.

Death neither laughed nor was hideous, but implacably stared me down. I fled into the depths of my own eyes, but he outflanked my defenses and reappeared in the optic nerves, freezing them. My Nirmanakaya dissolved into the mothering, all-encompassing Sambhogakaya, but death still lurked within, and I, astounded, leapt to empty space and found him as a black hole vacuuming God's antechamber.

Cornered in nothingness, I reversed myself and lunged at death, plummeting into him with all the vibrance of my life. There was a stunning relaxation and I fell with open eyes into a terminal reality.

I sat like a flame on a candle of stone and watched the exquisitely beautiful world dissolve under the impact of the new vision. The vast mountainscape became ashes, then, phoenix-like, it arose from itself, pondered its fate for a cosmic instant, and turned to ash again. I watched without pain, but not without compassion, and the tears dripping from my eyes fell away into the knowings of eternity.

Sometime later, my protoplasm resumed its mundane functions and busied itself with an inventory. I was a body slumped against a rock, exuding awe, but still seemingly alive. I straightened myself, wobbled to a more comfortable position, and reached into the pack for my notebook. The experience had left a verbal residue, and I was possessed with the desire to write something down. I fumbled awkwardly to do so. I held the pen differently than ever before, and the handwriting did not seem to be mine. I saw the page as a white cloud and the tracing of blue ink as the sky breaking through, crafting its meaning on my lap.

So now I sit awaiting my body's readiness to move.

I have been forcing myself through death and the intensity of the brilliance enlightens everything, which then wishes so very greatly for the so accustomed darkness to again envelop it, so thus does my body appear. And its animated otherness, its being dead to me who so like a ferret do inhabit it. Thus the monk-monks of the Monuments.

How so incredibly humbling is the marvelousness of the Experience. And the joint has gone out. O Holy Father My God Aum Tao.

The notebook closed on the pen and slipped from my fingers. Later, my legs became sturdy again and lifted me up. I stretched like a cat after napping, until surges of new vitality coursed through my body, telling me it was ready to move. I dressed and repacked. The remnant of the joint lay on the rock, so I picked it up, kissed it, and tucked it away, thinking to smoke it later in the Chalice, under the stars.

I bid the Serpent Tower good-bye and climbed from the platform. I was not steady enough to be venturesome on the crossing to the ridge, so I stayed to the middle of the causeway. Halfway across, a small, beautifully proportioned spruce grew like a Christmas tree from a fissure in the rock. Its aura was so tangible I was sure I could capture it on film, but while trying to do so, I became caught up again in the consciousness of serpents. The vision began with the diamondback rattlesnake of the Waterfall. His phantom spiraled about the tree, then metamorphosed. Its sensuous form replaced by the electromagnetic gridwork of his species' Sambhogakaya. We talked of arcane things, but when I later awoke to myself, I remembered only that I had conversed with the Great Serpency and dallied again in his company.

Bedazzled, I Aum'd my way onward. The end of the causeway abutted on a low tangled forest of oak. There were murmurs among the trees as I approached, and as I stooped low to pass beneath the branches of the first, it very distinctly said: "Hello, sir!" It sounded like a navy bo'sun and took me completely by surprise. I stood up in amazement, poking my head through his branches and leaves. This made the nearby trees chortle, and soon the whole grove was laughing.

I could not help but join in, and by the time I got clear of them, tears of hilarity were streaming down my cheeks, and a full crew of rollicking oaks was guffawing behind me.

The laughter was a catharsis, but as it died down with distance, it left me empty, and I experienced my walking as though I were pure space moving through itself. This, in turn, tuned me to a specific cognitive set that I already knew as my navigator's head. The mountain in its totality was a topographical space within me, and I could see exactly where I was in relation to anywhere I wanted to go. I remembered a large outcropping of dark rock shaped like the three pyramids of Giza, which I had seen from the Serpent Tower, so I used my reawakened positional sense to take me there. I found it and explored its environs. The pyramid shapes were huge, solid chunks of granite with crevices and overhangs, but no caves or hollows to probe. They did, however, push the forest back, providing an unobstructed view across the amphitheater to the broken Serpent. While photographing it, I remembered the full-flowering yucca by the trail to the spring. I also wanted its picture and realized that I could probably get back in time to catch it at its best, just before the sun dropped behind the ridge.

Calling on my navigator's head, I set off more or less directly through the forest. I detoured to check other outcroppings, but tarried nowhere for long. I was completely conscious of myself as a path-following animal with a sure instinct. When I eventually happened on the trail, I followed it without breaking stride. Almost immediately thereafter, however, I became lost. The path went off, and I went off it, and when I finally realized what had happened, the trail was nowhere to be found.

I was out of the forest, somewhere on the backside of the second ridge. The terrain was steep, occasionally terraced, dotted with huge boulders, and covered with scrub, shin daggers, and cactus. I knew that somewhere below me the trail curved, so I continued down through the brush. En route, I came on an outcropping that acted as a retaining wall. I climbed to the bottom where the feeling of the place slowed me. There were flowers everywhere, smells, and cool shadows among the rocks, which themselves seemed more like the walls of a temple garden than an accumulation of rubble. I had no intention of stopping and hesitated only to breathe deeply of its fragrance. But then I noticed a melon-sized hole in the wall, and a sparkle within caused me to examine it more closely. Sprinkled inside like the constellations of heaven were hundreds of tiny crystals.

The hole was just large enough for my head, so I doffed pack and canteens and knelt before it. I led with my chin, then followed gingerly with my skull until I was embedded in stone up to my ears. My cheeks and forehead pressed into crystals, and as I grew accustomed to the darkness, my mind opened out like an organic planetarium encompassing aspects of deep space. Brightly colored lines, like laser beams, sliced through my vision and toyed with other dimensions. Gradually the lines faded; the space solidified to star-encasing crystal, then shattered silently to void, where energy bedazzled thinking and all dreams fell away.

Later, no memory remained, and it seemed as though a snippet had been cut from the veil of my life. But through that hole light poured, and when I came to myself on the ground, sitting before the marvelous womb in the rock, I was tingling with astonishment. Aware that I was a guest in a sacred grove on a sacred mountain, I paid what obeisance I could to its reigning spirits, thanked them for their magic, and left the place in awe. I had delayed fifteen or twenty minutes and was not sure I could still get to the yucca before sunset, but I decided to assume that if I hurried I could make it. Fifty yards farther down, however the way became impassable. I could see the trail some distance below, but the way between was choked with vegetation, and I had to backtrack.

I skirted the denser scrub and was passing about twenty yards from the magical grove when suddenly, very emphatically, I was filled with the sense that I had not done the place justice. The force of the realization startled me into reassessing my position. If I went back to the grove, I would miss photographing the yucca, but now this seemed unimportant, so I altered heading and returned to the rock with its keyhole to eternity.

The grove welcomed me like the smile of a friend. I had little water left, but I poured some on the flowers and took a last mouthful. The sun was behind my shoulder as I gazed again into the bejeweled niche. The crystals sparkled, casting tiny, peaked shadows, which, as I drew closer, looked like mountains on the moon. As my head slipped into the stone, the shadows were replaced by my own, and jeweled peaks pressed into my flesh. There was a moment of adjustment, a pause, then the birth of sentient light. The crystal consciousness of the earth shone all around. Pure and transparent to its depths, utterly clear, it surpassed conciseness, for it fathered each distinction and mothered every contradiction. An invisible wave undulated through it, ringing like a silent bell which, resonating, rang me.

The wave receded. I steadied to stillness, and motion departed. All about was frozen wonder which, at a pointless point in its centerless center, turned through itself and involuted reality.

I awoke in the Sambhogakaya and there saw a being of vast and eternal aspect, who presented herself as the sky-encompassing figure of a great lady contemplating the universe within her. She turned and, as a mother on awakening sees first to her infant, looked at me. Then she, too, dissolved, and a resplendent reality revealed itself as brilliance.

Time departed. Light pulsed inward. Returning to its source, it collapsed on itself and ignited as a small sphere of plasma in the breathlessness of space. A nebula condensed around it, and planets appeared to weave a filament of energies about their shining lord. The stellar system twisted toward me, and I, fascinated, drew nearer.

The star and its dancing planets moved through me as a family of intelligent orbs, omnidimensionally involved with themselves and their galaxy. Beams of force pierced the Dharmakayaic blackness, which, through a visionary finesse, muted the tones of the fiery universe to the soft colors of life and tended the development of civilizations.

The sun-star sparkled like a perfectly sentient diamond, taking pleasure in his children. They basked in his stimulating, life-giving rays and swirled through my center as an eternally joyful expression of God's mind. But suddenly, from out of the pregnant emptiness, came another, similar to the lord, but smaller, older by far in the cycle of present existence, dark, and fallen in upon itself in the consummation of immense age: a cold star, tiny, barely radiating, lightless for a billion years, almost without memory, adrift in the ancient wonder of space, and falling through time to the compelling lusters of the young and shining sun.

The old one reached for the younger and entered the circles of his family. Strange eddies coursed through the ether, attractions and welcomings; but there was also care, consternation. Guided by their dexterous lord, the family of planets shifted to accept the newcomer.

Regal fingers reached out, touching the visitor, guiding his fall, and leading him to a safe orbit in the space newly created for him.

The ancient one approached in a gallant arc and dove past his new lord. Passing perihelion, he made a courtesy obeisance, and started away again, but the forces in the near vicinity of the young giant were too strong, or perhaps the ancient wanderer himself too weak, for he shuddered beneath their impact and wavered. Immense fields of power, like those once his, now tore at his innards. Astounded to wakefulness, he lunged on, but lagged also, with one part pulling ahead, another hanging back. He quivered and stretched, pulled oblong and exploded into pieces, spewing plasma across the sky.

A shock wave coughed through my space, distorting it. Remnants of the ancient one spun away from each other, loosed as belching demons into space. Throughout the family, disharmonies erupted, and long-standing resonances were overwhelmed. The lord struggled for control, but it was as though he held scorpions in his hands, their stings paralyzing his fingers.

The surging spheres of galactic plasma wreaked havoc among the children of the sun. Planets were pulled out of orbit, and satellites ripped from their hosts. One world was swallowed, another seared, another smothered, another sliced by swords of primal fire, as the wrathful demons thundered through the startlement of space and feasted on the efforts of aeons.

Stupendous was the destruction! Awesome and awful the contortions, the shriekings of rendered worlds, the death screams of planetary lives. Existential pain, like some great ecstasy exceeded crackled through every fiber of my being and preconative suffering shredded my heart. I could endure no more. My mind was obliterated, and my body of its own weight fell backward.

When I came to myself, my nervous system was smoldering, my memory shattered, and nothing remained but awe in the face of eternity and amazement at the mysteries of the earth. I was propped against a nearby boulder, weeping, but everything around me shone, and the light itself was my healing companion.

I bowed to the Presence and started on my way again. I found the trail without difficulty and shortly thereafter encountered a reddish brown rattlesnake. He crossed my path and slipped in among the branches of a manzanita. He was the color of the bark, and disappeared even as I looked at him, but his ability to control my sight seemed more than camouflage, for I felt him turning my eyes off and on at will. We held a conversation that climaxed in a medley of rattles and Aums. Spellbound, I spun on my heel and careened off down the trail. I laughed aloud and started singing to the smiling Presence:

> Aum Tao, Brother
> Thank you for the marvelous touch!
>
> Aum Tao, Brother
> Thank you for the marvelous touch!

A hundred yards further on, my singing conjured up yet another rattlesnake, this time a small diamondback coiled on the trail. He was very mellow, disturbed neither by my footfalls, nor by my taking his picture, and when I Aum'd good-bye, he caught the sound from the air with the tips of his tongue and slipped it inside for inspection.

Another twenty yards, and I was bitten. I saw it happen from hypertime, where both my organic and electromagnetic perceptual systems were functioning simultaneously, and the event, which to eye and ear alone was quite startling, left me unperturbed. I had been lustily singing my new song when I stepped on a stick whose other end jumped out of the bush and struck me on the wrist. Although I registered the sequence of events in extreme slow motion, the action was far too fast for my body to avoid. The tip of the branch was forked, and its two sharp points punctured my flesh, leaving a perfect imitation of fang marks. As twin drops of blood oozed out, I licked them away, wondering what strange karma had been repaid with a stickbite.

I crossed the Lion's back singing and descended along his rib cage with a chant. At the Monuments, I drank my fill and watered the flowers of the Chalice; then I set off for the spring. The yucca was already in shadow, but I took his portrait anyway, thanking him for his foot-guiding function in my day. He was a friendly yellow giant, who spoke fragrances through his thousand-petalled lips and responded by drenching me with perfume.

Twilight in the Chalice overtook me scribbling in my notebook, and I finished with the flashlight propped on a stone at my side. A curious moth played in its light until her shadow dance wooed me from my own. I remembered the remnant of DMT, but knew I was too tired to smoke it. Instead, I made a cup of bouillon and savored it on top of the Pedestal; then, wishing the stars good night, I melted back into earth.

NINETEENTH DAY

Return

My night of sleep and wakings was a tortuous road that tunneled through successive crests of the mountain. An aching body and vacuous mind followed the road, and when it ended in morning I was sore everywhere, though still very stoned. A few cobwebs had collected in my brain, so I took the hashish to the Chalice and offered a morning pipe to the Mountain Lady. The smoke reanimated my electromagnetics and wonderland reassembled around me. The air was laden with fragrances and utterly still, but I heard a humming coming from above, as though a breeze was caressing a forest. I looked up. The old derelict pine of the Chalice was singing a song to the mountain.

The music wove a filigree of images through my mind's eye, into which the pine projected herself, saying she could see as well as I, for her bark was no different than my turned-on skin: a transparent eyelid through which she saw her guides and mentors who were the force fields of the mountain. They revealed other objects in space, their relationships to her, and, if mobile, their intentions toward her. This seemed quite marvelous, so I confided that her lidded eye saw a dimension beyond mine, for I only saw things, not intentions. But she pointed out that in the Presence, intention and movement are the same, and everyone is exactly where he is due to his intention to be there. She said the real difference between us lay in how we reacted to the constantly shifting energies of the cosmos. She, being well rooted, had perfect faith in them; whereas I, rootless and footloose, was moved by them according to my attraction to their wiles. She accepted change, while I ignored it by embodying it, and I used it to leap from place to place, forever chasing my perception of the past.

I lay on my back and noted the inverted imagery of the pine tree, rooted to heaven with branches and upholding the Chalice as though it were an offering from above. The picture conjured up the image of "Contemplation", a tree on earth intelligently commingling the biosphere with the downpourings from Dharmakayaic space. I explained to her that she embodied one of our species' sacred metaphors and asked if being rooted was responsible for the elegance of her communion. She replied that digesting earth directly made one appreciate existence before life, but that to her understanding, animals were no different, for the empty space within each particle of everything is the same, and it is there that God exists. The accomplishment of animals, she continued, is their ability to move about while keeping an immovable center. Reference to this center shows them how to conduct themselves. She paused for a moment, then assured me that loss of contact with one's center was not really loss of contact, but merely a perceptual breakdown caused by sensory overload. However, since this immovable center is the vortex of the Dharmakaya, any loss of perception concerning it is a drastic fall and diminution of capability.

The matriarch of the Chalice was vibrantly alive and exquisitely beautiful, yet more than half of her was snag, and weathered to dead, gray wood. She told me this in no way lessened her capacity to see, nor would it when she was all dead wood, for every expression of creation experiences the creative force differently, but completely. I was impressed, but could not overlook the fact that she was bereft of pine cones while other trees were covered, and it occurred to me to plant a cone among her roots. She approved and told me of a tree in a turret on the desert side of the Monuments, which was her seed-mate, and from whom she would accept an offering.

The tree she spoke of was one I had frequently sat under. I remembered it having three large cones, and when I went there, I found the largest had fallen from the top. I carried it to the Chalice and set it on a gnarled root, then settled back with pipe in hand to further contemplate the image of "Contemplation". The tree nurtured a tranquil space into which Amitabha Bird flew like a mountain song clothed in iridescent feathers.

The three of us merged as perspectives on a single unfolding, wherein the Mountain Lady showed herself in communion with the Divine Mind. Roused from her rapture, she reached out for a moment as the great mother and whispered to her children. The Chalice lit up; all of its dark places ignited. I felt the brilliance and saw again that the darkness of ordinary awareness was, by comparison, the blackness of primal unconsciousness teasing itself with specks of light . . .

Amid this abundance, the coins of the *I Ching* fell and constructed the hexagrams of "Return" changing to "Approach". The first concerns the re-accumulation of energies after periods of depletion. It told me what my aching body already knew, that my returning strength should be renewed by rest. The book compares this time to that of the winter solstice, when ancient kings closed the passes and no one moved about. I assumed some solar flow was being inhibited by my body's fatigue, but although tired, I was committed to leaving the mountain. The changing line acknowledged my decision, for it says simply:

Quiet return.
Good fortune.

"Approach" depicts the ascent of the light-giving power, so I knew my energies would pick up with the day. The commentary notes that the hexagram is the inverse of "Contemplation". This prompted me to see myself much like the old Chalice pine: an upside-down tree, with my trunk growing into branchlike legs and my roots disappearing into the sphere of my head.

I buried the pinecone beneath a piece of quartz and then went off on one last climb around the Monuments. The day fit like a gossamer glove woven of visual beauty, perfumes, and mountain music. For lunch, I climbed the Pedestal, taking with me the three little statues from the shrine, to show them the view from the top again and together to thank the Presence.

I felt the immanence of my departure from the mountain, but was beyond caring. Each moment was its own wonder. I looked toward Garner Valley along the road I would soon be walking. The world at the end of it loomed into view for a moment, then faded away. I looked to the other side, where the desert lay with the San Bernardinos beyond. A large jet was landing at Palm Springs, and I wondered absently if it might be Air Force One or Two, with the dean of America's criminal element or his heavy aboard, come to hobnob with the nation's greedy.

My mind toyed with a dour comparison, pitting the president and his charade of shysters against the concept of the superior man delineated in the *I Ching*. In essence, there was no contest, for the Nixonian ethic was that of the inferior man, a category included in the book as a referential subspecies. To the *I Ching*, ethics is the science of proper neural circuiting and the art of living in the electromagnetic mode of consciousness. As such, it encompasses the more limited, often contradictory imperatives of defined behavior, much as the Einsteinian universe encompasses that of Newton.

I thought of Vietnam where Asia and America had met and we used men like Nixon to bear factional daggers; and how, bested in a vainglorious war, the same men remained lethally in power at home, calling sternly for more repressive laws, more fraudulent operations, and more sectarian fears to cradle them in their incompetence. It was the mentality of downers, and I was struck again by the irony of psychedelic substances being outlawed by the same authorities who prescribed depressants for every public ill.

Below me, the big jet touched down at Palm Springs, and I wondered why the leaders of corporate America were so at home in the plush, air-conditioned California desert. The answer wafted up like smog. The gambling was private, the women discreet, but far more was involved. Palm Springs was Pompeii, the monied capital of the nation's legal drug culture, where tranquilizers, barbiturates, narcotics, and alcohol were freely prescribed to subtract the wealthy from their worries.

The breeze snapped at my brow, calling me back to my own reality. The Mountain Lady, having attended my philippic, now soothed me with her healing breath. She lingered while I packed, and escorted me to the edge of the Saddle, where I, covered with six layers of dirt, scruffy bearded, and shiny eyed, departed from her foot. I nodded to my yucca friend in passing, stopped briefly to fill a canteen at the spring, and pushed on toward the ranch. The buildings were visible most of the way down; they were deserted, and only the wind in the yard raised an occasional wisp of dust.

I dropped my gear by the fence and continued to the main house. The door hung open, so I entered quietly. Daylight made it no worse than I remembered, and I saw the familiar place as though in a multilevel dream, with its many past faces superimposed on the new grimace. I walked the short hall to the kitchen. A pack of squirrels were routing through the mess on the floor and shelves. My sudden appearance startled them, and we all froze for a few breathless moments, staring at each other. Then, softly, I Aum'd, bursting the bubble. As though of one muscle, they all scurried off, disappearing into the floor, up the chimney, and out the windows.

The commotion disturbed a bird trapped in the house. He took to the air and sailed past my ear into the living room. I followed, then by dancing a bit and waving my arms, managed to usher him out a broken window. On the cornice were two postcards and a book I had picked up from the litter on the floor two weeks earlier. The postcards were a Madonna and Child, and a Buddha. The book was a pocket edition of Gideon's *New Testament, Psalms and Proverbs,* presented, as the flyleaf told in a child's hand, to the Vietnam Soldiers, by the Sixth Class of Wilson Methodist Church, on Thanksgiving Day, 1966. It seemed a notation appropriate to my surroundings, except it was the wrong year, the wrong country, and the wrong war.

I pocketed my souvenirs and picked my way back out through the debris of the house. The pack was less of a burden than what I had left behind so I shouldered it and headed to the reservoir, eager for a swim. The water had enticed me all the way down from the Saddle, and I had savored it a dozen times in my imagination. When I threw off my clothes and stepped in, however, I stopped cold, for the pond was brimming with the mountain's icy runoff and far more frigid than I had fantasized. For a few minutes, I stayed in the shallows watching little blue gills and perch play about my toes. When I finally slipped into the water, I was pleasantly surprised to feel no cold at all. I seemed rather to be enclosed in an envelope of self-generating heat.

I swam to the middle of the pond and floated on my back. The sky was sentient blue, so I called out Aum Tao, and the mountain sent it back in triplicate. I called again, conjuring up a sound vision, which I chipped to conciseness with BU-DA! The energy spiraled down in echoes and soon had me swimming in circles. I dove, surfaced, and dove again, twisting through the murky brown depths and breaking for air with the genetic rhythms of the water creature I once had been.

I stood atingle in the afternoon breeze, then took the tarpaulin from the pack and sat for a while on the beach, spacing out on the rippled reflections of the mountain. I lay back, better to see the original, and soon fell asleep. No dreams intervened and I awoke to a lowering sun pointing west. I got myself together, Aum Tao'd the ranch, and set off to the Waterfall. The way was largely downhill, so I arrived still refreshed and re-established my first campsite. The advancing season had tinged the glade with summer, turning green to yellow, and flowers to seed, but the immediate environs of the stream were lush and vibrant with life. I found a dry spot near the falls and sat to listen. My ear was tuned for music, and the moist whispers from the mountain's throat did not disappoint it. I took the Gideon Bible from my pocket and opened it randomly. Happenstance selected the Eighteenth Psalm, a song of David's illumination. I mused on the passage over dinner, then, taking the pipe, whiled away evening, listening for night.

The Final Oracle

I awoke to the sentient stars of morning enacting the sky: above, the Swan swam the Milky Way, and further south, Sagittarius as an old-fashioned kettle poured celestial water on the Scorpion's tail. I watched dawn with a practiced eye and waited for warmth as the sky rainbowed to blue. The waterfall played the prelude, and orchestrating day added songs of awakening. I rose on a crescendo and cavorted among the rocks, playing in my own way with the water and trees, with the mysterious flowings and flowerings of the Tao.

For breakfast, I savored the last of my protein and milk powder and the final crumbs of chocolate. Then I rolled the remaining marijuana into four joints and smoked half of one. The *I Ching* took over and guided me to a smooth rock shelf above the falls. Every feature of the canyon shimmered intelligently as a living metaphor of the book's wisdom, and the prescient coins spoke as they fell on the stone.

This was my last *I Ching* reading of the trip, so I hoped for some counsel to steer me back to the world. I also needed advice about what to do with all I had been given. The first hexagram was "Increase". It says the time resembles a marriage of heaven and earth, when what is above gives generously to what is below, making it full, and thereby demonstrating that spirit which alone has power to help the world. It adds that times such as these do not endure and must be utilized while they last. I took this as confirmation of an earlier decision that I should try to make a book of the things I had experienced. The changing line cheered me on by saying:

> It furthers one to accomplish great deeds.
> Supreme good fortune.
> No blame.

The second hexagram was the culminating image of my trip, the sacred mountain, "Contemplation", appearing a final time as a farewell and summation. The book, as mediator between mountain and man, told of its pleasure in the encounter. I took the judgment on the hexagram to indicate an interlude in my life for writing, for it pointed out that the ablution had been made but not yet the offering.

By midmorning I had broken camp, assembled the pack, and smoked the rest of the joint. I elected to follow the canyon to Garner Valley, not knowing how difficult this might prove to be with the pack. The way was often tangled, steep, or abrupt, but the stream was my guide. During the course of our traveling together, it taught me the way of water: how it flowed, filled up the deep places, and went on, following its gravitational intuition. Taking its advice, I chose the easiest way. When confronted with an obstacle, I waited before it until my mind had analyzed its perceptions and offered the result to the unknown arbiter of such riddles, who, in turn, lighted a way ahead.

My body also learned from the stream, for it moved almost without effort and relaxed with every step. The result was a funny, ambling gait, but a most enjoyable way to walk requiring virtually no energy, for only the muscles needed at any particular moment were activated. It was a state of animated relaxation, from which I was able to see my usual tension as the residual poisonings of a chemically encapsulated ego.

The way of water embodied itself in other animals. Birds swam the sky; water striders strode the stream. As I crawled through some bushes, an inchworm dropped to the back of my hand and demonstrated a protoplasmic wave by jogging toward my elbow. Later, in a grassy meadow, I was intercepted by a huge gopher snake, a true master in the ways of organic fluidity. He was by far the largest snake I had encountered on the trip, and his aura informed me that he embodied the Great Serpency, come graciously to bid me good-bye. Thoroughly atingle, I sang him a song, and he, in the mellow tones of our hybrid intimacy, spoke of water's simple ways and its enlivening spirit.

I passed the last of the deep pools and left the final bluff of sculpted rock behind. The streambed widened, and the canyon walls became hills settling into Garner Valley, where the sparse forest had been logged and bulldozed, leaving the delicate earth torn up and blowing away. It served as a reminder of what lay ahead in the uncertain and secular world, where every sacrament that worked was prohibited and every voice of dissent overwhelmed. I sat to make a final entry in my notebook; then, bowing to the mountain, I shouldered my pack and headed out across Garner Valley to rejoin my brothers.

Epilogue

The mountain still slumbers in the troubled beauty of its nighttime. The earth sleeps below. I, like a dream, have drifted away, and bedeck myself with words, hoping somehow to trigger a memory of that which is never recalled. Time is not a sequence, but a field; space is empty of everything, including distance. The mind that stands beyond such limits invests the universe with manifold possibilities for its extension, focus, and incarnation in form. All creation is its temple, wherein man wanders at will along the corridors of his being. Immortality is ungrasping acceptance of what is given, a relinquishment of expectation in the certainty of perfection.

I learned many things from my sky-clad mountain, but how paltry they seem when cast into thought and left hanging like a veil before its Lady. I discovered my body was a much better instrument than any I carried with me, and its proper use implied blissful awareness. Equally accessible were other levels of experience with distinct characteristics and unique patterns of vibratory response, which bespoke a transcendent intelligence expressing its immanence. Not confined to a single form, it imbued the least to the greatest with its essence. The sacred mountain molded the field that molded me, and I had but to listen through the stillness of my own astonishment to sample its cosmic attunement.

A temple is where creatures join together at the apex of creation and one mind is focused in God. Presence becomes reality, time-space is transcended in the rapture of heaven, and the essence of life is self-consciously returned to its source. The mode of those who experience this unfolding is compassionate awareness of otherness in unity, a state which, when noticed, is called love—when unnoticed, contemplation. This experience is the archetypal temple: the pole, axis, and center of earth, and the supreme pole of the universe.

In the early days of humanity, the whole earth was a temple tuned to her creatures, but bad times befell us and the surface consciousness of the planet became constricted. As a three-million-year-old species, it is clear we have a history mostly untold, and the few thousand years we lay claim to are like the remnant of a tapestry from a house burned down. Both science and mythology preserve memories of our more distant past, but the data from their various disciplines are seldom correlated. A moment on which they seem to agree, however, is of both scientific and historical importance: it is an event recalled in Hopi myth as the destruction of the Second World, and in science as the last major reversal of the earth's magnetic field. This occurred about 700,000 years ago, and the time since has been marked by four great ice ages. According to the Hopi, the catastrophe happened when Sotuknang relieved Poqanghoya and Palongawhoya of their responsibilities:

> The twins had hardly abandoned their stations when the world, with no one to control it, teetered off balance, spun around crazily, then rolled over twice. Mountains plunged into the seas with a great splash, seas and lakes sloshed over the land; and as the world spun through cold and lifeless space it froze into solid ice. (Waters 1963)

Scientifically, we can only speculate about the secondary effects that might accompany a reversal of the earth's magnetic field, either with respect to the structure of the earth or of ourselves. It has been conjectured that at some point the planetary magnetic shield would disappear, leaving her surface prey to the blastings of the solar wind and the antiseptic radiations of Dharmakayaic space. This would certainly be destructive and produce mutants, but it would hardly be enough to initiate the effects remembered by the Hopi. Indeed, we might even assume that under normal conditions, the reversal could proceed with no destructive activity at all. The earth, one day asleep, would reawaken and resume her daytime activities. But according to some fragmentary scientific evidence, 700,000 years ago was not a normal time for the solar system or any of its inhabitants.

Meteorites and meteoritic dust originate within the solar system, and each year the earth sweeps up about 5 million tons of them. Most of this debris is dissolved by the atmosphere and sprinkles to earth as tiny cosmic spherules, whose extraterrestrial origin can be recognized under a microscope. In deep ocean sediments, whose layers create a geologic clock, these spherules gradually accumulate and provide a link between the history of the earth and that of its solar environment. Most meteoritic activity took place in the very distant past, when the original solar system was still condensing out of its mothering nebula and the planets were building by the violent accretion of particles. Eventually the system stabilized and most of the afterbirth was swept up. Then, sometime between one and two million years ago, very recently on the geologic time scale, the meteoritic activity over earth picked up dramatically. The ocean sediments became dark with spherules, telling us that somewhere back in our species' mid-history, the solar system unaccountably became much dirtier than before.

It is possible that this sudden littering of our solar environment included the event the Hopi describe as the destruction of the First World. This climactic occurrence, the initial shock in the awful series of catastrophes that have befallen us, was initiated by the Godhead,

> . . . for Taiowa commanded Sotuknang to destroy the world. Sotuknang destroyed it by fire because the Fire Clan had been its leaders. He rained fire upon it. He opened up the volcanoes. Fire came from above and below and all around until the earth, the waters, the air, all was one element, fire, and there was nothing left except the people safe inside the womb of earth. (Waters 1963)

What the Hopi remembered reminded me of the galactic visions I had experienced on the mountain, culminating with what I saw when my head was in the crystal-sprinkled rock on the afternoon of the eighteenth day. I had witnessed a series of cosmic events, which at the time, though profound, were without relevance. However, it is possible that under the prodding of psychedelics I had seen further into my genetic past, to a long-forgotten time when the dwarfed remnant of an ancient star fell into orbit around the sun, causing devastation. Under the fierce pull of the sun's gravitational field, the tiny wanderer ripped apart and swirled out through the solar system as a satanic bola. Before its major fragments settled into separate orbits as the massive sun-like planets Jupiter and Saturn, cosmic gore was scattered behind them, and utter havoc wreaked on a once peaceful system of worlds.

The solar system today is a strangely anomalous place. There are 8 planets, 35 known satellites, 2,000 sizable asteroids, and an estimated

400,000 minor asteroids more than a kilometer in diameter. The number of comets is unknown. Four of the satellites are larger than the planet Mercury, while others are little more than chunks of debris. Some of them travel in one direction around their planets, some in the other. Jupiter, Saturn, and Neptune have satellites going in both directions.

Most asteroids are found in orbit between Mars and Jupiter, but some are eccentric, like the Apollo objects, which by crossing the earth's orbit, give rise to probabilities of collision. The total mass of the asteroids is less than that of a large moon, and, for the most part, they are chunks of ice and rock, but why they are there is a puzzle. Comets are dirty ice circling the sun in vast, elliptical orbits. Each time they pass within the orbit of Mars, they melt away as streaming tails of vapor. Had they been with us long, they would not be with us at all, yet their recent origin is a mystery, so they are hypothesized to have hibernated in deep space.

The planets are as baffling as the rest of the debris-ridden system. Of the eight, we are the only one with a living surface. Venus, long thought of as our twin in both poetry and cosmology, is more like hell to our heaven. Its atmosphere is a hundred times as massive as our own, yet it contains neither water nor oxygen. It is composed primarily of burn products: carbon dioxide and carbon monoxide, and generates sulphuric acid thunderstorms to ravish the lands below.

Mars is burned red, shows surface signs of massive, violent wrenching, and wobbles badly on its track. It has areas of water erosion more extensive than the Grand Canyon, but little water remains. Like the earth's moon, Mars is preferentially cratered, with a great deal of recent activity apparent in one section, as though something nearby exploded, blasting the face turned toward it. Many of the planet's surface features are sharply defined, indicating that they were recently formed, for Mars is subject to corrosive planetwide dust storms.

Jupiter is two and a half times as massive as the rest of the planets combined and emits twice as much energy as it receives from the sun, thus classifying it as a small, virtually dormant star. Like the sun and Saturn, it is composed primarily of metallic and molecular hydrogen and has an atmosphere of turbulent ammonia. A persistent, visible feature is the Great Red Spot, which is a single storm large enough to swallow several earth-sized planets. We do not know what it is, but it has been there since before telescopes were first used to see it 300 years ago. Both Jupiter and Saturn have a permanent, unexplained smog of small dark particles in their atmospheres; and though Saturn has virtually no water in its composition, it is unaccountably ringed with ice. Uranus, too, has rings, and spins on its side, having presumably been struck by a comparable sized neighbor. The dwarf planet Pluto, though having a moon, is thought to be an escaped moon, as is our own satellite. With our own moon, we are not so sure, and astronomers, like lovers, find it veiled in mystery.

What may have preceded this chaotic state of affairs is, of course, hypothetical, but the flotsam could indicate that one or more now extinct planets once completed a harmonious system of life supporting worlds. But into this family, a cosmic dumbbell fell, and each planet in its turn confronted doomsday. Venus was boiled in star-stuff, Mars was roasted, and Uranus and Neptune were embalmed. Another, nameless world was swept up in the crossbar of the dumbbell and ripped apart, its oceans and continents pulled into space as moons, asteroids, comets, planetary rings, and cosmic dust, while the body of the planet fell into Jupiter, where it still bobs up and down in an ocean of liquid hydrogen, with a bloody red storm as its headstone.

In this epic of destruction, the earth fared better than her solar siblings, for she was not gobbled by a hungry giant, nor was her life-bearing envelope obliterated. We know there were fire storms and columns like napalm from heaven, for these events are recorded among such peoples as the Hopi and the Aztec, but more specific evidence of this catastrophe may still linger on the earth as Helios, the sun god himself, in his manifestation as helium.

The sun, Jupiter, and Saturn are gigantic concentrations of the first and second constituents of primal matter. Within stars, hydrogen fuses in its own furnace, producing vast amounts of energy and helium as ash. Neither hydrogen nor helium remain long on the surface of the earth, for under these conditions they are the lightest gases. Hydrogen, however, is abundant, for it readily combines with other elements, stabilizing in compounds such as water. Helium, being inert and unable to combine, floats off into space. Small amounts of it are found together with other gases in deep underground wells in various parts of the world. One of the anomalies of earth science is that 90 percent of the world's helium is found within 250 miles of Amarillo, Texas. Why this is so and how it got there are scientific puzzles, but it could be the residue of the day when a torrent of star stuff fell from the sky and burned a hole through the belly of North America.

For some time after the cataclysmic event, the solar system was a shambles. Surging gravitational and electromagnetic fields buffeted the debris, and orbits were rearranged. Meteorites and fireballs continued to fall to earth, while comets dazzled her skies. Eventually, the power of the sun settled the unruly family, and a semblance of stability returned. In wounded misery, the dazed earth gazed about. She alone had survived. Her siblings were replaced by balls of seeming insentience, to whom she could speak only at the levels of physical law and fields of force. Though stunned, she strove to bring order to her being and establish her new identity as a daughter among three suns.

We, the creatures of her surface, were as stunned as she. The Garden of Eden was irretrievably lost, for the cosmic serpent had breathed destruction on it. During the Second World, the earth succored her children, but this world also ended, for she either fell asleep or was knocked out. According to the Hopi, the latter occurred, for the cataclysm they record indicates that the reversal of the planetary magnetic field was induced by a collision with a significant piece of debris.

In this evaluation, modern science concurs, again through studies of meteoritic phenomena. When a large meteorite strikes the earth, it momentarily melts the impact area and splashes terrestrial material, mostly silicon, into the atmosphere. The splash solidifies as glass droplets called tektites, which sprinkle back to earth some distance from the impact site and are found throughout an area known as a strewn field. The largest of these is the Australasian strewn field, which covers about 10 percent of the earth's surface and is estimated to contain 100 million tons of tektite glass. Using sediment stratigraphy, potassium-argon, and fission-track dating methods, the event causing the strewn field has been placed 700,000 years in the past.

The earth's orbit is still a dangerous place. As recently as 1972, a huge meteoroid was observed to graze the atmosphere above Montana and skip across Canada like a flat stone bounced on a lake. A similar event occurred in 1965, and in 1937, the Apollo asteroid, Hermes, passed within two lunar distances of the earth. Hermes is a chunk of rock about a kilometer in diameter, and had it struck, its impact would have been equivalent to an explosion of many thousand hydrogen bombs. The probability of being hit by one of the 30 or so known Apollo asteroids has been calculated at about once every 250,000 years. The odds on our intercepting a comet, however, cannot be so readily estimated. An unknown number of them already come within the earth's orbit, and any of the others could be deflected toward us by the gravitational fields of the outer planets.

With the destruction of the Second World, the earth slept, but her sleep was not without dreams, and dangers still lurked in the tumblings of space. Although she had turned within to heal, the earth maintained contact with her surfaces through her sacred mountains. She showed how these could bring power from heaven to stabilize the climate of their environments, and through them she talked in a subdued way with those who could hear her. In this fashion, enclaves powered by the earth's magnetosphere withstood the rigors of the ice ages. I had seen something of this on the mountain, when beams from the sky poured down into the Lady's eye, bedazzling her with an aura of energy. It seems probable that Atlantis was another of these enclaves, as was Hyperborea, fabled as the northern abode of the sun god, a tropical paradise ringed in ice and centered on a mountain tuned to heaven.

Slowly, through millennium after millennium of the Third World, the earth swept up the debris in her path, occasionally being seared by a migrant chunk. Then, 11,000 years ago, while she still slept, another huge meteorite struck her, and the long nighttime of coping on her surfaces was shattered. Again she reeled, tilted, her magnetic sleep disturbed, and waters, like cold sweat, rolled across her face. Atlantis was swamped; Hyperborea, buried in ice; the Mountain Lady, blown apart.

This catastrophe, the Deluge, was also cosmic, but since that time, strangely enough, representatives of our species from every corner of the planet have laid the blame for the tragedy on ourselves. The Hopi, like the authors of the Old Testament, call it the result of human wickedness, while Hindus and Buddhists see it as the outcome of our ignorance. Both judgments imply culpability—one of the heart, the other of the head—but even accepting our excessive egocentricity, it seems unlikely that these gloomy conclusions from the keepers of our species' continuum would be so pervasive if the fall of the great meteorite had been a random event, rather than one associated with the purposive behavior of man.

The Chinese legend of Kung-Kung, the mythic villain who tilted the earth's axis by running his head against Mount Pu Chou, states that he was a minister of the earth sovereign, and his destructive frenzy is termed a rebellion. This might indicate that Kung-Kung was an Apollo asteroid pulled out of orbit to crash into the planetary surface. If the enclaves of the Third World powered their civilizations with energy extracted from the earth's magnetosphere, it is possible that they altered it into some kind of electromagnetic vortex, which acted as a pulling magnet. This could be dangerous in a solar system amply speckled with huge chunks of iron, for one might eventually be drawn to earth. If this possibility was known but discounted, then the technological manipulation of the earth field would have to be termed wickedness. If the possibility was unsuspected, however, it could subsequently be seen as ignorance. Since some traditions claim the one, and others the other, we may conclude that both are probably true, that some knew of the technological deception, and others did not. Perhaps a place like Hyperborea overloaded the system in order to maximize its own opulence, and instead called down the judgment of heaven on us all.

This hypothesis may be taken further, for it implies that some would have had knowledge of the impending collision. The question naturally arises, what could they do under the circumstances? Today, probably everyone who could would try to be airborne at the time of the impact, hoping their vehicle would withstand the atmospheric shock. Others would take to submarines and boats, while the United States and the Soviet Union would probably launch fifty or a hundred couples into orbit, leaving it up to them to come down at a suitable place. The rest of us would get to pray, become violent, or have an orgy, all of which are usual human responses to a threatening catastrophe, as well, mysteriously enough, as to the approach of an unknown and unanticipated catastrophe, for it seems that the lemmings in us all know their fate.

It is perhaps wiser to seek for knowledge than blame from our heritage. Unlike today's proponents of social evolution, wise men at the beginning of our history maintained that the people of previous civilizations were mentally and psychologically more adept than they, so we may assume that the sophisticated technological capability of the antediluvian world allowed its inhabitants, to some extent, to avert the doom they brought on themselves. Indeed, we might assume that they were able to extract results from the universe quite different from those we achieve or aspire to. How their technologies operated we do not know, but the traditions concerning them were never lost, for they were written on sacred mountains long before the Deluge, and since then have been chiseled into the stone of pyramids, temples, and stelae.

My experience with the mountain has left me with a deep respect for the abilities of our ancestors. Combined with what I understand of today's laws of physics, this has led me to some rather interesting conclusions. Ancient cultures tell of the Sambhogakaya as unadorned intelligence, as cosmic presence and earth mind, as father, mother, and repository of all human potential, whose wisdom is the universe. Into this mind, ancient people merged, and losing themselves in its immenseness, emerged elsewhere; for there is a golden matrix within our universe along which we as dream creatures of earth may travel. In the contemplative state, formal creation falls away and with it goes the attachment of mind to the limited locus of individuality. From this state, every point in time-space is equidistant, and the re-emergence of a projected consciousness anywhere is possible. Certain sites, both in time and space, are more probable, however, for their coordinates are built into us as aspects of human consciousness. Thus the mind in meditation may reappear wherever its affective nexus takes it. With billions of galaxies, trillions of stars, and a quadrillion worlds, heaven is an unendingly splendored realm.

Within heaven, earth is one member in a living gridwork of worlds, all tuned to a certain, complex thought which, including ourselves as participants in a greater whole, links these places as a psychic subfield within the galactic intelligence. Our sister worlds, though often dissimilar to earth, are fully complementary, and our ways of functioning appropriate to their ambiance. Some are even compatible with our bodies, and we could go and live on them, subject only to the laws of the relativistic universe.

During the epochs of the mountain's efflorescence, it served the purpose of linking the earth, through us and others, with her sisters in space. A symbiotic mind composed of compatible contemplatives appeared as a concise expression of earth on another world. There, as within our sacred mountains, it incarnated in a form made available for it on arrival and participated as an honored earth-being in the life of the place. An actual physical body was rarely sent anywhere, though this could be done by encoding it in light and projecting it to a world suitable for its emergence. The difficulty, besides being for the most part unnecessary, was that those so projected were effectively dead during the light-years of transit time, though, on arriving at their destination, they would experience no time lapse. Occasionally, individuals were sent to establish the species on a new world that had evolved to the point of sustaining them; or, if a cosmic catastrophe threatened, a world could be physically evacuated by those capable of the transition through Dharmakayaic space.

Such, I believe, was the option exercised by some of the Third World survivors, who, as refugees from the earth, projected themselves as light through the relativistic universe to a place of suitable emergence, thousands of light-years away. Where they went, we do not know, though the knowledge is probably contained in the astronomical temples of historical antiquity, for these were built by those who returned. Since the great civilizations of Sumer, Egypt, and China burst into prominence around 3000 BCE, some 6,000 years after the fall of the Hudson Bay meteorite, we might assume the turnaround planet to be about 3,000 light-years off toward the center of the galaxy.

Since that time, other civilizations: Greek, Vedic, Japanese, Mayan and Inca, have claimed that their culture bearers came from the sky, so it appears that the ancient pathways have been activated now and again during historical times, leading me to wonder about my mysterious Iboga people, encased in living crystal, spinning slowly, dreamily, through empty space. I wonder if they still move outbound, or whether, having found their place of emergence, they might now be returning to rejoin us in the next world. Their re-emergence here would imply that the earth's tuning is again proper for this kind of transference, and some old mountain, like a diamond in morning sunlight, would sparkle again for the moment of their coming and remind us of our origins in eternity.

Works Cited

Evans-Wentz, W.Y., trans. 1957. *The Tibetan Book of the Dead: Bardo Thodol.* Oxford: University Press.

Govinda, Lama Anagarika. 1966. *The Way of the White Clouds.* London: Hutchinson & Co.

Graham, A.C., trans. 1990. *The Book of Lieh-Tzu: a Classic of the Tao.* New York: Columbia University Press.

Morgan, Evan S., trans. 1933. *Huai-nan Tzu.* Shanghai.

Leary, Timothy, Ralph Metzner, Richard Alpert. 1964. *The Psychedelic Experience.* New York: University Books.

Le Blanc, Charles, trans. 1985. *The Masters of Huainan.* Hong Kong: University Press.

Jowett, Benjamin, trans. 1892. *The Dialogues of Plato, vol.3—Timæus.* London: Oxford University Press.

Shelley, Percy Bysshe. (1818). *The Golden Treasury.* Edited by Francis T. Palgrave. London: Macmillan, 1875.

Waters, Frank. 1963. *Book of the Hopi.* New York: Viking Penguin Inc.

Wilhelm, Richard, trans. 1950. *The I Ching, or Book of Changes.* New York: Bollingen Foundation.